The Electric Vegetarian

THE ELECTRIC VEGETARIAN

Natural cooking the food processor way

PAULA SZILARD AND JULIANA J. WOO

DAVID & CHARLES
Newton Abbot   London

Dedicated to

My mother Pansy, who guided me through the preparation
and cooking of many meals, and to the memory of my
father, Joel.

Julie

My parents, who have farmed or gardened organically as
far back as I can remember, and who have taught me the
simple pleasures of homegrown, homecooked food.

Paula

British Library Cataloguing in Publication Data
Szilard, Paula
  The electric vegetarian: natural cooking the
  food processor way.
  1. Vegetarian cookery 2. Food   processor cookery
  I. Title II. Woo, Juliana J.
  641.5′63   TXB37

  ISBN 0–7153–8821–5

Edited by Rosemary Moon

Phototypeset by P&M Typesetting Ltd, Exeter
Printed in Great Britain
by Redwood Burn Ltd, Trowbridge, Wilts
for David & Charles Publishers plc
Brunel House Newton Abbot Devon

Contents

Introduction   7
Basics of Vegetarian Nutrition   10
Keeping a Vegetarian Kitchen   21
Appetisers   27
Soups   31
Salads and Dressings   34
Main Dishes   42
    Grains and Pulses   42
    Eggs, Milk and Cheese   48
    Pastas and Sauces   57
    Pizzas and Turnovers   73
    Quiches, Pies and Tarts   76
    Crêpes and Enchiladas   88
    Tofu   93
Side Dishes   96
    Vegetables   96
    Grains and Pulses   99
Breads   102
    Yeast Breads   110
    Quick Breads   126
    Unleavened Breads   134
Pancakes and Waffles   136
Desserts   140
Appendices   147
Subject and Recipe Title Index   151
Major Ingredient Index   156

Introduction

Traditional vegetarian cooking is as old as cooking itself. Modern Western vegetarian cooking has often tried to imitate the traditional, but has not been totally successful. Both are time-consuming, and though the traditional has been both tasty and nutritious the contemporary has often not been. We therefore consider this book a departure point for a new, less time-consuming style of vegetarian cooking – a style that maximises taste, nutritional value and ease of preparation. We emphasise taste because too often it has been neglected in the attempt to achieve nutritional soundness. We stress nutritional soundness because it has frequently been disregarded in the pursuit of taste. And we underline ease of preparation because the vegetarian cook has often had to sacrifice both nutritional value and taste to save time. With the advent of the food processor none of these values need be slighted in an attempt to realise the others.

The food processor is without doubt the most revolutionary kitchen appliance to appear in the last twenty years. In a vegetarian kitchen, where most cooking is done from scratch, it is nothing short of miraculous and has given us a sense of freedom we hope you will soon share. It has opened up a whole new world of good cooking and eating where the imagination is unconstrained by conventional techniques, and the dull, repetitive tasks no longer take up so much time that they inhibit our creativity. Chopping, slicing, shredding, grating, puréeing, mixing and kneading take only a few seconds or minutes now. And the processor allows us to do things that were difficult, if not impossible before, such as pulverising chillis for an enchilada sauce or grinding sesame seeds into a crêpe batter.

Here are only a few of the tasks that can be performed by this modern miracle machine using each of the major blades or discs.

METAL BLADE
Finely chopping onions and other vegetables
Making nut flours and nut butters
Making mayonnaise
Making pasta dough
Mixing quick breads, cakes and pancakes
Mixing and kneading bread dough
Making pastry
Making breadcrumbs
Puréeing chick peas for hummus
Making pesto sauce
Grating hard cheeses

SLICING DISC
Slicing vegetables and fruits
Slicing cabbage for coleslaw
Cutting vegetables into julienne strips
Frenching beans

SHREDDING DISC
Shredding carrots and other vegetables for salads
Shredding potatoes for potato pancakes
Shredding or grating cheese

We adhere to the complementary protein approach to vegetarian cookery. From the beginning we wanted to make this a cookbook with a real difference. We wanted to emphasise nutritional values in a very concrete way and decided to do this chiefly by providing detailed information on the protein content of each dish. We focused on protein because the supposed lack of it is often viewed as a problem when trying to achieve a well balanced but meat-free diet. You will notice that all of our main dishes contain at least 10g of protein per serving.

We decided to include a chapter on the 'Basics of Vegetarian Nutrition' to provide a framework for interpreting our protein calculations. It contains information on protein and on other nutrients which are difficult to obtain in some vegetarian diets. We decided not to expand this chapter to include a discussion of all major nutrients as they relate to a vegetarian diet because this is primarily a cookbook with supplementary nutritional information – not a nutritional book containing a few recipes.

Although experienced vegetarians will find some new information here, the nutritional chapter may be most useful to those just starting out. It is, however, possible to use the recipes without reading the entire chapter. Simply follow the suggestions at the end of the chapter on 'How to Get a Balanced Diet Using This Book' and familiarise yourself with the various groups or families of complementary foods. It will then be easy for you to complement the major protein source served at every meal. Complementing without worrying about precise proportions is so simple that it will quickly become second nature to you.

Vegetarian cuisine has been dominated by what we euphemistically refer to as 'the health food school of cooking', where a few foods are emphasised to the exclusion of others because they are viewed as health-promoting. Food is regarded as medicine, and questions of taste are largely irrelevant. Our approach is quite different. We believe that nutritious food must taste delicious and to this end we have tested all of our recipes with the food processor until we felt they were as good and as tasty as possible.

Other than pleasing the palate, irresistible food can provide an incentive for family members to be at home when meals are served instead of grabbing a bite on the run. Good food also furnishes a pleasurable atmosphere for socialising with friends, and looking forward to a sandwich made with home-made bread for lunch certainly makes the work day pass a bit more quickly. So, if you expect another volume of nondescript recipes, seemingly designed to be morally uplifting, rather than satisfyingly tasty, you will be pleasantly surprised.

You will also be surprised if you expect to be subjected to ethical arguments for becoming a vegetarian. Although there are some good arguments we do not make them here for two reasons. The first and most important is that this is a cookbook, not a philosophy text. Secondly, we believe the change to vegetarian eating is usually a long term process, barring some traumatic incident, which must come from within and not from without. We have observed that those individuals who remain vegetarians have made the transition gradually. They progressively eat less and less meat until they completely lose their taste for it. On the other hand, if the conversion involved the overnight giving up of meat, the new style of eating is usually short-lived because the resulting sacrifice and self-denial are difficult to sustain. While not trying to convince you to become a vegetarian, if you are ready to make the change, this book will help you to do so.

Whether you are making the transition or have already made it, we can help you to prepare pleasurable and nourishing meals in a reasonable length of time. Although our recipes are aimed chiefly at ovo-lacto vegetarians, vegans (pure vegetarians) will also be able to use a large number of them. Also, those committed to a natural style of eating will find that, whenever possible, we use unrefined or minimally processed foods. And those who, for economic or health reasons, are attempting to cut back on their meat intake will be pleased to discover that we include an extensive section of main dishes. In addition, our numerous recipes and detailed directions for making whole grain breads and pastas will be useful to all cooks who want to prepare these foods using only the most wholesome ingredients.

Although all of our recipes use the food processor we do not view this book as a basic manual on how to use these machines. There are a number of such books available already. Food processors differ slightly and directions for the basic procedures may vary, depending on the make of the machine. It is best to familiarise yourself thoroughly with the capabilities, directions for use, and safety precautions that come with your machine.

We developed all our recipes with a Cuisinart processor, but the directions for preparation apply equally well to other machines. If you have not yet purchased a machine, the best advice we can give you is to consider very carefully all of the tasks you will want it to perform. For bread making, for instance, it is wise to have a heavy base so that your machine does not travel when it kneads the heavier whole grain bread doughs. A machine with direct drive is preferable to a belt-driven model because the belts may break under a heavy load. It is best to consult an independent consumer test magazine for details of test results on various machines. Talking to food processor owners is also a good idea, but remember that the same features are not equally important to everyone.

Basics of Vegetarian Nutrition

Vegetarian Diets Can Be Healthy

Though much has been written about vegetarianism and vegetarian nutrition, not all of it is reliable. There are, for instance, a number of books based on principles totally foreign to sound nutrition, such as those advocating extreme macrobiotic diets. Numerous vegetarian cookbooks contain recipes for main dishes clearly without a major protein source. In 1974 anxiety about vegetarian diets had reached such a level, particularly among parents concerned about the health of their vegetarian offspring, that the Committee on Nutritional Misinformation of the Food and Nutrition Board in the National Research Council (USA) considered it necessary to issue a brief statement explaining that a well-planned vegetarian diet could be nutritionally adequate.

A nutritionally sound diet can be attained by a balanced approach to vegetarian cooking such as we present in this book. However, a word of caution is in order for the new vegetarian. It is unwise to stop eating meat without changing dietary habits as a whole. When it comes to a matter of health we recommend a conservative stance. We have had friends who have experimented with vegetarian diets without otherwise changing their eating habits. They suffered from health problems as a result, or returned to a meat-centred diet because it made them feel better. If you see yourself inching towards vegetarianism, approach it gradually and eat a balanced diet! If you follow our suggestions and adhere to our recipes you will find them healthy and no more demanding than the cooking that you do now.

Making the transition from a meat-centred diet to a vegetarian diet means examining all of your assumptions about what constitutes a balanced diet and an adequate protein source. People often think of different foods as being composed of, or representative of, major nutrient classes – carbohydrates, fats or proteins – when in fact most unrefined foods contain two or all three. These misconceptions are due to established dietary habits in our culture. Meat, eggs, cheese, fish and milk are thought of as providing the protein in our diet: grains and pulses are commonly thought of as starchy and as contributing only carbohydrate. Actually, meat and fish contain both protein and fat, and milk and cheese contain protein, carbohydrate and fat. Grains and pulses also contain three nutrient classes.

Natural Is Best

We are committed to foods which are as close to their original state as possible. It is true that most food is 'natural' in the sense of coming from nature, but the important point is how much processing it has undergone, what percentage of the edible portion remains, what nutrients are left and what additives have been introduced to make the food easier to process, more colourful or longer lasting. Our preference is for unrefined whole grain cereals, fresh fruits and vegetables, naturally aged cheeses and dried, not canned, pulses. We use sugar and even honey conservatively.

The following are some reasons why natural foods are preferable to refined foods:

1. They taste better. Westerners are used to poor tasting and denatured food because too much stress has been placed on convenience and increased shelf life. Our taste has become perverted toward the artificial.

2. Whole grain foods, such as brown rice and wholewheat flour, contain more protein and a better balance of amino acids than their counterparts. Vegetarians can ill afford such losses because of their dependence on plant protein sources.

3. Most whole foods are higher in vitamins and minerals than refined foods. Of all the nutrients removed in the refining process only a few are replaced by enrichment. Checking any standard table of food values for vitamins and minerals contained in wholewheat flour as against those in enriched white flour should convince even the most sceptical.

4. It is best to eat wholefoods to ensure obtaining nutrients which have not yet been identified. Since nutrition is a relatively young science we really do not have any guarantee that all the essential nutrients have been discovered. It makes sense to avoid highly refined foods from which many important, but as yet unknown, nutrients may have been removed.

5. Wholefoods, especially grains, pulses and vegetables, are much higher in dietary fibre than refined foods. Although some of the claims made for high fibre diets are as yet unsubstantiated, fibre has been shown useful in the prevention and treatment of constipation, diverticulosis and the irritable bowel syndrome. Although some physicians still maintain that bowel movements at two to three day intervals are normal some researchers have demonstrated that the refined foods eaten in industrial societies are responsible for some of our digestive problems. Native peoples who eat a high-fibre diet have larger, heavier stools that absorb more water and therefore pass without strain. In short, being normal in a constipated society means only that you are as constipated as everyone else.

What Is Protein?

The body needs a continuous supply of protein for growth, maintenance and repair of tissues, as well as for the production of enzymes, hormones and antibodies.

Protein is composed of twenty-two amino acids. These are literally the building blocks with which all plant and animal proteins are constructed – including those required by the human body.

Nine of these amino acids cannot be produced in the body and must be obtained in the food we eat. These are referred to as the essential amino acids. Not only must these be present in our food, but each must be available in the quantity the body needs and in the correct proportion to the others. The body is capable of utilising only a certain limited 'profile' of amino acids. If one of the nine essential amino acids is in short supply, it limits the extent to which all of the others are used and is therefore called the limiting amino acid.

The protein quality, or usability, of a food is largely determined by its amino acid profile and its digestibility. The protein in the egg is generally considered the highest in quality because it closely resembles the amino acid pattern required by human beings. This is why the egg is frequently used as the standard for evaluating the quality of other proteins.

To Complement or Not To Complement?

The question of protein is generally uppermost in people's minds whenever vegetarianism is discussed. We feel some complementing is necessary at each meal because the body can compensate only partially for poor quality proteins by recycling amino acids from within.

Too Much Protein?

Many Westerners daily consume at least twice the recommended amount of protein. Most of this is animal protein, making the typical diet very high in saturated fat which has long been implicated as a possible factor in coronary heart disease. Unsaturated fat is somewhat superior, but even it requires caution since there is a correlation, though not necessarily a cause-effect relationship, between high total dietary fat intake and breast and colon cancer rates. Moreover, consuming excessive fat not only displaces other valuable nutrients but can also lead to obesity, as can an excess of calories in either of the other nutrient classes. Remember that a gram of fat contains nine calories, while a gram of carbohydrate or protein contains about four calories.

Popular opinion has it that excess protein will not result in weight gain. This could not be farther from the truth. There is simply no way for the body to store protein as protein. If the body gets more than it needs the excess is either broken down and used as an energy source, like the carbohydrates and fats, or it is stored in the adipose tissue as fat. To use protein as a source of energy is both expensive and extremely wasteful.

Where Do You Get Your Protein?

The following families or groups of foods serve as the major protein sources in a well-balanced vegetarian diet:

Pulses: includes all dried beans, peas, lentils, soybeans and soybean products such as tofu.

Grains: includes all whole grain cereals and cereal products such as wheat, rye, oats, barley, millet, rice, buckwheat and corn.

Seeds: includes sesame, sunflower and pumpkin seeds.

Nuts: this group is limited chiefly to those nuts which are not excessively high in fat content, such as peanuts and cashews, and nut butters made from these nuts. Other nuts, such as pistachios and walnuts, are excluded only because they are now too expensive to serve as major protein sources for the vegetarian.

Milk and Milk Products: in addition to liquid milk this group includes dried milk and all cheese except very fatty cheeses, such as cream cheese.

Eggs: these should be used conservatively until the dietary cholesterol-heart disease controversy is resolved.

Vegetarians Do Not Live By Vegetables Alone

Although all plant foods contain all of the essential amino acids, pulses, nuts, seeds and grains are the best sources of plant protein. Fruit and vegetables are generally not good sources because their total percentage of protein is quite low and their amino acid balance is frequently poor. There are, however, a few notable exceptions, such as potatoes and certain leafy green vegetables, which can constitute acceptable supplementary sources of protein, but they do not contain enough protein to be considered adequate sources by themselves. Vegetables and fruits are, of course, extremely good sources of vitamins and minerals and should be eaten in liberal quantities to satisfy our requirements for these nutrients.

We have done some calculating to illustrate the futility of trying to meet protein requirements by eating vegetables alone. Let's assume that you are the mythical average female between the ages of 19 and 50 and that you weigh 120lb. You need roughly 44g of high quality protein (around 75% usable) per day. If you should try to meet this need with cooked carrots alone, you must take into account that 100g (approx 3½oz) provides less than 1g of protein, and that it is not of high quality. To make up for this, you would need to consume approximately 8kg (17½lb) of carrots a day to obtain your required amount of high quality protein. For most people that would be a feat indeed – not to mention that it might change the colour of your skin!

Contrast this with the amount of protein contained in grains and pulses. The same 120lb woman can obtain her daily requirement of protein from 1.25 small loaves of bread, if the bread is made with 325g (12oz) wholewheat flour per loaf. If she obtained all her protein from cooked chick peas alone, she would need roughly 800g (1lb 12oz). Either approach is much better than eating 8kg (17 lb) of carrots.

These extreme examples illustrate the two major dimensions of our concern with protein intake – the percentage of protein in the food and its amino acid composition. While it is possible to live on foods which contain a very small percentage of protein and a relatively poor amino acid balance, we must consume them in large quantities to make up for these deficiencies.

The Tradition of Complementing

Foods vary widely in the amounts of essential amino acids they contain. Combining two or more foods in one dish, or at a single meal, allows them to complement one another, bringing the amount of each amino acid up to a higher level in relation to the others and results in a higher quality protein. Consequently, the number of protein grams the body can use is greater than when the foods are eaten separately.

Interestingly, most traditional cuisines have evolved some time-tested complementary dishes. Yet these evolved before there was any conceptual framework to hang them on. They were made up of the basic foods available to a large percentage of the population where meat was either in short supply or inequitably distributed. People used their imaginations to combine these foods in appetising ways. In Mexico, the beans with rice and beans with corn (tortillas) combinations occur in a large number of staple dishes and meals. In India, dals (pulses of all types) are served with rice and chapatis, a whole grain bread. In Italy, numerous pasta dishes feature noodles and some type of cheese. Some Middle Eastern combinations are sesame, chick peas and wheat, found in hummus and pitta bread. In Switzerland, cheese fondue with bread is a national favourite. In China and Japan, tofu and other soy products are always eaten with rice.

What To Combine and Why

Animal proteins frequently contain a somewhat better amino acid balance and a higher percentage of protein than plant sources. Liquid foods like milk are an exception because they contain a great deal of water, and therefore a lower percentage of protein than solid foods, such as meat and cheese.

Amino acids in most foods are distributed in such a way that if we concern ourselves with supplying three or four of the essential amino acids, the others will automatically be present. This applies to animal and vegetable proteins alike. Foods may be deficient (low in relation to the egg or other standard) in any of the following amino acids: tryptophan, isoleucine, lysine, and the combination of sulphur-containing amino acids, methionine and cystine.

Fortunately, however, amino acid strengths and weaknesses generally occur in patterns that apply to entire groups or families of foods. Most pulses (beans, peas, lentils and soybeans) are generally deficient in tryptophan and the sulphur-containing amino acids. They are reasonably strong, on the other hand, in isoleucine and exceptionally strong in lysine. Most grains are deficient in isoleucine and lysine, but higher in tryptophan and the sulphur-containing amino acids. Combining the two foods in adequate proportions raises the level of the sulphur-containing amino acids and tryptophan and results in a larger percentage of usable protein by increasing the amounts of the limiting amino acids in the mixture. (See the appendix for a detailed discussion of amino acids.)

The following are some important general principles relating to the complementing of protein foods.

Combinations of Entire Food Families where most members combine interchangeably with other members.
1. Milk or a milk product with or in any dish complements all grains, pulses, seeds, nuts and certain vegetables, such as potatoes. In other words, milk products complement all vegetable proteins.

2. Pulses in dried form, such as all peas, beans, lentils, soybeans and soybean products complement grains such as rice, millet, rye and corn as well as flours and other products made from these grains.

3. Seeds, such as sesame and sunflower seeds, complement pulses.

Combinations of Individual Foods which cannot be extended to other members of the family:

1. Peanuts with sunflower seeds
2. Sesame seeds with rice

Multiple Combinations used less frequently:

1. Peanuts with wheat and milk
2. Soybeans or soybean products with sesame seeds and wheat
3. Soybeans or soybean products with peanuts and sesame seeds
4. Soybeans or soybean products with peanuts and wheat

How Much Protein Is Enough?

As we have indicated, the amount of protein required varies considerably with the quality of the protein consumed. Populations living primarily on an animal protein diet require fewer grams of protein a day than populations consuming a diet of vegetable proteins. If a vegetarian diet is complemented in part by animal protein sources such as milk and milk products, its usable protein equivalent will be close or identical to the animal protein based diet.

An ovo-lacto-vegetarian diet relies to a considerable extent on animal protein sources, such as milk and milk products of all types. We estimate that its protein usability is somewhere in the region of 70-75%, using the egg as a standard.

Like the protein content in a diet, the protein requirements of an individual can be stated in two ways: in terms of usable protein grams per day or total protein grams per day. In our view, the former is much more important in a pure vegetarian diet than in an ovo-lacto-vegetarian diet. Because our diet is so close to the national norm, we prefer to base our calculations on the number of total protein grams as expressed in the Recommended Dietary Allowances issued by the Food and Nutrition Board of the National Research Council (USA).

Since it is nitrogen that makes protein different from other nutrients, estimates of the amount of protein required for maintenance of the healthy adult are based on nitrogen balance studies. If the total amount of nitrogen (protein) consumed is equivalent to the amount eliminated in the faeces and urine and lost through the hair, perspiration etc one is said to be in a state of low nitrogen equilibrium. This means that no new protein tissues are being built, nor is the body forced to deplete muscle tissue to maintain vital organs, as in negative nitrogen balance. Growing children and pregnant women are said to be in a positive nitrogen balance because they retain more nitrogen than they lose. All nitrogen (protein) lost from the body must be replaced or nitrogen equilibrium cannot be maintained. These nitrogen losses are used by the Food and Nutrition Board as a basis for calculating the recommended dietary allowance for protein.

The adult allowance for protein is .8g per kg, or .36g per lb of body weight. This means that the average 154lb man should be consuming about 56g of protein a day, and the average 120lb woman around 44g.

This allowance is intended to keep most healthy individuals in the population in nitrogen balance. It is arrived at by totalling all known protein losses, adding a margin of safety to allow for individual differences, allowing for the reduced usability of protein when consumed at or near requirement levels, and then making adjustments for the protein quality of the typical diet.

Nitrogen balance studies indicate that a man weighing 154lb sustains nitrogen losses roughly equivalent to 24g of protein a day. A woman weighing 120lb loses approximately 19g a day. These losses are equivalent to .34g per kg or .15g per lb of body weight. It cannot be overemphasised, however, that these are averages only, and that the precise amounts vary a great deal from individual to individual. About half of the population loses more nitrogen daily, and half loses less. Since the Food and Nutrition Board is supposed to make recommendations that apply to almost all healthy people in America, these amounts are increased to meet the needs of 97.5% of the population.

One of these increases takes into account the reduced usability of even high quality (egg) protein when intake approaches requirement levels. It is recognised that because of this reduced usability, an amount exceeding the required level is needed to maintain nitrogen balance.

The other increase allows for the protein quality or usability of the American diet. The mixed animal and vegetable protein diet of the United States is assumed to be 75% usable. In a country where plant protein diets are the norm, the usability of the diet is approximately 55%.

It is true that the recommended allowances for protein exceed the needs of most normal individuals, but they are actually not high enough for the 2% of the population with abnormally high needs. Even though it is possible to make statistical generalisations about the population as a whole, it is virtually impossible for a given individual to know what his or her particular needs are. When viewed in this light, the somewhat conservative approach taken by the Food and Nutrition Board makes a great deal of sense.

An individual's need for protein varies throughout the life cycle. During the first year of life an infant triples its body weight. Its increase in body protein is over 3g a day. This growth must be adequately provided for in a diet consisting only of milk. As children become older, less and less protein is needed for growth, and more is used for maintenance.

The protein allowance for pregnant women must be liberal enough to provide adequately for the growing foetus, the placenta and the support tissue, as well as meeting the mother's requirement for maintenance. No wonder it is set so high! During lactation the mother's protein intake must be high enough for maintenance and an adequate supply of milk for the infant, with some allowance for a loss of efficiency during the conversion process. (The table of recommended dietary allowances in the appendix contains detailed information on the protein requirements for infants, children, adolescents and adults.)

Other Nutrients

It is outside the scope of this book to discuss each essential nutrient as it relates to the vegetarian diet. Our concern in this section is to alert the reader to those vitamins and minerals which tend to be inadequately supplied in a vegetarian diet: namely, iron, zinc, calcium and vitamin B-12.

Iron: The recommended allowance for a woman in her child-bearing years is 18mg per day. This is about twice the amount recommended for men, because iron is regularly lost in the menstrual flow. This allowance is inadequately supplied even by the typical Western diet, which is much higher in usable iron than a vegetarian diet. The iron intake of rapidly growing children and adolescents of both sexes may also be inadequate.

Until recently, it has been assumed that approximately 10% of all dietary iron is absorbed. Now that we have more data, we know that we must clearly differentiate between heme iron, a highly absorbable form derived from animal tissues, and nonheme iron, derived from both animals and plants. An estimated 40% of the iron in animal tissues is heme iron, and this is absorbable in amounts ranging from 25 to 35%. Nonheme iron, the only source of iron in a vegetarian diet, is much more plentiful in all diets than heme iron, yet absorption may be as low as 2%. Its absorption in any particular meal is markedly influenced by the following factors:

1. The amount of animal tissue consumed, in

other words, the amount of meat, fish or fowl.

2. The level of vitamin C in the meal. This vitamin has the effect of reducing iron in the ferric state to ferrous iron, a much more absorbable form. Since vitamin C is destroyed by heat, the cooked food itself cannot be relied upon to provide a sufficient amount of this vitamin.

3. The iron status of the individual. The more limited the iron stores of an individual, the larger the fraction of dietary iron absorbed, and vice versa.

Since vegetarians do not have the option of consuming animal tissue, they must rely on other ways of increasing the amount of absorbed iron – for example, eating fresh vitamin C-rich fruits and vegetables at the same meal with iron-rich foods, such as dried beans, peas and lentils. It is assumed that 1mg of vitamin C promotes iron absorption as well as 1g of meat. This means that in terms of its enhancing effect, 100mg of vitamin C should be equivalent to a typical 100g (3½oz) serving of meat. Absorption of iron in a meal containing only nonheme iron and minute amounts of vitamin C is calculated at roughly 3%, whereas the consumption of at least 90 mg of vitamin C increases absorption to approximately 8%.

Another way of increasing the quantity of absorbed iron is to eat liberal amounts of yeast-risen bread. Much of the iron in wheat and other grains is bound up tightly in the form of a chemical substance known as phytate. While the dough is rising, the action of the yeast helps to activate the phytase, an enzyme which breaks this bond, and releases the iron for absorption by the body.

Cooking foods in cast iron pots and pans has also been suggested as a way of increasing iron intake. This practice results in some of the iron being leached out into the food. We only suggest this as a possible option. We do not do it ourselves because we do not like the taste of certain foods cooked in iron pots.

All of the above suggestions will help to bring the amount of absorbed iron to acceptable levels. It should be kept in mind, however, that individuals in groups which are likely to be deficient, such as women in their child-bearing years, should consider an iron supplement as the most reliable way of ensuring an adequate intake.

Zinc: This mineral, which is an essential constituent of the hormone insulin and of enzymes involved in the metabolic process, is in short supply even in a conventional diet. It is extremely scarce in a vegetarian diet. Recommended allowances are high because absorption is low. In vegetable sources absorption is limited because, like iron and calcium, this mineral is bound up in a form of phytate. Yeast-risen breads are a good source. However, to meet the daily adult allowance, a vegetarian would have to eat an uncomfortably large quantity of certain foods (3375g (7½lb) of chick peas, 1.75 loaves of wholewheat bread, 125g (4oz) of wheat germ, 4.2l (8½pt) of milk, etc). Supplementation is desirable.

Calcium: The equivalent of three glasses of milk per day is sufficient to meet the needs of most of the population. In a purely plant-based diet, though, this nutrient may be supplied in inadequate amounts and is inconsistently absorbed. Calcium in plants is frequently bound up in the form of phytate and oxalate, the same compounds that bind together other essential minerals. Phytate is chiefly found in whole grain cereals, while oxalate is found in certain vegetables such as spinach, rhubarb, chard and soybeans. These compounds are thought to form insoluble salts in the intestines and are difficult or impossible to break down under ordinary circumstances. The extent to which these substances make calcium unavailable is still controversial.

Other factors which are thought to decrease calcium absorption and retention are high levels of dietary protein – levels clearly exceeding twice the recommended allowance – and high levels of phosphate. Phosphates occur naturally in some foods, such as bran, wholewheat flour and unpolished rice, or may be introduced in the form of food additives.

It should be emphasised that calcium intake has virtually no effect on blood calcium levels, which remain relatively constant. The body simply withdraws what it needs from storage in the bones if dietary calcium is inadequate and redeposits it when blood levels begin to rise. If calcium is inadequate over a long period of time, these stores become depleted, resulting in porous, brittle bones. The whole system is a bit analogous to withdrawing from your savings account in time of financial crisis and then replenishing your savings when you have more income. Also, when calcium intake is high, less of it is absorbed, and as a result more is excreted in the faeces.

An adequate intake of vitamin D or exposure to sunshine is essential for the absorption of calcium. Other substances which increase absorption are lactose (milk sugar) and certain amino acids, such as lysine. All of these are contained in vitamin D fortified milk, making it the best possible source of this mineral. For the lactose intolerant, fermented milk products such as buttermilk and yogurt, which are low in lactose, may help. Alternatively, lactase (the enzyme that breaks down lactose) may be purchased in tablet form and added to milk.

Vegetable foods which can make a small, but significant contribution toward meeting our daily allowance for calcium are corn tortillas made from corn soaked in calcium hydroxide, those types of tofu precipitated using calcium compounds, and green vegetables like broccoli and kale which do not contain significant amounts of oxalate. Sesame seeds are frequently thought of as a good source of calcium but this calcium, unfortunately, is largely unavailable because most of it is bound up in the form of calcium oxalate in the outer husk of the seed. Calcium fortified soy milk is the best and most reliable source of this mineral for the pure vegetarian.

Vitamin B-12: This vitamin is found almost exclusively in foods of animal origin. As far as we know there are only two significant vegetable sources. Large amounts are found in tempeh, a fermented soybean cake common in Indonesia and increasingly available in the United States. A typical serving may contain more than the recommended allowance. Other soy foods containing this vitamin are miso, natto and naturally fermented soy sauce.

A mixed vegetable and animal protein diet such as ours is adequate in this nutrient. Our major sources are eggs, milk and cheese. Pure vegetarians must take care to eat generous amounts of the fermented soy foods mentioned above, or make liberal use of vitamin B-12 fortified soy milk. The only alternative is supplementation in moderate amounts.

How To Achieve a Balanced Diet Using This Book

Now that we have discussed requirements for protein and other critical nutrients, you may want to use the table of recommended allowances in the appendix to locate requirements for the major nutrients for your sex and age group. Adhering to the guidelines for a balanced diet outlined below should ensure an adequate intake of protein as well as vitamins and minerals.

People sometimes exceed calorific requirements because they equate individual foods with single nutrients. An awareness that most foods are rich in several key nutrients will help to keep calorific intakes within reasonable limits. For example, most dark green leafy vegetables are not only good sources of vitamin A, but also contain substantial amounts of vitamin C, riboflavin, folacin, potassium and other minerals. Milk, in addition to being an excellent source of calcium and protein, is a good source of vitamin B-12, vitamin A, riboflavin, phosphorous and zinc.

Major Protein Sources: Always include a major protein source and its complement at each meal. For the purposes of this book, a major protein source is defined as any single food, dish or combination of foods containing approximately 10g of protein per serving. It can consist of pulses, grains, nuts, seeds, eggs or milk or milk products. Because pulses are such excellent sources of major nutrients besides protein, try to include them in your diet as often as possible. They are excellent sources of thiamin, niacin, folacin, phosphorous, potassium and magnesium and are good sources of zinc.

The major protein source will usually be in the form of a main dish and will generally include its own complement. If a dish does not contain a complement, follow the serving suggestions in the recipe or check the list of combinations provided earlier in this chapter.

Each recipe containing a substantial amount of protein provides information on the total number of protein grams per serving. Our main dishes, by definition, have at least 10 protein grams per serving. Each recipe has symbols representing the groups or families of protein sources that are complementary. For example, our Bean and Raisin Enchiladas contain 16g of protein per serving, consisting of the following complementary protein combinations, corn plus beans, beans plus cheese.

Milk and Milk Products: Include a 250ml (10 fl oz) glass of milk or its equivalent three times a day, preferably at meals. Equivalents are: 25-40g (1-1½oz) cheese, 275g (10oz) cottage cheese, yogurt, buttermilk or calcium fortified soy milk. Concentrate on skimmed milk, non-fat dried milk, buttermilk, low fat yogurt, and the less fatty cheeses such as cottage cheese, mozzarella, Parmesan and Swiss cheeses. Avoid cream, cream cheese, soured cream and other very fatty dairy products.

If you have milk or cheese with or in your meal you are accomplishing two things at once – providing a complement for any of the major families of vegetable proteins and contributing toward meeting your daily allowance of calcium and other nutrients. It is a fiction that adults do not need milk. They certainly can do without the fat contained in whole milk, but they do need the calcium! That is why we suggest using skimmed milk and low fat milk products whenever possible.

Major Nutrients Supplied:
protein
vitamins: vitamin A, riboflavin (vitamin B-2),
                   vitamin B-12 (cobalamin),
                   vitamin D
minerals: calcium, phosphorous, zinc

Whole Grain Cereals: Include a whole grain cereal at each meal, preferably a whole grain, yeast-risen bread. Yeast-risen breads are an important staple in any vegetarian diet because the action of the yeast helps make iron and other minerals more readily available to the body.

The whole grain cereal may be in the main dish or served as a complement to the main dish. If you are serving a whole grain pasta dish complemented with plenty of Parmesan cheese, you have provided for your major protein source and its complement, have contributed toward meeting your calcium requirement and have provided for a whole grain cereal product at the same time. If you desire, you may serve a yeast-risen bread with this meal, but it is not essential if you have already had several servings of yeast-risen bread that day.

Major Nutrients Supplied:
protein
vitamins: thiamin (vitamin B-1), niacin
                   (vitamin B-3), vitamin B-6
                   (pyridoxine), folacin (folic acid),
                   vitamin E
minerals: iron, magnesium, zinc,
                   phosphorous (all more available in
                   yeast-risen breads).

Vegetables: Include at least one serving of a leafy green or dark yellow vegetable per day. The general rule is the darker the better. This includes carrots, spinach, kale, some squash, sweet potatoes, turnip greens, chard and other dark salad greens. When fresh papayas (paw-paw), mangoes and cantaloupe melons are available, they may be substituted for the above vegetables. Include one or more servings of other types of vegetables, such as green beans, fresh peas, celery, cabbage, corn, alfalfa or mung bean sprouts, courgettes, tomatoes, broccoli and sweet peppers. We serve at least one salad a day, preferably as an accompaniment to our evening meal. Good, fresh spinach is available so rarely in the markets that when we find some, we almost invariably use it in a fresh green salad. Use iceberg lettuce as little as possible. Other salad vegetables have much more to offer nutritionally.

Major Nutrients Supplied:
vitamins: vitamin A (leafy green and dark
                 yellow vegetables only), riboflavin
                 (vitamin B-2), vitamin B-6
                 (pyridoxine), folacin (folic acid)
                 thiamin (vitamin B-1), vitamin C
                 (raw or carefully cooked
                 vegetables only)
minerals: potassium, iron and calcium (the
                 latter two being largely unavailable
                 to the body)

Fruit: Include three or more servings of fresh fruit per day, preferably with meals. If possible, try to include at least one generous serving of citrus fruit or juice, papaya or guava when available. Berries and melons, such as watermelons, cantaloupes and honeydew melons also count as fruit.

Major Nutrients Supplied:
vitamins: vitamin C, folacin (folic acid)
minerals: potassium

Following these suggestions means nothing more than applying the basic principles of a good diet to foods usually consumed by vegetarians. Basically, all we are suggesting is that you have an adequate amount of protein at each meal, that you try to complement this protein, that you serve plenty of whole grain foods, a sufficient amount of milk, and lots of fresh fruits and vegetables.

Note: As the recipes contained in this book are converted from the American system of measuring, the protein calculations must be regarded as a very rough guide only, as calculations may have been affected by the measurement conversion.

Symbols For Major Protein Sources

Milk, cheese, and yogurt

Whole grain cereals and cereal products, such as wheat, rye, triticale, oats, barley, millet, rice, buckwheat, and corn

Dried beans, peas, lentils, soybeans, and soybean products, such as tofu

Sesame and sunflower seeds

Nuts, chiefly cashews and peanuts, but also almonds and walnuts

Potatoes

Eggs

Major Complementary Combinations

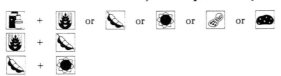

Because eggs are viewed by many nutritionists as the ideal protein, they are not considered as complementary in this book. Technically, they stand by themselves. Nevertheless, they do enhance the quality of all vegetable proteins eaten at the same meal.

Protein Calculations

The designation Protein g/s stands for protein grams per serving. Protein calculations are approximate and are for total rather than usable protein grams. They were arrived at using values obtained from *Food Values of Portions Commonly Used* by C. F. Church and H. N. Church and *Laurel's Kitchen: A Handbook For Vegetarian Cookery and Nutrition* by Laurel Robertson and others. A few values not contained in these sources were obtained from the producers. Most vegetables were not included in the calculations because their contributions to the protein content of a dish was considered insignificant. We made an exception in the case of fresh peas, fresh corn, and potatoes.

Keeping a Vegetarian Kitchen

In our grandmother's time it was common for women to spend a good part of the day preparing and cooking food. Today, either out of economic necessity or a desire to pursue a career, many women work outside the home. They have less time to devote to meal preparation and have become dependent on the 'instant' foods which predominate in our supermarkets.

A generation or two of women are convinced that cooking from 'scratch' is an impossible undertaking unless you have the greater part of the day to devote to it. We hope that in this chapter and throughout the entire book we help to dispel this myth. What we want to convey is that you and your family can be properly nourished without your spending an entire day in the kitchen. All that is required is some time-saving equipment, a kitchen well-stocked with staple foods and a certain amount of advance planning and preparation.

Equipment

After food processors, which are discussed in the introduction, pressure cookers are the most valuable kitchen technology you can buy. They can save considerable time and electricity, particularly in the preparation of beans and soups. For example, most beans can be cooked in 10-15 minutes at 15lb pressure, if pre-soaked overnight. Contrast this with 1-2 hours of cooking in a saucepan! Although some cookers can be set at 5, 10 or 15lb of pressure, there seems to be little point in using the lower pressures when the highest pressure setting will cook food more quickly and just as safely.

Manufacturers of some pressure cookers do not recommend their use for split peas or lentils because these pulses have a tendency to froth and clog the vent. Directions for others indicate that you may cook split peas or lentils provided that you fill the cooker no more than half full. Carefully follow the instructions for your particular make.

Pressure cookers come in a wide range of sizes. Because we cook large quantities of beans ahead of time for freezing, we prefer the 6-8l (12-16pt) size. We have learnt from past experience that it is a good idea to keep extra rubber gaskets and safety valves on hand in case these parts deteriorate.

Another important piece of kitchen equipment is a set of scales. In recipes for the food processor, ingredients to be processed are frequently weighed instead of measured. Our preference is for a scale that measures both ounces and grams and has a bowl large enough for weighing dry ingredients such as beans. When following these recipes adhere to either the metric or imperial measurements – do not mix measures within a recipe.

Staple Foods to Have on Hand

Beans, Peas and Lentils: Pinto beans, kidney beans, black beans, chick peas, lentils, yellow split peas, and mung beans for sprouting if you sprout your own.

Shopping Hints: Obviously dry beans are preferable to the canned type. The latter are generally considered more convenient, but you can achieve a similar degree of convenience at considerably less expense by cooking large quantities in your pressure cooker and freezing them for later use. Most beans, peas and lentils can be purchased at a wholefood shop or at the supermarket.

Storage: Store in tightly covered glass jars, preferably on the worktop, where you can see when your supply needs replenishing. Most pulses will keep for at least a year when stored in this manner.

Tofu: If you observed that soybeans were conspicuously absent from the above list, it's because we are not really fond of them. We prefer to use tofu instead.

Shopping Hints: The traditional Japanese style tofu is the most widely available in the UK, and is generally found in wholefood and health food shops. Long-life and fresh are sold, the fresh having the better flavour.

Storage: Remove the tofu from its packaging and place it in a bowl of fresh water. Cover and store in the refrigerator. It will stay fresh for a week if the water is changed daily. A sour taste indicates that it is past its prime.

Grains, Flours and Flour Products: Wholewheat flour, buckwheat flour, rye flour, soy flour, bulgur or cracked wheat, millet, brown rice, bran, wheat germ, non-instant rolled oats and an assortment of wholewheat pastas to use when you do not have time to make your own.

Shopping hints: Purchase your flour from a source which has a rapid turnover. We are not convinced that all the nutritional claims made for stoneground wholewheat flours are true. Their coarseness alone does not make them more wholesome. The process of stone grinding produces lower temperatures than standard milling of flour and may therefore better preserve a few of the vitamins which are affected by heat.

However, these gains are miniscule, considering that no one eats flour in the raw state. A loaf of bread must be baked and during baking it will be exposed to much higher temperatures for a much longer time than during milling. Besides, a finely ground 100% extraction flour can be used for all baking and cooking, whereas the coarser 100% extraction stoneground flours are used chiefly in yeast-risen breads. What is more,

they tend to cost more than the standard wholewheat flours. When shopping for rye flour, keep in mind that both light and medium rye flours are less desirable than dark rye flour, which is much higher in protein and other nutrients.

Storage: Whole grain flours should never be stored in the kitchen cupboards unless used almost immediately. Either freeze or refrigerate them or their natural oils will quickly become rancid. Remember to allow time to bring them to room temperature before using them in yeast-risen doughs. Wheat germ and grains which have been cracked must likewise be kept under refrigeration. Bran, rice and millet may be stored for longer periods of time in tightly sealed glass jars at room temperature. Wholewheat pastas should not be stored at room temperature for longer than a few days. Home made pastas may either be frozen or dried and refrigerated.

Seeds: Sunflower seeds, sesame seeds and alfalfa seeds, if you do your own sprouting.

Shopping Hints: Our recipes call for hulled sunflower and sesame seeds, both of which are available through health food shops and some larger supermarkets. We use the hulled sesame seeds because they are more digestible than the unhulled type. The hulled seeds are white and shiny in contrast to the pale-brown colour of the unhulled variety. Make sure that any seeds you buy for sprouting are intended specifically for that purpose. Some of the seeds intended for planting are treated with harmful chemicals.

Storage: Store sunflower seeds and sesame seeds in the refrigerator or freezer unless they will be used almost immediately. Store alfalfa and other seeds for sprouting in an airtight jar in a cool, dry place.

Nuts: Peanuts, cashew nuts and some walnuts for baking.

Shopping Hints: Purchase raw nuts in bulk and roast them yourself in the oven at gas mark 3/160°C/325°F for roughly 35-45 minutes.

Watch carefully so they do not become overdone. Peanuts with the skins on make very good peanut butter.
Storage: Refrigerate or freeze unless they will be used almost immediately.

Milk and Cheese: Dried skimmed milk, cottage cheese or curd cheese, and a selection of your preferred cured cheeses, such as natural white Cheddar, mozzarella and Swiss cheeses. Also skimmed milk, 2% milk or buttermilk for cooking and drinking.
Shopping Hints: Dried skimmed milk is generally available at supermarkets and most food shops. It is easily blended to a smooth consistency in the food processor. Insert the metal blade, place the dry milk in the work bowl and turn the machine on. Then slowly add the water. The yellow-orange cheeses are to be avoided for obvious reasons: they contain artificial colouring, but that is generally not indicated on the label.
Storage: All milk and milk products should be refrigerated. Even dry milk will deteriorate in several weeks' time after the container is opened. It is best kept in a tightly sealed container in the refrigerator.

Eggs:
Shopping Hints: Buy eggs as fresh as possible, preferably locally produced.
Storage: Refrigerate immediately. Eggs will keep in the refrigerator for approximately three weeks. They are less likely to absorb refrigerator odours if stored in the original carton.
Note: Grains, nuts, seeds and eggs do not require storage in the refrigerator in the UK except in exceptionally hot summers.

Sweeteners and Dried Fruit: Honey, brown sugar, molasses, 100% maple syrup and raisins.
Shopping Hints: Our preference is for honey and brown sugar, although excess sugar in any form is undesirable and this unfortunately includes sweeteners such as honey. This is probably a good time to mention the differences between sugars. Nutritionally there is little difference between white and brown sugar. The latter is only refined sugar with a little molasses added for colour. So-called raw sugar is actually partly refined sugar. Real raw sugar is seldom available. All honey is 'natural' so a word like 'natural' on the label tells you nothing. There is no law defining 'natural'. Buy unstrained, uncooked honey and do not worry if it has crystallised. It can be liquified again by placing the opened jar in a pan of simmering water and heating it until the crystals dissolve.
Storage: Honey may be stored for up to 18 months in your kitchen cabinet, molasses for two years and all types of sugar for several years if you use glass containers. We refrigerate our maple syrup because we have had problems with mildew forming on the top. Raisins will keep for approximately six months at room temperature in a sealed jar.

Oils and Fats: A good quality vegetable oil, high in polyunsaturated fat, such as safflower or soy oil and safflower margarine or butter.
Shopping Hints: In order to understand the difference between vegetable oils, it is necessary to know how they are produced. Oil is either pressed out of the seeds or beans, or extracted by use of a petroleum solvent. Oils which are pressed are expeller pressed, which means that the seeds are cut into small flakes or pieces and pressed at high pressures to extract the oil. Oils labelled 'cold-pressed' are actually pressed at temperatures ranging from 120°F-150°F. These are nutritionally superior to 'hot-pressed' oils, which are pressed the same way, but at much higher temperatures. Oils which are solvent extracted undergo the greatest losses of vitamin E.

After the oil is extracted from the seeds, it may or may not be refined. If it remains unrefined, it is simply filtered and bottled. If it is refined, it may undergo up to five additional processes. In one of these, most of the vitamin E in the oil is removed for use in vitamin supplements. Many natural oils which are totally unrefined may be rich in vitamin E, but they are difficult or impossible to cook with because they have such strong flavours of their own. We have tried making mayonnaise from unrefined sesame and safflower oils. It had to be discarded because it had too strong a taste. It is a trade-off. The less refined the oil, the more nutritious it is but the less people are willing to eat it.

Do not purchase cottonseed oils. These may have higher than normal pesticide residues, because cotton is sprayed rather freely.

The best olive oils are labelled 'virgin olive oil'. The lesser quality olive oils, which bear the designation 'pure olive oil', are pressed or solvent extracted from the pulp that remains after the 'virgin olive oil' is made.

The best butter is made from sweet cream. Commercially sold butter is often coloured with artificial or natural colouring, yet this information never appears on the label. Therefore, you might consider making your own, especially if you can get double cream directly from a local dairy at a reasonable price. Butter is easily made by whipping the cream in your food processor or mixer until the fat separates. Pour off the fresh buttermilk and carefully rinse the butter with cold water. Compress it into small pats and keep frozen until required.

Buy margarine made from polyunsaturated oil with the name of the oil listed first on the label. It should be coloured only with beta carotene, a precursor of vitamin A, and should be free of artificial flavours and preservatives.

Storage: Refrigerate all oils and fats. You may freeze butter and margarine for long-term storage. Even though olive oil does not become rancid as rapidly as other oils, it should be refrigerated because it is usually purchased in large containers and is used up more slowly. It will become semi-solid under refrigeration. Simply bring it to room temperature before using.

Vegetables: Several packets of frozen spinach, a green pepper or two, canned tomato sauce and paste and canned tomatoes. Also useful are lots of onions, including salad onions, potatoes, carrots, celery, lettuce and tomatoes.

Shopping Hints: Canned tomato products are best purchased in large quantities at the supermarket when they are on special offer. We shop for most of our vegetables at the local supermarket. We do appreciate the superior taste of home grown organic produce, yet under the present circumstances, the consumer who does not have a garden of his own has no guarantee that he is actually getting what he is paying for. Because there is no legal definition of 'organic', almost anything can be labelled 'organic' by an unscrupulous manufacturer or dealer. Since there are no assurances about growing conditions or pesticide residues, we prefer to spend less and buy conventional produce – at the same time wishing that it tasted as good as home-grown vegetables.

Storage: Celery can be kept for two weeks, and carrots for several weeks sealed in a plastic bag in the salad drawer of your refrigerator. Potatoes will keep for two or three months in the salad drawer unwrapped. Green peppers, tomatoes and lettuce will keep approximately ten days sealed in an airtight container in the bottom of the refrigerator. Salad onions stored in this manner will keep for up to a week.

Seasonings: In addition to the standard items like salt and pepper, you will need a good assortment of dried herbs and spices. Grow some of your own herbs, if possible, even if it is only on your window sill. Other useful items to have on hand are vegetable stock cubes, Dijon mustard, plenty of fresh garlic, red wine vinegar and malt vinegar.

Shopping Hints: Chemical analysis has revealed that sea salt is not nutritionally superior to plain iodised salt. Use it if you prefer the taste. Because the sodium content of the Western diet is high many people are making a conscious effort to cut down on their salt intake. Products to be used like ordinary salt but containing approximately half the sodium chloride are now widely available. The balance of the product is potassium chloride. Even these products should be used sparingly.

Storage: Certain vegetable stock cubes keep better when refrigerated – check the label. Dijon mustard should be refrigerated after opening. Garlic keeps well at room temperature, if air is allowed to circulate freely around it. Vinegars and dried herbs should be sealed tightly in glass jars. Spices are best when used freshly ground.

The staples discussed above are basic items to have on hand regardless of the type of cooking you do. Those listed below are commonly used foods you will need to prepare the many ethnic recipes in our book. The more perishable items are listed last.

Italian dishes: Basic Marinara Sauce (see index) from your freezer, frozen spinach, olive oil, Parmesan or Romano cheese, mozzarella cheese, ricotta, curd or cottage cheese, basil (fresh if possible).

Greek and Middle Eastern dishes: Cooked chick peas from the freezer, canned ripe olives, olive oil, lemons, feta cheese, aubergines.

Mexican dishes: Cooked pinto beans from your freezer, canned mild green chillis, canned black olives, an assortment of mild dried red chillis, chilli powder, ground cumin, tortillas, natural Cheddar cheese, avocados.

Japanese and Chinese dishes: Long grain brown rice, soy sauce, oriental sesame seed oil, fresh ginger, fresh mung bean sprouts, salad onions, tofu.

Indian dishes: A variety of dals (eg split peas, lentils, chick peas and other beans), long grain brown rice, ground turmeric, ground coriander, ground cumin, ground cardamom, fresh ginger. If you cook a lot of Indian food it may be useful for you to invest in a small electric grinder so that you can roast and grind your own spices for garam masala from whole seeds. This is much more flavourful than using commercially ground spices.

Advance Planning and Preparation

Cooking Ahead

The key to efficient and time-saving vegetarian meals is cooking large quantities of staple items from scratch and always having them on hand in your freezer. We have found the weekend best for this. Always cook two or three times the basic ingredients you need for a meal and freeze the rest or save some in the refrigerator to prepare a different dish two or three days later. Here are some general suggestions on how you can best use this book to organise your cooking more efficiently.

1. Bread can be made any time you spend three continuous hours at home. Bake all of your bread for the week at once, freeze all but one loaf, and remove what you need from the freezer during the week. This is much more energy-efficient than baking several times, because the oven is heated only once.
2. Pasta may be made ahead at the weekends. It may be frozen or dried and refrigerated in a plastic bag. If frozen, it should be put into boiling water for cooking without defrosting.
3. Our Basic Marinara Sauce makes approximately 3.5l (7pt) of sauce. If you make the full recipe as suggested you should have enough for the following dishes: Lasagne or Aubergine Lasagne, Oven or Lentil Spaghetti, Wholewheat Ravioli and Pizza. Freeze the sauce in amounts you are most likely to use at one time, for example 375ml (15fl oz) for pizza, 750ml (1½pt) for lasagne, etc. Just one quantity of this sauce will last you approximately five weeks if you serve one Italian dish per week.
4. Many of our recipes specify cooked beans

or lentils. We cook ours with vegetable stock cubes for better flavour. Never prepare beans or lentils without preparing at least two or three times the amount you need for a particular recipe. For example, if you are cooking chick peas for hummus, you will need only 200g (7oz) dry, or 325g (12oz) cooked peas. Consider boiling at least 900g (2lb) extra dry chick peas to give 1800g (4lb) extra cooked so you have them on hand for making the following dishes over a month or two: Arabic Moussaka, Curried Chick Peas, and Greek Chef's Salad. The same approach can be used with pinto beans. If you are making Bean and Raisin Enchiladas, consider cooking additional beans for our Mexican Chef's Salad and Vegetarian Tacos. Always check the major ingredient index to see what else you can do with a staple ingredient and then cook the amount you may need for a month or two.

5. Our recipe for Enchilada Sauce makes enough for four or five batches of enchiladas. Freeze it in containers of 375ml (15fl oz). It can be used in the preparation of the following dishes: Bean and Raisin Enchiladas, Fresh Corn Enchiladas and Enchiladas Coloradas.

6. When making crêpes, consider making your crêpe batter the night before and letting it stand in the refrigerator until ready to use. This will save you an hour of 'standing time' just before dinner.

7. Always prepare twice as much rice as you think you can use in one meal. Refrigerate it and use it within four or five days to make the following: Chinese Style Fried Rice and Moussaka.

8. Prepare salad dressing ahead of time. Vinegar and oil dressings are much better if allowed to stand for a day or two before using. They may be refrigerated for several weeks. Milk, egg or cheese based dressings will keep for up to four or five days.

Planning Your Menus

Give careful consideration to the rules for a balanced diet outlined in the chapter on the 'Basics of Vegetarian Nutrition' when planning your weekly menu. Be realistic and also consider the time you have available for cooking. When you are especially short on time, consider the following possibilities:

1. Serve a quickly prepared, stir fried tofu dish at least once a week.

2. Prepare a chef's salad or a quickly prepared main dish salad once or twice a week – any salad that has approximately 10g of protein per serving.

3. Cook quantities of main dishes at the weekends, and serve the left-overs once or twice a week.

4. Check our main dish recipes, make a note of those that are particularly fast to prepare and develop a repertoire of those your family likes.

Shopping

If you do most of your shopping at a supermarket, look for the special offers and then plan your menus for the week using the major ingredient index at the back of the book. If you prefer to shop locally then plan your menus around seasonal ingredients. Allow yourself enough flexibility to take advantage of especially good buys that you discover while you are shopping. Keep a continuous list of basic ingredients you are low on, so you know what items need replenishing when on special offer. We use small note cards attached to the refrigerator door with a magnet.

We hope that you will use the above short-cuts and advice for keeping a vegetarian kitchen and in due time develop some of your own. In this chapter we have tried to show that you can prepare nutritious and appetising meals without spending an undue amount of time in the kitchen. If you have found that what we have said is new to you, we suggest that you go about following our suggestions gradually.

Appetisers

Carrot Filled Courgettes

Makes 30 appetisers

Make these early in the day and refrigerate until serving time.

6-7 thin courgettes, approx 20cm (8in) long
10 medium carrots, about 675g (1½lb), peeled
3×15ml (tbsp) butter or margarine
3×15ml (tbsp) peanut butter

Place the whole courgettes in a pan of boiling water and simmer for 8 min. Refresh in cold water and drain well in a colander.

SLICING DISC: Cut the carrots to fit the feed tube vertically; stack and slice. Steam the carrot slices until just cooked, approx 17–20 min.

METAL BLADE: Place the steamed carrots, butter and peanut butter in the processor bowl. Process until smooth.

TO FINISH: Cut the courgettes into 4cm (1½in) lengths. Using a small knife, remove the pulp and reserve for another use. Place the courgette lengths, cut side down, on paper towels to drain. Fill with puréed carrot mixture. Serve warm or refrigerate for several hours to chill.

Preparation: 15 minutes
Cooking: 20–25 minutes

Aubergine Dip

This Middle Eastern salad is a good dip to serve with raw vegetables, taco chips or wedges of pitta or chapati bread.

1-2 aubergines, approx 675g (1½lb)
4-5×15ml (tbsp) tahini paste (creamed sesame)
3 large cloves garlic
salt
juice of 1 lemon
3 sprigs parsley
1 tomato

Preheat the oven to gas mark 6/200°C/400°F.

Line a baking tin with foil and oil it lightly. Prick the aubergines then place them in the tin and bake for 30–40 mins until very soft. Cool slightly then peel off the skin and chop the pulp into 5cm (2in) pieces.

METAL BLADE: Place the garlic in the processor bowl and pulse on/off until finely chopped. Add the aubergine pulp and process until smooth. Add the tahini, lemon juice and salt to taste. Process until well blended.

Pour the dip into a small bowl and garnish with parsley. Arrange the tomato, cut into wedges, around the edge of the bowl.

Preparation: 10 minutes
Baking: 30-40 min for aubergine

Mushroom and Broccoli Tartlets

Makes 18

Make these bite-size tartlets a day in advance and refrigerate. Bake uncovered in a preheated oven at gas mark 4/180°C/350°F for approximately 10 min to reheat.

Pastry

225g (8oz) wholewheat flour
50g (2oz) Parmesan cheese, at room temperature, in 2.5cm (1in) cubes
75g (3oz) butter or margarine, cut into 2.5cm (1in) pieces
1 egg
2-3×15ml (tbsp) iced water

METAL BLADE: Place the Parmesan in the processor bowl and process until finely grated. Add the flour and pulse on/off to mix. Add the butter and pulse on/off until the mixture resembles breadcrumbs. With the machine running, add the egg and enough iced water through the feed tube to form a ball. Stop the machine as soon as the ball forms. Wrap the pastry and refrigerate whilst preparing the filling.

Filling

2 salad onions, cut into 2.5cm (1in) lengths
125g (4oz) fresh mushrooms
225g (8oz) broccoli, trimmed, cut into 2.5cm (1in) pieces
2×15ml (tbsp) oil
1×5ml (tsp) dried thyme
1×15ml (tbsp) lemon juice
salt
125g (4oz) Gruyere cheese
2×15ml (tbsp) oil

METAL BLADE: Place the onions in the processing bowl and chop. Add the mushrooms and pulse on/off so the mushrooms are coarsely chopped.

Heat 2×15ml (tbsp) oil in a large pan, add the onion and mushroom mixture and cook quickly for 2 mins.

METAL BLADE: Add the broccoli to the processor bowl and pulse on/off until finely chopped. Add the broccoli, thyme, lemon juice and salt to the mushrooms and mix well. Cover and cook over a low heat until the broccoli is tender and the liquid has evaporated, about 10–15 mins. Stir occasionally to prevent sticking. Remove the pan from the heat and set aside.

SHREDDING DISC: Cut the cheese to fit the feed tube and grate, using light pressure.

Roll out the pastry and use to line 18 deep patty tins. Divide the mushroom and broccoli filling between the tartlets. Top each with a little of the cheese.

Preheat the oven to gas mark 6/200°C/400°F.

Custard

4 eggs
200ml (8fl oz) milk plus
50ml (2fl oz) dry white wine or vermouth OR
250ml (10fl oz) milk
pinch ground nutmeg
salt and pepper

METAL BLADE: Place the eggs in the processor
bowl; With the machine running add the
liquids and seasonings. Process until well
blended. Carefully spoon the custard into the
tartlets.

Place the tartlets in the oven and reduce the
heat to gas mark 5/190°C/375°F. Bake for 25–30
mins until the custard is set and the tops are
lightly browned and risen.

Cool in the tins for 10 mins. Serve warm or
remove to a wire rack to cool completely.

Preparation: 30 minutes
Baking: 25 minutes
Standing: 10 minutes
Protein g/s: 6.5

Cucumber Dip

Serves 10

Served with a variety of raw vegetables or
pitta wedges, this dip will be welcomed at any
party.

1 clove garlic
2 large cucumbers, peeled
500ml (1pt) thick yogurt
salt and pepper

METAL BLADE: Place the garlic in the processing
bowl and pulse on/off until chopped. Remove
to a mixing bowl and add the yogurt with
some salt and pepper.

SHREDDING DISC: Cut the cucumbers to fit the
feed tube vertically. Shred. Place half the
cucumber in a clean teatowel and squeeze to
remove as much moisture as possible. Repeat

with the remaining cucumber. Add to the
yogurt and stir gently to mix. Cover and
refrigerate for 1 hour.

Preparation: 10 minutes
Chilling: 1 hour
Protein g/s: 1.5

Parmesan Herb Dip

Serves 8

Serve with cauliflower florets, green pepper
strips, courgette strips or tiny tomatoes.

50g (2oz) Parmesan cheese at room
temperature
2 large cloves garlic
25g (1oz) parsley
1×5ml (tsp) dried basil
salt and freshly ground black pepper
2 eggs
3×15ml (tbsp) lemon juice
250ml (10fl oz) sunflower oil

METAL BLADE: Cut the Parmesan into 2.5cm
(1in) cubes and place in the processor bowl.
Process until finely grated. Add the garlic,
parsley, basil, salt and pepper. Pulse on/off
until the garlic and parsley are finely chopped.

Add the eggs, lemon juice and 1×15ml
(tbsp) of oil. Process for 30 secs. With the
machine running, add the remaining oil very
slowly through the feed tube until you can see
that the mixture has thickened. Remaining oil
can be added a little faster. This process is
similar to making mayonnaise. Process until
the dip is thick. Check the seasoning and place
in a serving bowl. Cover and chill for 1 hour.

Preparation time: 10 minutes
Chilling: 1 hour
Protein g/s: 4

Guacamole

Serves 4-6

Served on a bed of shredded lettuce and garnished with crisp corn tortillas or taco chips, this tasty dish makes an excellent salad.

2 large very ripe avocados, weighing approx 675g (1½lb)
2-3 salad onions, cut into 5cm (2in) lengths
½ green pepper, cut into small pieces
1 small tomato, quartered
3×15ml (tbsp) fresh lemon juice
pinch cayenne pepper
salt and freshly ground black pepper
2×15ml (tbsp) Vinaigrette Herb Dressing (see index) or similar vinaigrette

Scoop the avocado flesh from the skins using a spoon. The skins may be used for serving the guacamole.

METAL BLADE: Place the onions, pepper, tomato, avocado, lemon juice, salt, cayenne pepper and dressing in the processor bowl. Pulse on/off until the ingredients are finely chopped – do not process to a purée. Serve.

Preparation: 10 mins

Soups

Black Bean Soup

Serves 8

A generous serving of whole grain bread makes this a hearty main dish. It is especially attractive when garnished with a spoonful of yogurt surrounded by lemon slices.

450g (1lb) dried black beans, rinsed
2l (4pt) water
2 large onions
1 lemon, cut into 8 wedges
2 vegetable stock cubes
2-3×15ml (tbsp) olive oil
8 cloves
1×15ml (tbsp) Worcestershire sauce
1/2×5ml (tsp) nutmeg
pinch ground allspice
salt and freshly ground pepper
1×15ml (tbsp) + 1×5ml (tsp) molasses
500ml (1pt) water
1×5ml (tsp) distilled malt vinegar
50ml (2fl oz) dry sherry (optional)
yogurt
sprigs of parsley
lemon slices

Soak beans in 2l (4pt) water at room temperature overnight.

METAL BLADE: Place the onions, cut into 2cm (1in) pieces, in the processor bowl. Pulse on/off until finely chopped.

In a large pan or pressure cooker heat the oil. Add the onions and cook until soft and transparent. Add the beans, soaking water, lemon wedges, stock cubes, cloves, Worcestershire sauce, nutmeg, allspice, salt, pepper, molasses and additional 500ml (1pt) water to the pan.

Simmer for approximately 2 hours until the beans are tender. Alternatively, cook the beans at 15lb pressure for 10–15 minutes then allow the pressure to reduce slowly. When the beans are cooked, remove the lemon wedges then drain the beans, reserving the liquid.

METAL BLADE: Place the parsley in the processing bowl and pulse on/off until finely chopped. Remove from the bowl and set aside. Place half the beans in the bowl and process until puréed. Return to the pan with the reserved liquid. Process the remaining beans. Stir in the vinegar and sherry. Add to the pan and reheat as necessary.

Serve in bowls, garnished with yogurt and 2 lemon slices and sprinkled with parsley.

Preparation: 15 minutes
Cooking: 20-40 minutes pressure cooking
          2 hours on the hob
Protein g/s: 14

Minestrone

Serves 10-14

This recipe makes sufficient for 10–14 servings so you will require a very large pan. We like to serve this soup with whole grain bread and herb butter. This soup freezes well, making it an ideal make-ahead meal.

450g (1lb) dried kidney beans
5.5l (12pt) water (in total)
3 vegetable stock cubes
2-4×5ml (tsp) vegetable soup seasoning (optional)
salt, to taste
2 large onions
3 medium leeks
2-3×15ml (tbsp) oil
2-3 large carrots, peeled
2 large stalks celery, trimmed
2-3 large potatoes, peeled
225g (8oz) green beans, cut into 1cm (½in) lengths
50g (2oz) wholewheat macaroni, uncooked
½ small head of cabbage
4 small courgettes, washed
2-3 large cloves garlic
2×15ml (tbsp) freshly chopped basil or 2×5ml (tsp) dried
½×5ml (tsp) dried oregano
1×400g (14oz) can whole tomatoes
large bunch parsley
salt and pepper to taste
grated Parmesan cheese, 2×15ml (tbsp) per serving

Soak the beans in 2l (4pt) water at room temperature overnight. Combine beans, soaking water, 2l (4pt) additional water, stock cubes, soup seasoning (if used) and salt and simmer in a large pan until the beans are tender, for approximately 2 hours. Alternately pressure cook the beans at 15lb pressure for 15 mins, allowing pressure to reduce gradually at the end of the cooking time.

Wash the leeks thoroughly to remove all grit. Discard the tough upper portion of the tops.

METAL BLADE: Place the onions and leeks, cut into 2.5cm (1in) pieces, in the processor bowl and pulse on/off until chopped fairly finely.

Heat the oil in a very large pan, add the onions and leeks and cook until soft, approx 3–4 mins.

SLICING DISC: Cut the carrots in half lengthways then into lengths to fit the feed tube vertically; slice. Cut the celery to fit the feed tube vertically; slice. Add to the pan with the onions. Cook for 5 minutes. Stir the onion mixture into the beans with the remaining water. Simmer for 10 minutes. Quarter the potatoes and cut into lengths to fit the feed tube vertically; slice. Cook the potatoes and the green beans in a pan until just softened then add to the main pan with the macaroni. Cut the cabbage and courgettes to fit the feed tube vertically, slice and add to the pot. Wipe the processing bowl dry.

METAL BLADE: Place the garlic in the processing bowl; pulse on/off until finely chopped. Add the basil leaves and pulse on/off until finely minced. Stir this into the soup with the oregano. Simmer the soup until the potatoes are tender, approx 20 minutes. Place the canned tomatoes in the processor bowl and process until coarsely chopped. When the soup vegetables are tender, add the tomatoes and heat. Wipe the processor bowl and chop the parsley.

To serve, top the soup with parsley and Parmesan cheese.

Preparation: 20 min
Cooking: 1 hour pressure cooking or
2 hours on the hob
Protein g/s: 10 servings–17.5
12 servings–15.5
14 servings–14

Lentil Soup

Serves 8

When served with our Wholewheat French Bread (see index) and cheese, this makes a hearty main dish.

675g (1½lb) dry lentils, rinsed
2.5l (5pt) water
2 vegetable stock cubes
2×5ml (tsp) vegetable soup seasoning (optional)
3 large onions
2 stalks celery
3 carrots, peeled
2-3×15ml (tbsp) oil
1×300g (10.6oz) jar tomato paste
1-2×15ml (tbsp) molasses
2×15ml (tbsp) lemon juice
vinegar to taste
salt and pepper

In a large pan combine the lentils, water, stock cubes and soup seasoning if used. Simmer until the lentils are just tender but not mushy, 1-1½ hours.

METAL BLADE: Place the onions, cut into large pieces, in the processing bowl. Pulse on/off until roughly chopped. Remove the metal blade and insert the slicing disc.

SLICING DISC: Cut the celery and carrots to fit the feed tube vertically; slice.

Heat the oil in a large pan. Add the onions, carrots and celery and cook for 5 minutes. Stir the vegetables into the lentils and continue to cook until the vegetables are tender, 30–45 minutes. Stir in the tomato paste, molasses and lemon juice and heat through. Season to taste with vinegar, salt and pepper.

Preparation: 10 minutes
Cooking: 1½-2 hours
Protein g/s: 17.5

Salads and Dressings

Cauliflower with Creamy Parmesan Dressing

Serves 6

Both the vegetables and the dressing can be prepared in advance, refrigerated and combined just before serving.

1 medium cauliflower
2 salad onions
50g (2oz) radishes
200ml (8fl oz) whole milk yogurt
1×15ml (tbsp) grated Parmesan cheese
½ clove garlic, crushed
juice of ½ lemon
2×15ml (tbsp) olive oil
salt and white pepper

Trim the cauliflower and divide into florets.

METAL BLADE: Add the onions, cut into 2.5cm (1in) lengths, to the processing bowl. Pulse on/off until finely chopped.

SLICING DISC OR FINE SLICING DISC: Arrange the cauliflower in the feed tube, alternating heads and stems. Slice using light pressure. Stack radishes in feed tube; slice using light pressure. Remove to a mixing bowl, cover and chill until serving time.

In a small dish, stir together the yogurt, Parmesan cheese, garlic, lemon juice, oil, salt and pepper. Cover and refrigerate.

At serving time, pour the dressing over the salad mixture and toss to mix. Spoon onto lettuce lined salad bowls.

Preparation: 15 minutes
Chilling: variable
Protein g/s: 1.5

Hot German Potato Salad

Serves 8

Authentic in flavour and aroma but without the bacon. Complement the salad with a milk product.

1125g (2½lb) new potatoes, scrubbed
2 medium onions
3×15ml (tbsp) oil
2 vegetable stock cubes
250ml (10fl oz) boiling water
½×5ml (tsp) Dijon mustard
1×15ml (tbsp) soft brown sugar
5×15ml (tbsp) cider vinegar
dash pepper
1×15ml (tbsp) Aioli Mayonnaise (see index)
1 bunch chives
1 bunch radishes (optional)
parsley for garnish
salt and pepper to taste

Cook the potatoes until just cooked but still firm, 20–25 minutes. Drain and leave until cool enough to handle, then peel. Cut into slices 5mm (¼in) thick and about 2.5cm (1in) across. Place in a large bowl.

METAL BLADE: Place the onions, cut into 2.5cm (1in) pieces, in the processing bowl. Pulse on/off until chopped fairly finely.

Heat the oil in a pan and cook the onions until soft and lightly browned. Add the onions and any remaining oil to the potatoes and stir gently to mix. Dissolve the stock cubes in the boiling water and add the mustard, sugar, vinegar and pepper. Pour the mixture onto the potatoes. Add the mayonnaise and mix well with a wooden spoon. Season with salt and additional pepper.

METAL BLADE: Place the chives, cut into 2.5cm (1in) lengths, in the dry processing bowl. Pulse on/off until finely chopped. If you plan to reheat the potato salad for later use do not add the radishes.

SLICING DISC: Stack the radishes in the feed tube; slice and add to the salad. If the salad has cooled during preparation, heat briefly in a hot oven. Garnish with parsley and serve hot.

Preparation: 15 minutes
Cooking: 20–25 minutes
Protein g/s: 3

Red and White Coleslaw

Serves 8

Radishes contribute a bit of piquancy to this delightful variation of a traditional favourite.

125g (4oz) red cabbage
225g (8oz) white cabbage
4×10cm (4in) stalks celery
6 radishes, trimmed
140ml (5fl oz) Aioli Mayonnaise (see index)
2×5ml (tsp) malt vinegar
1×15ml (tbsp) lemon juice
2×5ml (tsp) soft brown sugar

SLICING DISC: Cut cabbage vertically into wedges, core and cut into sections to fit the feed tube. Wedge cabbage pieces upright in the feed tube; slice using moderate to light pressure. Place the celery in the feed tube vertically; slice.

SHREDDING DISC: Stack radishes in the feed tube; shred. Remove the vegetables to a large bowl. In a small jug or bowl combine the mayonnaise, vinegar, lemon juice and brown sugar. Pour the dressing over the cabbage mixture and toss gently to mix. Refrigerate, covered, until serving time.

Preparation: 10 minutes.

Dilled Egg Salad

Serves 8-10

This is a good recipe for a large group. The eggs can be cooked ahead of time and chilled in the refrigerator.

10 hard-boiled eggs, chilled or cooled to room temperature
3 medium dill cucumbers
2 stalks celery, trimmed
½ medium green pepper, quartered
½ small onion
2 sprigs parsley
125ml (5fl oz) plain or Aioli Mayonnaise (see index)
2×5ml (tsp) dry dill weed
salt and pepper to taste
radishes for garnish

METAL BLADE: Place 5 eggs, cut in half, in the processing bowl. Pulse on/off until coarsely chopped then place in a large mixing bowl. Repeat with the remaining eggs. Place the cucumbers, cut into 2.5 cm (1in) pieces, in the processing bowl; pulse on/off until finely chopped then add them to the mixing bowl. Cut the celery into 2.5cm (1in) pieces and place in the processing bowl. Pulse on/off until finely chopped; remove to mixing bowl. Place the green pepper in the processor and pulse on/off until finely chopped; add to the egg mixture. Place the onion, cut into 2.5cm (1in) pieces in the processor with the parsley and pulse on/off until finely chopped. Add to the mixing bowl with the mayonnaise, dill, salt and pepper. Toss gently to mix.

Cover and refrigerate for about 1 hour to allow the flavours to blend. Cut the radishes into flowers and soak in water to open. Arrange on top of the salad.

Preparation: 10 minutes
Cooking: allow time for the eggs
Chilling: 1 hour
Protein g/s: 8 servings–8.5
          10 servings–7

Mexican Chef's Salad

Serves 1

Assemble this tasty, colourful, meal-in-itself salad on a dinner plate. The quantities listed are for one serving. Corn tortillas are a nice accompaniment.

3-4 lettuce leaves, red if possible
½ tomato, chopped
¼-½ avocado, cubed
small piece of onion
50-125g (2-4oz) cooked kidney beans, chilled
25g (1oz) Cheddar cheese, well chilled
Honey French Dressing (see index)
Tabasco sauce (optional)
taco chips

Arrange the lettuce leaves, torn into bite-sized pieces, over the bottom of a dinner plate.

METAL BLADE: Place the onion, cut into 2.5cm (1in) pieces, in the processing bowl; pulse on/off until finely chopped. Sprinkle about half the onion over the lettuce, top with the beans and the remaining onion.

SHREDDING DISC: Cut the cheese to fit the feed tube; shred. Arrange over the salad. Top the salad with the chopped tomato and avocado. Pour over several spoonfuls of salad dressing and a few drops of tabasco sauce. Garnish with taco chips.

Preparation: 15 minutes
Cooking: allow time to cook the kidney beans
Chilling: allow time to chill the kidney beans
Protein g/s: 14-21

Greek Chef's Salad

Serves 1

Since it is easier to make individual salad plates, the quantities listed are for one

serving. Rinse the feta cheese and olives in water to remove some of the excess salt.

3-4 large lettuce leaves
50g (2oz) cooked chick peas, chilled
1×15ml (tbsp) red onion
½ small ripe but firm tomato
25-50g (1-2oz) feta cheese, cut into small pieces
50g (2oz) black olives
Tart Greek Salad Dressing (see index)

Line salad bowl with lettuce leaves, torn into bite-sized pieces. Spoon in the chick peas.

SLICING DISC: Place the onion in the feed tube; slice. Place the tomato in the feed tube; slice. Arrange over the chick peas. Top with feta cheese and olives. Pour on 2–3×15ml (tbsp) dressing.

Preparation: 10 minutes
Protein g/s: 16-22

Mexican Salad

Serves 6-8

Assemble the salad ahead of time, cover and refrigerate. Just before serving add the avocado slices, pour on the dressing and toss gently.

2 medium potatoes
1 medium head of lettuce
1 small onion
1 small green pepper, halved and deseeded
2 stalks celery
1×400g (14oz) can pitted black olives, drained
1 medium avocado
lemon or lime juice
75ml (3fl oz) oil
3×15ml (tbsp) red wine vinegar
1×5ml (tsp) chilli powder
½×5ml (tsp) dried oregano
salt and pepper

Early in the day, or the night before, cook the potatoes, peel if desired, and chill. Tear the lettuce into bite-sized pieces and line a salad bowl.

SLICING DISC: Cut the potatoes into quarters lengthways, place in the feed tube vertically and slice. Cut the onion into wedges to fit the feed tube and slice using light pressure. Cut the celery to fit the feed tube vertically; slice. Wedge the green pepper into the feed tube; slice. Stack the olives in the feed tube; slice.

Remove the sliced vegetables to the prepared salad bowl. Cover and refrigerate until serving time. Cut the avocado to fit the feed tube; slice. Sprinkle with lemon or lime juice. Remove to a small bowl, cover and refrigerate. In a small screw-topped jar combine the oil, vinegar, chilli powder, oregano, salt and pepper. Refrigerate the dressing for at least 30 minutes to allow the flavours to blend.

Shake the dressing well. Add the avocado to the salad bowl, pour the dressing over and toss gently to mix.

Preparation: 15 minutes
Cooking: 20-25 minutes
Chilling: allow time for the potatoes to chill
       30 minutes to chill dressing

Peanut Sunflower Waldorf Salad

Serves 6-8

Peanuts and sunflower seeds are a good complementary protein combination. Serve on lettuce leaves.

3 medium Red Delicious apples
2 stalks celery, trimmed
100g (3½oz) roasted, unsalted peanuts
100g (3½oz) unroasted sunflower seeds
25g (1oz) raisins
juice of ½ lemon
4-6×15ml (tbsp) mayonnaise

SLICING DISC: Core apples; cut into 8 wedges. Stack into feed tube vertically; slice. Cut celery to fit feed tube vertically, slice.

In a large bowl, combine apples, celery, raisins, peanuts, sunflower seeds, lemon juice and mayonnaise. Stir gently to mix well. Spoon into lettuce lined salad bowl or individual dishes.

Preparation: 10 minutes
Protein g/s: 6 servings–8.5
          8 servings–6.5

Mayonnaise

Makes 375ml (15fl oz)

There is just no comparison between freshly made mayonnaise and the bottled product. Instructions for making mayonnaise may vary with each processor so check your instruction manual and adapt the following accordingly. Lemon or lime juice may be substituted for the vinegar.

1 egg
1×15ml (tbsp) vinegar, lemon or lime juice
1×5ml (tsp) Dijon mustard
1×15ml (tbsp) oil
salt
310-330ml (12½-13fl oz) oil

METAL BLADE: Place the egg, vinegar, mustard, 1×15ml (tbsp) oil and salt in an absolutely dry processing bowl. Process for 1 minute. With the machine running, pour the oil very slowly through the feed tube until the mayonnaise has thickened. The remaining oil may be added a little faster. Process until thick. The longer you run the processor, the thicker the mayonnaise will become.

If your processor is supplied with a plastic blade, that should be used to make mayonnaise.

Store the mayonnaise in a covered container in the refrigerator for up to a week.

Preparation: 5 minutes

Aioli Mayonnaise

Makes 375ml (15fl oz)

A simple cheese, beansprout and avocado sandwich becomes a gourmet treat with this variation of the basic mayonnaise.

1 quantity of mayonnaise
2 large cloves garlic, crushed

When the mayonnaise is thick, add the crushed garlic and continue processing until blended.

Preparation: 5 minutes

Yogurt Herb Dressing

Makes 250ml (10fl oz) or 5 servings

Yogurt keeps this dressing low in fat and calories.

25g (1oz) Parmesan cheese, well chilled
2 cloves garlic
12 fresh basil leaves
25g (1oz) fresh chives, cut into 5cm (2in) leaves
1-2 sprigs parsley, torn into small pieces
freshly ground black pepper
juice of 1 small lime
250ml (10fl oz) natural yogurt

METAL BLADE: Place the Parmesan, cut into small pieces, in the processor bowl and process until finely grated. Add the garlic and continue to process until finely chopped. Stop the machine, add the basil, chives and parsley. Pulse on/off until herbs are finely chopped. Add the lime juice and yogurt; combine with 2-3 on/off pulses. Refrigerate in a covered container until serving time.

Preparation: 5 minutes
Protein g/s: 3

Tart Greek Salad Dressing

Makes 300ml (12fl oz)

The essential ingredient in the traditional Greek salad of lettuce, tomatoes, onions, Feta cheese and black olives.

2 large cloves garlic
3×15ml (tbsp) red wine vinegar
3×15ml (tbsp) lemon juice
250ml (10fl oz) olive oil
1/2×5ml (tsp) salt
1/2×5ml (tsp) freshly ground black pepper

METAL BLADE: Place the garlic in the processing bowl and process until finely chopped. With the machine running, pour in the vinegar, lemon juice, oil, salt and pepper. Process until well blended. Place in a covered container and leave to stand for 30 mins to allow the flavours to blend. Store in the refrigerator until serving time.

Preparation: 3 minutes
Standing: 30 minutes

Honey French Dressing

Makes 300ml (12fl oz)

You will get compliments when you serve this delicious creamy French dressing over a green or vegetable salad!

2 large cloves garlic
190ml (7 1/2 fl oz) oil
5×15ml (tbsp) distilled malt vinegar
2×15ml (tbsp) tomato paste
2×15ml (tbsp) honey
salt and pepper
1/2×5ml (tsp) paprika
1-2 drops Tabasco sauce, optional

METAL BLADE: Place the garlic in the processing bowl; pulse on/off until finely minced. Mix together the oil, vinegar, tomato paste, honey, salt and pepper, paprika and Tabasco. With the machine running, pour the tomato and honey mixture through the feed tube and process until well-mixed and creamy, about 15 seconds. Pour into a container, cover and refrigerate until serving time.

Preparation: 3-4 minutes

Vinaigrette Herb Dressing

Makes 300ml (12fl oz)

A delicious sweet-sour, salt-free dressing. A few drained capers may be added for a good variation.

1 large or 2 small cloves garlic
250ml (10fl oz) oil
60ml (2½fl oz) distilled malt vinegar
1×15ml (tbsp) freshly chopped thyme OR *1×5ml (tsp) dried*
1×15ml (tbsp) freshly chopped marjoram or 1×5ml (tsp) dried
1-2×5ml (tsp) soft brown sugar
salt (optional)

METAL BLADE: Place the garlic in the processor bowl and process until finely chopped. With the machine running, pour in the oil and vinegar. Add the thyme, marjoram, sugar and salt (if used). Process until well blended. Place in a covered container and leave for 30 minutes to allow the flavours to blend. Store in the refrigerator.

Preparation: 2-3 minutes
Standing: 30 minutes

Cheese Radish Salad

Serves 4

This high-protein salad is especially good when served with a whole grain rye bread. It is ideal for lunch or a light supper.

2 hard-boiled eggs, chilled and sliced
1 small bunch chives
1 bunch radishes, approx 325g (12oz) trimmed
175g (6oz) Gruyere cheese, cut into thin strips
2 sprigs parsley

lettuce leaves to line salad bowl
1×5ml (tsp) Dijon mustard
6×15ml (tbsp) oil
2×15ml (tbsp) cider vinegar
½×5ml (tsp) brown sugar
salt and pepper to taste

METAL BLADE: Place the chives, cut into 2.5cm (1in) lengths, in the processing bowl, pulse on/off until finely chopped. Remove the metal blade.

SLICING DISC: Stack the radishes in the feed tube; slice. Line a salad bowl with the lettuce leaves. Combine the radishes, cheese, eggs and chives in a mixing bowl and pile the mixture into the prepared salad bowl.

METAL BLADE: Place the Dijon mustard, oil, vinegar, brown sugar, salt and pepper in the processing bowl. Process until well mixed. Pour the dressing evenly over the salad and garnish with parsley. Toss gently to serve.

Preparation: 15 minutes
Protein g/s: 14

Tabouli Salad

Serves 4

A perfect salad to take on a picnic or serve at a buffet because it will not wilt. Rather than boiling the bulgur, which results in a sticky mess, we soften it in hot water. Serve with beans, lentils or a milk product.

125g (4oz) bulgur or cracked wheat
750ml (1½pt) boiling water
50g (2oz) parsley
50g (2oz) mint
3-4 salad onions
1 large or 2 small firm, ripe tomatoes
2-4×15ml (tbsp) oil
5×15ml (tbsp) fresh lemon juice
1 large clove garlic, crushed
½×5ml (tsp) salt

Cover the bulgur with the boiling water and stand for 1 hour. Drain then wrap in a clean teatowel and squeeze out the excess water. Place in a mixing bowl.

METAL BLADE: Pinch off the leaves from the parsley and mint and add to the processing bowl with the onions, cut into 5cm (2in) lengths. Pulse on/off until finely chopped. Combine with the bulgur, oil, lemon juice, garlic and salt. Chill, covered, until ready to serve or for at least 45 minutes. Quarter the tomato and place in the processing bowl; pulse on/off until coarsely chopped. Drain off any excess liquid then place the chopped tomato in a small dish and refrigerate, covered.

At serving time mix the tomatoes with the wheat mixture and serve in a large bowl or individual dishes.

Preparation: 10 minutes
Standing: 1 hour
Chilling: 45 minutes
Protein g/s: 5

 or

Chick Pea and Cheese Salad with Cumin Dressing

Serves 6-8

A good contribution to a barbecue Supper or picnic. The flavour is enhanced by chilling.

675g (1½lb) cooked chick peas (about 450g (1lb) dry), chilled
2 sprigs fresh parsley
2 firm ripe tomatoes
1 small cucumber, deseeded
125g (4oz) Cheddar cheese, well chilled
4×15ml (tbsp) olive oil
50ml (2fl oz) lemon juice
1×5ml (tsp) ground cumin
½×5ml (tsp) salt
ground white pepper

Place the chick peas in a serving bowl and add the remaining ingredients as they are processed.

METAL BLADE: Place the parsley in the processor, pulse on/off until finely chopped then add to the chick peas. Quarter the tomatoes and place in the processor, pulse on/off until chopped, then add to the salad. Place the cucumber, cut into 2.5cm (1in) pieces, in the processor; pulse on/off until chopped but not mushy.

SLICING DISC: Cut the cheese into strips and wedge them into the feed tube vertically then slice to make small cubes. Add to the salad.

METAL BLADE: Place the olive oil, lemon juice, cumin and salt and pepper in the processor. Process until well mixed then pour over the salad and mix well.

Cover and refrigerate for at least 30 minutes.

Preparation: 7–10 minutes
Cooking: allow time to cook the beans
Chilling: 30 minutes
Protein g/s: 6 servings–18.5
          8 servings–14

Carrot and Courgette Slices with Curry Dressing

Serves 8

This non-wilt salad is perfect for a picnic.

3 salad onions
4 medium courgettes, washed and trimmed
8 medium carrots, peeled
2×15ml (tbsp) lemon juice
75ml (3fl oz) oil
1×5ml (tsp) curry powder
pinch of salt
ground white pepper
3×15ml (tbsp) yogurt

METAL BLADE: Place the salad onions, cut into 2.5cm (1in) lengths, in the processing bowl. Pulse on/off until finely chopped. Remove the metal blade and insert the slicing disc.

THIN OR MEDIUM SLICING DISC: Cut the courgettes and carrots to fit the feed tube vertically; slice. When using the medium slicing disc, process using a light pressure to obtain thin slices.

Remove to a glass or ceramic mixing bowl.

In a jug, whisk together the lemon juice, oil, curry powder, salt, pepper and yogurt. Pour over the vegetables and toss to mix well. Cover and refrigerate for 3–4 hours to allow the flavours to blend.

Preparation: 10 minutes
Chilling: 3–4 hours

Main Dishes

Grains and Pulses

Lentil-Sunflower Burgers

Serves 3, 2 per serving

A quick meal if the lentils are prepared ahead. Serve with or without a wholewheat bun and your choice of condiments. These burgers go well with a tossed green salad.

225g (8oz) cooked lentils
75g (3oz) raw sunflower seeds
1 small onion
2 eggs, lightly beaten
1-2 cloves garlic, crushed
1×5ml (tsp) soy sauce
salt
2×5ml (tsp) tomato ketchup
oil

METAL BLADE: Place the sunflower seeds in the processing bowl; pulse on/off until fairly finely chopped. Remove to a mixing bowl and combine with the lentils. Place the onion, cut into 2.5cm (1in) pieces, in the processing bowl; pulse on/off until finely chopped.

Add to the mixing bowl with the eggs, garlic, soy sauce, salt and ketchup. Mix well with a wooden spoon. Divide into 6 burgers.

Heat a non-stick frying pan over a medium heat on the hob. Add 1-2 × 15ml (tbsp) oil. Spoon the burgers into the pan and cook until the first side is browned and the burger is firm, about 5 minutes. Turn and brown the second side.

Preparation: 10 minutes
Cooking: 10-20 minutes
　　　　　allow time to cook the lentils
Protein g/s: 17.5

Vegetarian Tacos

Makes 12, serves 6

Our version of this traditional favourite is quick and easy to prepare when the beans are cooked in advance.

1 medium onion
½ small green pepper, deseeded
1-2 canned green chillis, rinsed and deseeded
2-3×15ml (tbsp) oil
1 large clove garlic, crushed
325g (12oz) cooked pinto beans, drained
8×15ml (tbsp) tomato paste
1×5ml (tsp) chilli powder
salt
good pinch ground cumin
½ small iceberg lettuce
175g (6oz) Cheddar cheese, well chilled
2 medium tomatoes
12 taco shells
taco sauce

METAL BLADE: Place the onion, cut into 2.5cm (1in) pieces, in the processing bowl; pulse on/off until roughly chopped. Add the green pepper, cut into 2.5cm (1in) pieces; pulse on/off until roughly chopped. Pat the chillis dry with paper towel then add them to the processing bowl and pulse on/off until roughly chopped.

Heat the oil in a large saucepan, add the onion mixture and cook until the onions are soft, 3–5 minutes. Stir in the garlic, beans, tomato paste, chilli powder, salt and cumin. Cover and simmer until very thick, 5–10 minutes. Wipe the processor bowl dry with paper towel.

SLICING DISC: Cut lettuce into wedges to fit the feed tube vertically; slice. Heat the taco shells in a preheated oven at gas mark 4/180°C/350°F for about 5 mins.

SHREDDING DISC: Cut the cheese to fit the feed tube; shred. Remove the cheese from the bowl and set aside.

METAL BLADE: Place the tomatoes, cut in quarters, in the processing bowl; pulse on/off until roughly chopped. Remove the tomatoes and set aside.

To serve, place 2–3×15ml (tbsp) bean mixture in each taco shell; top with chopped tomato, lettuce, cheese and taco sauce to taste.

Preparation: 10 minutes
Cooking/baking: allow time to cook beans
               plus 20 minutes
Protein g/s: 17.5

Curried Chick Peas (Chana Dal)

Serves 4-6

Yellow Rice Pilaf and Chapatis (see index) make good accompaniments as well as complementary protein sources.

450g (1lb) cooked chick peas +
200-250ml (8-10fl oz) cooking liquid
3×15ml (tbsp) oil
1/2×5ml (tsp) cumin seeds
1 large onion
1 small piece root ginger
1 large clove garlic, crushed
1×5ml (tsp) ground turmeric
1/2×5ml (tsp) ground cumin
1×5ml (tsp) garam masala*
pinch cayenne pepper
fresh coriander leaves for garnish

In a 3-4 litre (6-8 pint) saucepan, heat the oil over a moderate heat. Roast the cumin seeds for 1 minute to bring out the flavour. Be careful not to let them burn.

METAL BLADE: Place the onion, cut into 2.5cm (1in) pieces, in the processor bowl. Pulse on/off until finely chopped. Add the onions to the pan and cook for 3 minutes. Peel and cut the ginger into small pieces. With the processor running, drop the pieces onto the moving blades to chop finely. Add the ginger and the garlic to the pan with the turmeric, ground cumin, garam masala and cayenne. Cook, stirring constantly, for 1 minute. Add the chick peas and cooking liquid. Cover and cook for 15 minutes or until the sauce has thickened and the flavours are blended. Garnish with coriander leaves.

Preparation: 8–10 minutes
Cooking: allow time to cook the chick peas
               plus 20 minutes
Protein g/s: 4 servings–20.5
             6 servings–13.5

* Garam masala is a blend of spices which varies from region to region in India. Make your own by roasting spices in the oven at gas mark 6/200°C/400°F for 30 minutes. Use a spice grinder or blender to make a fine powder. DO NOT USE THE FOOD PROCESSOR AS DAMAGE MAY RESULT.

1 part whole coriander seeds
1-1½ parts whole black peppercorns
2 parts whole cumin seeds
2 parts whole cloves
4 parts cardamom pods or 2 parts cardamom seeds
1 part cinnamon stick, broken into small pieces

Rice and Vegetable Torte

Serves 8

A slice of this torte reveals a layer of herbed vegetables between two layers of brown rice. The filling can be made the night before. Refrigerate until you are ready to assemble the torte.

675g (1½lb) cooked brown rice (about 275g (10oz) raw)
150g (5oz) Parmesan cheese, at room temperature
225g (8oz) mozzarella cheese, well chilled
1 clove garlic
1 medium onion
450g (1lb) aubergine, unpeeled
350g (12oz) courgette, washed and trimmed
1×5ml (tsp) dried basil
1×5ml (tsp) dried oregano
½×5ml (tsp) salt
freshly ground pepper
325g (12oz) tomatoes
2 eggs
paprika

METAL BLADE: Place the Parmesan, cut into 2.5cm (1in) pieces, in the processing bowl. Process until finely grated. Remove the cheese from the bowl and set aside.

SHREDDING DISC: Cut the mozzarella cheese to fit the feed tube, shred using light pressure. Remove from the bowl and set aside.

METAL BLADE: Place the garlic and the onion, cut into 2.5cm (1in) pieces, in the processing bowl. Pulse on/off until finely chopped. In a large frying pan heat 3×15ml (tbsp) oil. Add the onion and cook for 2 minutes.

THIN OR MEDIUM SLICING DISC: Cut the aubergine into quarters to fit the feed tube; slice. Add the aubergine to the frying pan. Cook over a medium heat, stirring frequently, until the vegetables are soft, about 10 minutes. Cut the courgettes to fit the feed tube vertically; slice, then add to the frying pan. Add the basil, oregano, salt and pepper. Continue to cook, stirring frequently, until the courgettes are soft, about 6 minutes.

METAL BLADE: Place the tomatoes, cut into wedges, in the processing bowl. Pulse on/off until roughly chopped. Remove the tomatoes to a colander and allow to drain.

Add the tomatoes to the frying pan and simmer until all the liquid has evaporated, about 15 minutes. Stir frequently. Remove the pan from the heat and allow to cool. In a large mixing bowl combine the rice, 1 egg, 125g (4oz) Parmesan and half the mozzarella cheese. Press half the rice mixture into the bottom of a well oiled 22cm (9in) springform tin. Preheat the oven to gas mark 4/180°C/ 350°F.

Add 1 egg and the remaining Parmesan to the vegetable mixture. Spoon over the rice. Top with the remaining rice mixture; press to form an even layer. Scatter the remaining mozzarella cheese over the top and sprinkle generously with paprika. Bake for 1 hour. Remove from the oven and allow to stand for 10 minutes before removing the sides of the pan. Cut into wedges and serve.

Preparation: 15 minutes
Cooking/Baking: 1½ hours
Standing: 10 minutes
Protein g/s: 17.5

Boston Baked Beans

Serves 8

A tossed green salad and a grain or milk product are perfect accompaniments to this classic bean dish. Soak the beans in 1.5l (3 pints) water overnight and pressure cook at 15 pounds pressure for about 15 minutes then allow the pressure to reduce slowly. Cooking in a pan on the hob will take about 2 hours. Add 2 vegetable stock cubes to the water to enhance the flavour of the beans.

675g (1½lb) cooked haricot beans (about 325g (12oz) dry)
1 large onion
2×15ml (tbsp) oil
1×5ml (tsp) salt
3×15ml (tbsp) molasses
2×15ml (tbsp) honey
6×15ml (tbsp) tomato paste
1×15ml (tbsp) tomato ketchup
1×15ml (tbsp) prepared mustard
few drops vinegar

METAL BLADE: Place the onion, cut into 2.5cm (1in) pieces, in the processing bowl. Pulse on/off until finely chopped.

Heat the oil in a frying pan, add the onions and cook until soft and transparent but not browned, 5–8 minutes. Preheat the oven to gas mark 4/180°C/350°F. In a large mixing bowl combine the beans, onions, salt, molasses, honey, tomato paste, tomato ketchup, mustard and vinegar. Grease a large baking dish, approximately 25cm (10in) in diameter and 8cm (3in) high, or any similar sized dish. Pour in the bean mixture, cover with foil and bake in the preheated oven for 30 minutes. Uncover and bake for a further 30 minutes.

Preparation: 10 minutes
Cooking/Baking: 1 hour,
                 allow time to cook the beans
Protein g/s: 11.5

Arabic Musakka'a

Serves 6

Ordinary ingredients – aubergine, tomato and the chick pea – are combined in this traditional dish with the not-so-ordinary flavour! Serve with pitta bread and a Greek salad topped with Feta cheese and olives.

2 aubergines, approx 450g (1lb) each, unpeeled
olive oil
2 large onions
4×400g (14oz) cans whole tomatoes, drained and liquid reserved
325g (12oz) cooked chick peas
1½×5ml (tsp) salt
100ml (4fl oz) reserved tomato liquid

Quarter the aubergines and, with a sharp knife, cut into large cubes, about 5×5cm (2×2in). Heat about 5mm (¼in) oil in the base of a heavy saucepan over a moderate heat. Add the aubergine pieces and cook until all sides are golden brown, taking care not to let them burn. Add extra oil if needed. Remove the aubergine from the pan and drain on paper towels.

SLICING DISC: Cut the onions into quarters, place them vertically in the feed tube; slice.

In the same pan, heat 1-2×15ml (tbsp) olive oil, add the onions and cook until golden brown, 3-5 mins. Remove the pan from the heat. Preheat the oven to gas mark 4/180°C/350°F.

Pour the reserved tomato juice through a sieve to remove any seeds. Measure out 100ml (4fl oz) and set aside.

METAL BLADE: Place the tomatoes in the processing bowl; pulse on/off until coarsely chopped. In a large casserole dish layer the ingredients as follows: all the aubergine, ½×5ml (tsp) salt, all the onions, chick peas, ½×5ml (tsp) salt and tomatoes. Pour in the tomato liquid and sprinkle with the remaining ½×5ml (tsp) salt. Cover with foil and bake for 40 minutes.

Preparation: 10 minutes
Cooking/Baking: 1 hour to 1 hour 15 minutes
Protein g/s: 10

Curried Lentils

Serves 4

Serve with Yellow Rice Pilaf, Chapatis (see index) or millet.

675g (1½lb) cooked lentils, 175g (6oz) dry,
plus about 125ml (5fl oz) cooking liquid
1 small piece fresh root ginger
1 large clove garlic
1 large onion
2-3×15ml (tbsp) oil
1×5ml (tsp) ground turmeric
½×5ml (tsp) ground cumin
¼×5ml (tsp) ground coriander
1×5ml (tsp) garam masala (see Curried Chick Peas)
pinch cayenne pepper, optional
salt

METAL BLADE: Peel the ginger and cut into 8 pieces. Start the processor and drop the ginger through the feed tube. Let the processor run until the ginger is finely grated. Remove from the bowl and set aside.

Place the garlic in the processor bowl and pulse on/off until finely chopped. Add the onion, cut into 5cm (2in) pieces and pulse on/off until chopped.

Heat the oil in a large pan. Add the garlic and onion and cook until soft and transparent in 3–5 minutes. Add the ginger and cook for a further 30 seconds. Stir in the spices and continue to cook for 1 minute. Stir constantly to prevent burning. Add the lentils and the cooking liquid, cayenne pepper and salt. Cook for about 5 minutes or until the liquid has evaporated. Season to taste.

Preparation: 5 minutes
Cooking: 10–15 minutes
            allow time to cook the lentils
Protein g/s: 12

Lentils Burgundy

Serves 8

A hearty main dish when complemented by a thick slice of whole grain bread. The aroma of the lentils during cooking will bring your family to the table without coaxing.

450g (1lb) dry lentils
1.5l (3pt) water
1 bay leaf
2 vegetable stock cubes
2 large onions
2-3×15ml (tbsp) oil
3 large carrots, peeled
2 large leeks
1 large clove garlic, crushed
½-1×5ml (tsp) dried thyme
375ml (15fl oz) Burgundy wine
salt and pepper to taste

Rinse the lentils and soak overnight in 1l (2pt) water at room temperature. Combine the lentils, soaking water, remaining water, bay leaf and stock cubes in a large pan. Bring to the boil, reduce the heat to a simmer and cook until the lentils are tender, about 30 minutes.

METAL BLADE: Place the onions, cut into 2.5cm (1in) pieces, in the processing bowl; pulse on/off until roughly chopped.

SLICING DISC: Cut the carrots to fit the feed tube vertically; slice. Heat the oil in a pan over a medium heat. Add the onions and carrots and cook until just tender. Stir the vegetables into the lentils.

Wash the leeks thoroughly, removing all the grit. Discard the tough upper portion of the leaves. Slice into 5mm (¼in) pieces and cook in about 1×15ml (tbsp) oil until soft. Add to the lentils. (If you are not concerned with evenly cut leeks, roughly chop in the processor with the metal blade in place.)

When the vegetables and the lentils are tender, add the garlic, thyme and Burgundy. Simmer for 25–30 minutes until thick. Season to taste and serve.

Preparation: 10 minutes
Cooking: 1 hour
Protein g/s: 15

Eggs, Milk and Cheese

Broccoli Rice Bake

Serves 6

Have the rice cooked ahead of time and dinner will be ready before you know it! Reheat leftovers, covered, in a preheated oven at gas mark 4/180°C/350°F for 20–25 minutes.

275g (10oz) cooked brown rice, cooled
(about 75g (3oz) raw)
450g (1lb) broccoli, untrimmed
175g (6oz) mature Cheddar cheese
1 small onion
25g (1oz) butter
1×5ml (tsp) salt
pepper
3 eggs
250ml (10fl oz) skimmed milk

Trim the broccoli and break into florets. Cut the stalks into 2.5cm (1in) pieces. Steam until just cooked then set aside.

SHREDDING DISC: Cut the cheese to fit the food tube; shred. Place in a large mixing bowl.

METAL BLADE: Place the onion, cut into 2.5cm (1in) pieces, in the processing bowl. Pulse on/off until finely chopped. Heat the butter in a small pan then add the onions and cook until soft. Add salt and pepper. Preheat the oven to gas mark 4/180°C/350°F. Place the broccoli in the processing bowl and pulse on/off until roughly chopped. Combine the rice, broccoli and onion in a mixing bowl with the cheese. Toss to mix. Place the eggs in the processing bowl; process for 5 seconds. With the machine running pour in the milk. Stop the machine as soon as the milk is added. Pour the custard into the broccoli mixture. Stir gently to mix.

Pour the mixture into a greased 20×20cm (8×8in) baking tin. Bake, uncovered, for 35–40 minutes or until the custard is set. Allow to stand for 10 minutes then cut into squares to serve.

Preparation: 15–20 minutes
Cooking/Baking: allow time to cook the rice
plus 35–40 minutes
Standing: 10 minutes
Protein g/s: 13

Moussaka

Serves 8

This tastes surprisingly authentic even without the lamb. Serve with a tossed green salad made with lettuce, olives, tomatoes, sliced red onions, small cubes of Feta cheese and Tart Greek Salad Dressing (see index).

Tomato Sauce

3 medium onions
2 cloves garlic, crushed
2×15ml (tbsp) olive oil
2-3 sprigs fresh mint or 1×15ml (tbsp) dried mint
2 sprigs fresh parsley
1-2×5ml (tsp) honey
salt and pepper
1×400g (14oz) can sieved tomatoes
¼×5ml (tsp) dried rosemary

METAL BLADE: Place the onions, cut into 2.5cm (1in) pieces in the processing bowl. Pulse on/off until finely chopped. Heat the oil in a saucepan and add the onions and garlic, cooking until soft and transparent in 5–8 minutes. Wipe the processor bowl with a paper towel.

METAL BLADE: Place the mint leaves and parsley in the processing bowl and pulse on/off until finely chopped. Add to the onions with the honey, salt, pepper, sieved tomatoes and rosemary. Cover and simmer for 30 minutes.

Aubergine-Rice Base

675g (1½lb) aubergines
450g (1lb) cooked brown rice, cooled (150g (5oz) raw)
½–1×5ml (tsp) ground nutmeg
½–1×5ml (tsp) ground cinnamon
½–1×5ml (tsp) ground allspice
olive oil

Preheat the oven to gas mark 6/200°C/400°F.

SLICING DISC: Cut the aubergines to fit the feed tube; slice. Place the slices on a well oiled baking sheet and bake for 15 minutes or until the slices are tender. Remove from the oven and set aside. Reduce the heat to gas mark 5/190°C/375°F.

Custard Topping

50g (2oz) Parmesan cheese, at room temperature
4 large eggs
225g (8oz) curd cheese
250ml (10fl oz) milk
¼×5ml (tsp) ground nutmeg
ground nutmeg to finish

METAL BLADE: Place the Parmesan cheese, cut into 2.5cm (1in) pieces, in the dry processing bowl. Process until finely chopped. Add the eggs, curd cheese, milk and nutmeg. Combine the ingredients with 2–3 on/off pulses. Stop the machine and scrape down the sides of the bowl. Process until mixed.

ASSEMBLY: Arrange the aubergine over the bottom of a well greased baking dish, approx 23×33cm (9×13in). Sprinkle with half the

nutmeg, cinnamon and allspice. Spread the rice over the aubergine and press down gently to form an even layer. Sprinkle with the remaining nutmeg, cinnamon and allspice. Spoon on the tomato sauce then pour the custard over the sauce. Sprinkle with a little extra nutmeg. Bake at gas mark 5/190°C/375°F for 40–45 minutes.

Preparation: 20 minutes
Cooking/Baking: 1½ hours
　　　　　　allow time for the rice to cook
Protein g/s: 11

Green Chilli and Pepper Bake

Serves 6

This has a soufflé-like consistency . . . light and spicy.

225g (8oz) sharp Cheddar cheese
1 small onion
1 medium green pepper
1×125g (4oz) can green chillis, rinsed and deseeded
4 eggs
125ml (5fl oz) yogurt
150g (5oz) cottage cheese
salt and pepper
good pinch chilli powder
1×15ml (tbsp) oil

Preheat the oven to gas mark 4/180°C/350°F.

SHREDDING DISC: Cut the cheese to fit the feed tube; shred. Remove the cheese to a mixing bowl.

METAL BLADE: Place the onion, cut into 2.5cm (1in) pieces; green pepper, cut into 2.5cm (1in) pieces; and the chillis in the processing bowl. Pulse on/off until coarsely chopped.

Heat the oil in a pan and add the onion mixture, cooking for 3–5 minutes or until the vegetables are soft and the liquid has evaporated. Remove the pan from the heat and allow to cool slightly.

METAL BLADE: Place the eggs, yogurt, cottage cheese, salt, pepper and chilli powder in the processing bowl. Process for 5 seconds. Stop the machine, remove the cover and scrape down the sides of the bowl. Process for 10 seconds or until smooth.

Combine the cheese, cooked vegetables and egg mixture in the mixing bowl. Pour into an oiled 20×20cm (8×8in) baking dish. Bake, uncovered, for 35–40 minutes or until the custard is set. Allow to cool for 10 minutes then cut into squares to serve.

Preparation: 15 minutes
Cooking/Baking: 35–40 minutes
Standing: 10 minutes
Protein g/s: 17.5

Egg Fu Yung Omelette

Serves 3

This dish is ideal when you want a meal in a hurry.

1 medium onion
2-3 stalks celery
2×15ml (tbsp) oil
225g (8oz) fresh mung bean sprouts
1 clove garlic, crushed
1×15ml (tbsp) soy sauce
6 eggs
chopped chives or spring onions for garnish

SLICING DISC: Cut the onion in half to fit the feed tube; slice with light pressure. Cut the celery to fit the feed tube vertically; slice.

In a small saucepan heat the oil over a moderate heat. Add the onions and celery and cook for 3–5 minutes. Add the beansprouts and garlic; cook for about 1 minute or until the sprouts are limp. Add the soy sauce and cook until the liquid has evaporated. Do not overcook the vegetables; they should still be crisp.

PLASTIC MIXING BLADE OR METAL BLADE: Place 2 eggs in the processing bowl and process until beaten. Pour into a lightly oiled 20cm (8in) non-stick pan and cook over a moderate heat until the eggs are cooked to your liking. Spoon one third of the filling down the centre, fold and slip onto a serving plate. Repeat with the remaining eggs. Garnish with chives or spring onions.

Preparation: 5 minutes
Cooking: 10 minutes
Protein g/s: 16.5

Stuffed Aubergine

Serves 4

Aubergines may be stuffed ahead of time. If refrigerated, add 10–15 minutes to the baking time. These also freeze well.

2 small round aubergines, approx 225g (8oz) each
50g (2oz) Parmesan cheese, at room temperature
2 slices wholewheat bread
3 sprigs parsley
½×5ml (tsp) dried basil
75g (3oz) Gruyere cheese
3 cloves garlic
1 small onion
2×15ml (tbsp) olive oil
pinch paprika
salt
1 large tomato
dried oregano

METAL BLADE: Place the Parmesan cheese, cut into 2.5 cm (1in) pieces, in the processing bowl. Process until finely chopped. Add the wholewheat bread, torn into small pieces, and process to make coarse crumbs. Add the parsley and basil. Process until the parsley is finely chopped. Remove the mixture from the bowl and reserve.

SHREDDING DISC: Cut the Gruyere to fit the feed tube; shred. Remove from the bowl and set aside. Reserve 2×15ml (tbsp) for topping. Cut the aubergines in half and scoop out the pulp, leaving a shell approximately 5mm (¼in) thick. Reserve the pulp for the filling.

METAL BLADE: Place the garlic cloves and onions, quartered, in the processing bowl. Pulse on/off until finely chopped. Heat the oil in a pan, add the onions and cook for 2 minutes. Place the aubergine pulp in the processing bowl and pulse on/off until finely chopped.

Add the aubergines to the onions, continue cooking for 2 minutes. Remove the pan from the heat. Add the breadcrumb mixture, paprika, salt, lemon juice and the majority of the Gruyere. Stir to mix well. Fill the aubergine shells, mounding into the centre.

SLICING DISC: Cut the tomato to fit the feed tube; slice with firm pressure. Top each filled shell with tomato slices, overlapping slightly. Sprinkle on the remaining Gruyere and a pinch of oregano. Cover and bake at gas mark 5/190°C/375°F for 40–50 minutes, until hot and the aubergine is tender.

Preparation: 15 minutes
Cooking/Baking: 40–50 minutes
Protein g/s: 11.5

Swiss'n'Broccoli Bake

Serves 4

325g (12oz) broccoli
125g (4oz) Gruyere cheese
1 small onion
2×15ml (tbsp) oil
1 slice wholewheat bread
2 sprigs fresh parsley
salt and pepper
½×5ml (tsp) dried oregano
4 eggs
50ml (2fl oz) skimmed milk

Preheat the oven to gas mark 5/190°C/375°F. Trim the broccoli, break into florets. Steam the broccoli until just cooked. Do not overcook. Remove from the heat and set aside.

SHREDDING DISC: Cut the cheese to fit the feed tube; shred with light pressure. Remove to a large mixing bowl and set aside.

METAL BLADE: Place the onion, cut into 2.5cm (1in) pieces, in the processor bowl. Pulse on/off until finely chopped. Heat the oil in a small pan and cook the onion until soft in 3–5 minutes. Place the broccoli in the processing bowl. Pulse on/off until coarsely chopped. Combine the broccoli and onion with the cheese in the mixing bowl. Wipe the processing bowl clean with paper towel. Place the bread, torn into pieces, in the processing bowl and process to make fine crumbs. Add the salt, pepper, oregano and parsley and process to chop the parsley. Stop the machine and add the eggs. Combine with 3 on/off pulses. With the machine running, pour in the milk. Turn the processor off as soon as all the milk has been added.

Pour the mixture into the vegetables and mix gently. Turn into a lightly oiled 1.5l (3pt) baking dish. Bake for 40 minutes or until the custard is firm and lightly browned. Stand for 10 minutes before serving.

Preparation: 10–15 minutes
Cooking/Baking: 55 minutes
Standing: 10 minutes
Protein g/s: 16

Nut Cheese Loaf

Serves 8

Serve with a tossed green salad and steamed green vegetables.

225g (8oz) cooked brown rice (about 40g (1½oz) raw)
4 large sprigs parsley
175g (6oz) walnuts
450g (1lb) Cheddar cheese, well chilled
1 small onion
1 clove garlic
125g (4oz) fresh mushrooms
4 eggs
1 quantity Two-in-One Tomato Sauce (see index)
or similar sauce

Preheat the oven to gas mark 4/180°C/350°F. Place the cooked rice in a large mixing bowl.

METAL BLADE: To maintain the individual texture, process the remaining ingredients separately and add to the rice in the bowl. Toss to mix. Pulse on/off to finely chop the parsley, coarsely chop the nuts, finely chop the garlic and onions, coarsely chop the mushrooms.

SHREDDING DISC: Cut the cheese to fit the feed tube; shred. Add to the rice mixture.

METAL BLADE: Place the eggs in the processing bowl. Process until well blended. Pour into the rice mixture and mix.

Butter a 23×13cm (9×5in) loaf tin and line with baking parchment. Spoon the rice mixture into the prepared pan. Bake for 1 hour. Let stand for 10 minutes before turning out. Serve slices topped with Two-in-One Tomato Sauce.

Preparation: 15–20 minutes
Cooking/Baking: 1 hour to bake the loaf
allow time to cook the rice
Standing: 10 minutes
Protein g/s: 22

Cheese Scalloped Potatoes with Mushrooms

Serves 6-8

Serve this hearty family favourite with a tossed green salad and freshly baked rolls.

1 bunch spring onions
2×15ml (tbsp) oil
450g (1lb) mushrooms
salt
225g (8oz) Cheddar cheese, well chilled
1350g (3lb) potatoes, peeled
50g (2oz) butter
300ml (12fl oz) hot milk

METAL BLADE: Place the onions, cut into 5cm (2in) lengths, in the processor. Pulse on/off to chop. Heat the oil in a saucepan, add the onions and cook for 1–2 minutes.

SLICING DISC: Stack the mushrooms in the feed tube; slice. Add to the pan and cook until soft and the liquid has evaporated. Add salt to taste. Remove from the heat.

SHREDDING DISC: Cut the cheese to fit the feed tube; shred. Remove from the bowl and set aside.

SLICING DISC OR THIN SLICING DISC: Cut the peeled potatoes to fit the tube; slice.

Use half the butter to grease a 23×33cm (9×13in) or similar baking tin. Arrange half the potato slices in the bottom of the tin. Sprinkle with a few pinches of salt. Cover with half the cheese and all the mushroom mixture. Finish layering with the remaining potatoes, a pinch or two of salt, and the cheese. Carefully pour in the hot milk and dot with the remaining butter. Bake at gas mark 5/190°C/375°F, covered, for 40 minutes. Remove cover and continue baking for 20 minutes or until the potatoes are tender.

Preparation: 20 minutes
Baking: 60–70 minutes
Protein g/s: 6 servings–16
8 servings–12

German Potato Pancakes

Serves 4, 2 pancakes per serving

The addition of dried milk powder increases the protein power of our version of this traditional recipe. Serve with red cabbage and apples (see index) and a slice or two of rye bread.

50g (2oz) fresh parsley
1 medium onion
450g (1lb) potatoes, peeled
2 eggs
25g (1oz) milk powder
4×15ml (tbsp) wholewheat flour
2×15ml (tbsp) sour cream or yogurt
salt
oil for frying
yogurt and chives for garnish, optional

METAL BLADE: Place the parsley in the processing bowl. Pulse on/off until finely chopped. Remove to a mixing bowl. Place the onion, cut into 2.5cm (1in) pieces, in the processing bowl. Pulse on/off until finely chopped. Drain off any excess liquid and add the onion to the parsley.

SHREDDING DISC: Cut the peeled potatoes to fit the feed tube; shred. Remove to waxed paper.

METAL BLADE: Place the shredded potatoes in the processing bowl and process until finely chopped or puréed. In Germany the potatoes are so finely shredded that they resemble a purée. Add the potatoes to the onions. Stir together the milk powder and flour. Place the eggs in the work bowl and process for 5 seconds. Scrape down the sides of the bowl. With the machine running, add the milk powder and flour mixture, sour cream and salt. Process until smooth. Pour into the mixing bowl; stir to mix well.

In a non-stick pan heat 1-2×15ml (tbsp) oil. Use the mixture to make 8 pancakes, cooking for about 10 minutes, turning once, until golden brown. Serve with yogurt and chives or a little apple sauce.

Preparation: 15 minutes
Cooking: 30 minutes
Protein g/s: 12.5

Tomato and Mozzarella Pie

Serves 4-6

A layer of cooked shredded potatoes holds a tasty tomato and mozzarella filling. Cook the potatoes the night before or earlier in the day.

900g (2lb) red potatoes
2 sprigs parsley
50g (2oz) butter or margarine
60g (2½oz) Parmesan cheese, at room temperature
225g (8oz) mozzarella cheese, well chilled
3 tomatoes
1×5ml (tsp) dried oregano
butter
flour

Earlier in the day, cook the unpeeled potatoes until just tender and refrigerate. Preheat the oven to gas mark 7/225°C/425°F. Lightly butter and flour a 20×20cm (8×8in) baking dish or tin.

METAL BLADE: Place the parsley in the processing bowl and pulse on/off until finely chopped. Remove from the bowl and set aside. Place the Parmesan cheese, cut into 2.5cm (1in) pieces, in the processing bowl. Process until finely chopped. Remove from the bowl and set aside.

SHREDDING DISC: Cut the unpeeled, chilled potatoes to fit the feed tube; shred with firm pressure. Toss with the parsley. Spread the potatoes evenly over the bottom of the prepared baking tin. Dot with 50g (2oz) butter. Cut the mozzarella cheese to fit the feed tube; shred. Spread half the cheese over the potatoes, reserving the remaining cheese.

SLICING DISC: Cut the tomatoes to fit the feed tube; slice with firm pressure. Arrange the tomatoes in a single layer over the cheese. Sprinkle the oregano over the tomatoes. Top with the remaining mozzarella and Parmesan cheeses. Bake for 25 minutes, until the cheese is melted and lightly browned. Cut into squares and serve.

Preparation: 10 minutes
Cooking/Baking: 25 minutes
                 allow time to cook the potatoes
Protein g/s: 4 servings–26
             6 servings–17

Cheese and Broccoli Bake

Serves 4

This dish is light in texture and taste. Serve with steamed carrots and a tossed green salad.

450g (1lb) broccoli
125g (4oz) mature Cheddar cheese
575g (20oz) cottage cheese
2 eggs
1/2×5ml (tsp) dry dill weed
1×15ml (tbsp) lemon juice
2×15ml (tbsp) wholewheat flour
2×15ml (tbsp) bran
salt and pepper to taste

Trim the broccoli; break into florets and steam until just cooked. Broccoli should be crisp.

SHREDDING DISC: Cut the cheese to fit the feed tube; shred. Remove the cheese to a mixing bowl and set aside.

METAL BLADE: Place the broccoli in the processing bowl. Pulse on/off until coarsely chopped. Remove from the bowl and add to the cheese. Place the cottage cheese, eggs, dill weed, lemon juice, flour and bran to the bowl. Combine with 2 or 3 on/off pulses. Scrape down the sides of the bowl and process until

smooth. Pour the mixture into the mixing bowl and stir gently to mix.

Turn the broccoli mixture into a lightly oiled 1l (2pt) casserole. Bake, uncovered, in a preheated oven at gas mark 4/180°C/350°F for 35–40 minutes or until set. Allow to stand for 5–10 minutes and cut into squares to serve.

Preparation: 20 minutes
Cooking/Baking: 35–45 minutes
Standing: 5–10 minutes
Protein g/s: 26.5

Cauliflower Basil Mushroom Bake

Serves 4-6

1 small cauliflower (450g – 1lb) broken into small florets
2×15ml (tbsp) oil
175g (6oz) mature Cheddar cheese
1 clove garlic
1 small onion
225g (8oz) fresh mushrooms
1 slice wholewheat bread
salt
pinch dried basil
3 eggs
125ml (5fl oz) skimmed milk

Steam the cauliflower until just cooked; remove from the heat and set aside. Preheat the oven to gas mark 4/180°C/350°F.

SHREDDING DISC: Cut the cheese to fit the feed tube; shred using light pressure. Remove from the bowl and set aside.

METAL BLADE: Place the garlic in the processing bowl and pulse on/off until finely chopped. Add the onion, cut into 2.5cm (1in) pieces. Pulse on/off until finely chopped. In a large pan heat the oil then add the onions and garlic and cook until soft, about 5 mins.

SLICING DISC: Stack the mushrooms in the feed tube; slice with firm pressure. Add the mushrooms to the pan and continue cooking until they are soft and the liquid has evaporated, about 5 mins. Remove the pan from the heat and set aside.

METAL BLADE: Place the bread, torn into small pieces, in the processing bowl and process to make fine crumbs. Add the salt, basil, eggs and milk. Pulse on/off to mix well. Stop the machine and add 125g (4oz) cheese. Pulse on/off until just mixed then stir into the pan.

Arrange the cauliflower in a single layer in a lightly oiled 20 × 20cm (8×8in) baking dish. Spread the mushroom and onion mixture over the cauliflower and top with the remaining cheese. Bake, uncovered, for 20–25 minutes or until set. Cut into squares and serve.

Preparation: 15 minutes
Cooking/Baking: 25 minutes
Protein g/s: 4 servings–18
          6 servings–12

Courgette Lasagne

Serves 6

Crisp steamed courgette slices are the 'noodles' in this quick-to-assemble dish.

2 slices wholewheat bread, toasted
900g (2lb) courgettes, scrubbed
175g (6oz) mozzarella cheese, well chilled
575g (20oz) cottage cheese
2 eggs
1×15ml (tbsp) dried parsley
1 clove garlic, crushed
1×200ml (7fl oz) can chopped tomatoes
½×5ml (tsp) salt
½×5ml (tsp) dried oregano
pinch dried basil
pinch dried rosemary

Preheat oven to gas mark 4/180°C/350°F.

METAL BLADE: Place the bread, torn into pieces, in the processing bowl and process to make fine breadcrumbs. Remove from the bowl and set aside.

SLICING DISC: Cut the courgettes into the largest pieces that will fit the feed tube; slice. Steam until just cooked in 3–5 minutes. Remove from the heat and allow to drain.

SHREDDING DISC: Cut the mozzarella cheese to fit the feed tube, shred using light pressure. Remove from the bowl and set aside.

METAL BLADE: Place the cottage cheese and eggs in the processing bowl. Combine with 3–4 on/off pulses. Add the parsley, process to mix. In a bowl, stir together the garlic, tomatoes, oregano and basil.

ASSEMBLY: In a greased 20×20cm (8×8in) baking dish layer the ingredients as follows: half the courgettes, half the breadcrumbs, half the cottage cheese mixture, half the tomatoes and half the mozzarella cheese. Repeat the layering with the remaining courgettes, breadcrumbs, cottage cheese and tomatoes. Reserve the remaining cheese.

Bake, uncovered, for 25 minutes. Sprinkle with the reserved cheese. Return to the oven and bake until the cheese melts, 4–6 minutes. Let stand for 10 minutes. Cut into squares to serve.

Preparation: 20 minutes
Cooking/Baking: 35 minutes
Standing: 10 minutes
Protein g/s: 21

Mushroom Olive Bake

Serves 6

Serve with brown rice and a tossed green salad. This dish is definitely for mushroom lovers! To clean mushrooms, wipe with a damp paper towel. Do not soak in water.

3 slices wholewheat bread, toasted
225g (8oz) Cheddar cheese, well chilled
450g (1lb) mushrooms
1×400g (14oz) can black olives, drained and pitted
50ml (2fl oz) milk

Preheat the oven to gas mark 4/180°C/350°F.

METAL BLADE: Place the bread, torn into small pieces, in the processing bowl. Process to crumbs. Remove from the bowl and set aside.

SHREDDING DISC: Cut the cheese to fit the feed tube; shred with firm pressure. Remove from the bowl and set aside.

SLICING DISC: Stack the mushrooms in the feed tube; slice with firm pressure. Remove from the bowl and set aside. Add the drained pitted olives to the feed tube; slice.

Lightly grease a 20×20cm (8×8in) baking dish. Sprinkle one third of the breadcrumbs over the bottom of the dish. Layer half the mushrooms, half the remaining crumbs, half the sliced olives and half the cheese. Repeat the layers of mushrooms, crumbs, olives and cheese. Add the milk. Bake for 35–40 minutes. Allow to cool for 5–10 minutes. Cut into squares and serve.

Preparation: 8–10 minutes
Baking: 35–40 minutes
Standing: 5–10 minutes
Protein g/s: 11.5

Cheese Soufflé

Serves 4-6

The ingredients for this elegant dish are usually available in any well-stocked kitchen. Although it can be prepared quickly, it is not suitable for large groups as it needs special care and last minute attention.

225g (8oz) Cheddar cheese
125g (4oz) butter or margarine
4×15ml (tbsp) wholewheat flour
250ml (10fl oz) hot milk
4 eggs, separated
salt to taste
butter or margarine to grease the soufflé dish

Preheat the oven to gas mark 5/190°C/375°F.

SHREDDING DISC: Cut the cheese to fit the feed tube; shred. In a 2l (4pt) saucepan, melt the butter then add the flour and stir well. Cook until the mixture becomes a smooth paste in 1–2 minutes. Gradually stir in the milk. Continue cooking and stirring until the sauce is thick. Add the cheese by the handful and cook, stirring constantly, until the cheese is melted. Remove from the heat and allow to cool to room temperature, 15 minutes.

METAL BLADE: Place the egg yolks in the processing bowl and process until well blended. Slow stir into the cooled sauce. Using an electric or hand beater, whisk the egg whites until stiff. Carefully fold into the cheese mixture. Pour into a well greased soufflé dish, measuring 16cm (6½in) across and 8cm (3in) high. Bake in the preheated oven for 30–35 minutes. The soufflé will rise about 5cm (2in) above the rim of the dish. Serve immediately; it will begin to sink very quickly.

Preparation: 10 minutes
Standing: allow 15 minutes for the sauce to cool
Cooking/Baking: 40–45 minutes
Protein g/s: 4 servings–24
            6 servings–16

Pastas and Sauces

We have begun to appreciate the taste of homemade pasta. However, making it by hand is a difficult and very time-consuming craft and it is only for connoisseurs who value the subtle differences in texture produced by hand kneading, rolling and stretching the dough. The use of a food processor and pasta machine requires less time and experience and makes an excellent-tasting pasta.

Our pasta dough is prepared instantaneously in the food processor. It is then rolled into thin, narrow sheets and cut into ribbons by a pasta machine. The taste is exceptional, and the ingredients – whole grain flours and fresh eggs – make it nutritionally superior to anything you can buy. Pasta easily serves as the focal point of a meal when served with any of our sauces and topped with Parmesan or Romano cheese. You will find that there is no limit to the ingredients that you can use for a good sauce – a little olive oil, onion, garlic, and whatever fresh vegetables are available.

Pasta Machines

Ours is a simple machine, turned by hand, which can produce noodles of two different widths. Manual machines are available with detachable cutting rollers, allowing a larger choice of cutting widths. Electric machines are a temptation because they are easier to use, and some people think that the pasta produced has a better (rougher) texture. But they are more expensive, sometimes work too fast to keep up with, and are insufferably noisy.

Basic Techniques

Mixing the Dough: The metal blade of your food processor does an excellent job of mixing and kneading the dough to the right consistency. We make three types of noodle doughs: doughs made of flour and eggs, without water or oil; those made of flour, eggs, water and possibly oil; and those containing spinach or other vegetables or herbs. The techniques for each of these doughs differ slightly.

Flour/Eggs: Place the flour, salt and any other dry ingredients in the processing bowl. The amount of flour is approximate because the precise amount is determined by the size of the eggs. Add the eggs and process the dough until it forms a ball. To produce a firm but elastic ball of dough, it may be necessary to add 1-4×15ml(tbsp) of flour.

Flour/Eggs/Water or Oil and Water: Put the flour and any other dry ingredients in the processing bowl. With this type of dough the amount of flour is fixed because the desired changes in the consistency are made by adjusting the amount of water. Add the eggs and the oil, if used. Process until the mixture resembles crumbs. With the machine running gradually add the water in small amounts according to the directions in the individual recipe until the dough begins to form a ball. Stop adding water and process until ball is firm and elastic.

Flour/Eggs/Spinach or Other Vegetables or Herbs: Vegetables should be cooked and squeezed totally dry. Herbs, such as parsley or basil, are best left raw. Both must first be processed with the metal blade until they are puréed or very finely chopped. The flour, salt and eggs are then added. At this point directions for individual recipes vary, with some requiring the addition of flour, and some the addition of water to produce a ball of dough of the right consistency. Carefully folllow the directions in the recipe you are using.

Problems: If the ball seems too 'loose' it contains too much liquid. With the machine running, add flour by the 15ml (tbsp) until the dough is firm but still elastic. A ball which is too 'tight' is an indication that too much flour has been worked into it. It will usually crumble when run through the pasta machine. When this happens, break it into small pieces and put it back into the processing bowl. With the machine running, slowly add water by the 5ml (tsp) until the dough has the right consistency. When the dough made from fresh herbs comes apart when run through the pasta machine, it usually means that you did not chop or purée the herbs finely enough, or that you failed to work a sufficient amount of flour into the dough. In the former case, just put the ball back into the machine and process it until the herbs are more finely chopped. In the latter, put the ball back into the machine and process, slowly adding flour by the 15ml (tbsp) until the ball of dough is the right consistency.

Pasta Machine Technique: The instructions that come with the machine are often of little help as the English translation of the Italian is frequently inaccurate. Most pasta machines have an adjustable roller mechanism with settings for rolling flat sheets of dough of different thicknesses. Usually setting number one is the widest and setting number six is the narrowest and makes the thinnest noodles.

1 *Rolling the Dough*: Divide the dough into 8 pieces. Form it into balls and flour well. Do not use cornflour because it will eventually cause the cutting rollers to stick, and is extremely

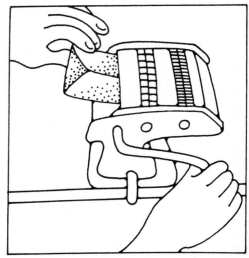

difficult to remove. Our machine techniques do not require resting time to relax the gluten to make the dough more stretchy, but if you are rolling the dough by hand, allow it to rest for 15–20 minutes. Place the dough in a plastic bag to keep it from drying out and remove one ball of dough at a time, flour it, flatten it with the ball of your hand, and pass it through the roller mechanism lengthwise as follows, flouring as necessary:

1st Setting: Pass through the rollers. Fold dough into thirds and pass through two more times.
2nd Setting: Fold dough into thirds and pass through once.
3rd-5th Settings: Pass through each setting once without folding.
6th Setting: Use only if you like your pasta very thin.

2 *Drying*: The dough must be partially dried or the noodles will stick together when they are cut. Drying time depends both on the amount of humidity in the air and on the amount of flouring that you have done. It may take any time from 15 to 35 minutes. You can drape the sheets of dough over chairbacks covered with kitchen towels, or place them on a specially designed pasta rack. If you purchase a pasta rack, make certain that it holds at least eight

sheets of dough. If you want the dough to dry quickly, place it near a sunny window. Be careful not to dry it for too long so that the dough becomes brittle and cracks when run through the cutting rollers.

3 *Cutting the Noodles*: Flour the partially dried sheets of dough and feed them through the cutting roller of your choice, making sure that you catch them as they come out the other side. Hang the noodles to dry until you are ready to use them. Some machines have optional attachments for making lasagne sheets, but they are hardly worth the expense as these large pieces are so easy to cut by hand. An interesting 'square cut' can be achieved by stopping at the fourth setting and then cutting the noodles on the narrow cutting roller.

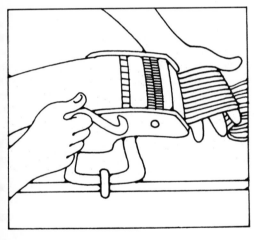

Manual Rolling and Cutting: Mix the dough in the processor as directed above. Divide it into four pieces. Flour well and allow it to rest for 15–20 minutes to relax the gluten for easier stretching and handling. Keep the pieces in a plastic bag to prevent them from drying out. Remove one ball of dough at a time, flatten it with the ball of your hand, and roll it into a circle 30cm (12in) in diameter and 1.5mm (1/16in) thick, or thinner, using a rolling pin or pasta dowel. This is a real art and takes considerable practice. Allow the dough to dry

as above. Flour well, roll up as for a Swiss roll, and cut thin slices with a sharp knife. Unroll and hang up or lay flat on a floured board until ready to use.

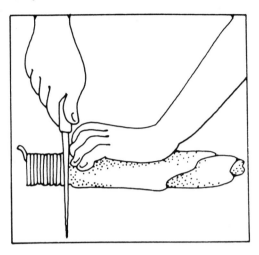

Storage: If you will be using the noodles the same day, just leave them out to dry until you need them. If you will not use them the same day you have two options – freezing them while they are still moist, or allowing them to dry out completely and refrigerating them in a tightly sealed plastic bag.

Cooking: Bring a large pot of water to the boil. Add salt and 2×15ml (tbsp) oil. The oil prevents the noodles from sticking. Add the noodles and boil for 4–7 minutes. To cook frozen noodles, remove from the freezer and drop directly into boiling water without defrosting. If allowed to thaw, the noodles will stick together. Cook the pasta until there is a slight resistance to the bite – this is referred to as cooking *al dente*. The cooking time varies with the degree of dryness and the thickness of the noodles. Moist, freshly made noodles cook in the shortest time. It is best to test them several times to avoid overcooking. Let individual preference be your guide. Remove the pasta with a pasta rake or drain in a colander. Rinsing is not recommended as nutrients are washed away.

Rich Egg Noodles

Serves 4-8

This is our best plain egg noodle recipe. It is unusual because it has no oil or water. The total amount of flour used is determined by the size of the eggs.

225g (8oz) wholewheat flour
½×5ml (tsp) salt
3 eggs, size 2
1-4×15ml (tbsp) additional flour, as required

METAL BLADE: Place the flour and salt in the processing bowl; pulse on/off until well mixed. With the machine off, pour in all the eggs at once. Turn the machine on; process until the dough forms into a solid ball. Stop the processor and feel the dough – it should be firm and elastic. Add extra flour if required. Remove the dough from the processor and flour well. Proceed as in the basic instructions for making pasta at the beginning of this chapter.

Preparation: 45–55 minutes
Protein g/s: 4 servings–11
        6 servings–7.5
        8 servings–5.5

Wholewheat Egg Noodles

Serves 4-6

A good basic recipe for those wanting to cut down on their consumption of eggs.

175g (6oz) wholewheat flour
2 eggs
1×5ml (tsp) oil
½×5ml (tsp) salt
1-9×5ml (tsp) water, as required

METAL BLADE: Place the flour, eggs, oil and salt in the processing bowl. Pulse on/off until the mixture has crumbed, in 3–4 seconds. With the machine running, slowly pour in the water

by the 5ml (tsp) spoonful until the dough begins to gather into a ball. Stop adding water and continue processing until the ball of dough is firm and elastic. Remove the dough from the processor; flour well. Proceed as in the basic instructions for making pasta at the beginning of this chapter.

Preparation: 45–55 minutes
Protein g/s: 4 servings–9.5
        6 servings–6.5

Carrot Noodles

Serves 6-8

Top these orange-yellow noodles with Cacciatore Sauce (see index) and you will be in for a visual and tasty treat!

350g (12oz) carrots, peeled
250ml (10fl oz) water
1×15ml (tbsp) oil
½×5ml (tsp) salt
250g (9oz) wholewheat flour
15g (½oz) milk powder
1 egg
1-5×15ml (tbsp) wholewheat flour, as required

SLICING DISC OR THIN SLICING DISC: Cut the carrots to fit the feed tube vertically; slice with light pressure to produce extra thin slices. Combine carrots, water, oil and salt in a small saucepan. Bring the water to the boil and cook, covered, until the carrots are tender. Drain well and allow to cool slightly.

METAL BLADE: Place the carrots in the processing bowl and process until puréed. Stop the machine and scrape down the sides of the bowl as required. Add the flour, milk and egg. Process until the dough forms a firm, elastic ball, adding extra flour as needed. Remove the dough from the processor and flour well. Proceed as in the basic instructions for making pasta at the beginning of this chapter.

Preparation: 1 hour
Protein g/s: 6 servings–9
　　　　　 8 servings–6.5

Spinach Noodles (Pasta Verde)

Serves 6-8

These noodles are a beautiful grass green when served fresh. Top the noodles with our Basic Marinara Sauce or use when making Baked Green Fettucine (see index).

1×275g (10oz) package frozen leaf spinach, cooked OR
leaves from 450g (1lb) fresh spinach, cooked and cooled
250g (9oz) wholewheat flour
½×5ml (tsp) salt
2 eggs
1-4×15ml (tbsp) wholewheat flour, as required

Allow the spinach to cool enough to handle. Place in a clean tea towel and squeeze out as much liquid as possible.

METAL BLADE: Place the spinach, cooled to room temperature, in the processing bowl. Pulse on/off until finely chopped. It will resemble a purée. With the machine off, add the flour, eggs and salt. Process until the dough forms a firm, elastic ball, adding flour as required. The dough will be slightly sticky. Remove the dough from the workbowl; flour well. Proceed as in the basic instructions for making pasta at the beginning of this chapter.

Preparation: 55–60 minutes
Protein g/s: 6 servings–8.5
　　　　　 8 servings–6.5

Chinese Style Stir-Fried Noodles

Serves 6

Tofu turns this tasty noodle dish into a complementary main course. Excellent when served with Stir-Fried Vegetables and Cashews (see index).

1 quantity Wholewheat Egg Noodles (see index) OR
¾ quantity Rich Egg Noodles (dry or freeze the remainder) OR
225-275g (8-10oz) purchased noodles or spaghetti
1 large carrot, peeled
2-3 medium stalks celery, trimmed
3-4×15ml (tbsp) sesame oil (or similar)
1 small piece root ginger
1 large clove garlic, crushed
2-3×15ml (tbsp) soy sauce
125g (4oz) mung bean sprouts
4 salad onions, cut into 2.5 cm (1in) lengths
½×5ml (tsp) soft brown sugar
275g (10oz) tofu, drained and cut into 2.5cm (1in) cubes

Bring a large pan of water to the boil. Add 2×15ml (tbsp) oil and a pinch of salt. Boil the noodles until cooked *al dente*, 4–7 minutes for fresh noodles, 8–14 minutes for dried noodles. Drain, set aside and keep warm.

SHREDDING DISC: Cut the carrot to fit the feed tube horizontally; shred.

SLICING DISC: Cut the celery to fit the feed tube vertically; slice. In a large pan heat 2×15ml (tbsp) oil. Stir fry the carrots and celery for 1 minute. Wipe the processing bowl completely dry.

METAL BLADE: Cut the ginger into 8 pieces. Start the processor and drop the ginger through the feed tube. Let the processor run until finely grated. Add the ginger and garlic to the pan and stir-fry for 1 minute. Add soy sauce, bean sprouts, salad onions, sugar, tofu and any remaining oil as needed. Stir gently to mix and cook until tofu is hot and bean sprouts are just cooked. Do not overcook; the vegetables should remain crisp. Season to taste with soy sauce. Spoon over warm noodles.

Preparation: 5–10 minutes plus time to prepare the noodles
Cooking: 15–25 minutes
Protein g/s: 10

Lasagne

Serves 8

The food processor takes the work out of shredding and grating the cheese for this classic dish.

1 quantity Wholewheat Egg Noodles (see index) OR
quantity Rich Egg Noodles (see index) OR
225g (8oz) purchased wholewheat lasagne
50g (2oz) Parmesan cheese, at room temperature
225g (8oz) mozzarella cheese, well chilled
750ml (1 pt) Basic Marinara Sauce (see index) or other similar tomato-based sauce
450g (1lb) curd cheese

Prepare the pasta dough according to instructions. Do not allow to dry. Cut by hand into two 36cm (14in) strips. Bring a large pan of water to the boil. Add 1-2×15ml (tbsp) oil and a pinch of salt. Cook the noodles in rapidly boiling water until cooked in 4–8 minutes. Drain and set aside. Cook bought lasagne according to package directions. Drain. Preheat the oven to gas mark 4/180° C/350°F.

METAL BLADE: Place the Parmesan, cut into 2.5cm (1in) pieces, in the processing bowl and process until finely chopped. Remove and set aside.

SHREDDING DISC: Cut the mozzarella cheese to fit the feed tube, shred using light pressure. In a greased 23×33cm (9×13in) or similar size dish, layer half the lasagne, one third of the

sauce, all of the curd cheese, half the mozzarella, one third of the sauce, the remaining lasagne, sauce and mozzarella cheese. Top with grated Parmesan. Bake, covered, for 25–30 minutes or until hot and the cheese is bubbly.

Preparation: 10–15 minutes
allow time to prepare the noodles
Cooking/Baking: 40–55 minutes
Protein g/s: 22

Lentil Spaghetti

Serves 6

Having plenty of cooked lentils and marinara sauce in the freezer speeds up the preparation of dishes like this. Good when served with our wholewheat French bread and a tossed green salad.

350g (12oz) cooked lentils (approx 125g (4oz) dry)
1125ml (2pt) Basic Marinara Sauce (see index) OR
similar tomato-based sauce
125ml (5fl oz) red wine
1 quantity Wholewheat Egg Noodles (see index) OR
Rich Egg Noodles, cut to spaghetti noodle thickness OR
225-350g (8-12oz) purchased wholewheat spaghetti
2×15ml (tbsp) oil
salt
50g (2oz) Parmesan cheese, at room temperature
125g (4oz) mozzarella cheese, well chilled

In a large saucepan, combine the lentils, marinara sauce and wine. Simmer for 5 minutes or until heated through. Keep hot until the noodles are ready. Bring a large pan of water to the boil. Add oil and a pinch of salt.

oil the noodles for 4–7 minutes or until ooked *al dente*. For bought spaghetti, follow e cooking instructions on the packet, 10–15 inutes. Drain.

ETAL BLADE: Place the Parmesan cheese, cut to 2.5cm (1in) pieces, in the processing owl. Process until finely chopped. Remove om the bowl and set aside.

IREDDING DISC: Cut the mozzarella cheese to fit e feed tube; shred using light pressure. To erve, place spaghetti on individual serving lates, top with sauce and generous rinklings of mozzarella and Parmesan eese.

reparation: 10 minutes
        allow time to prepare the noodles
ooking: 15–20 minutes
rotein g/s: 18.5

Two-In-One Tomato Sauce

Makes 500ml (1 pt)

This tomato-based sauce is an excellent opping for pizza. Make up a large quantity nd freeze in small portions for later use.

*medium onion
×15ml (tbsp) olive oil
cloves garlic
×400g (14oz) can whole tomatoes
×15ml (tbsp) tomato paste
×5ml (tsp) dried basil
×15ml (tbsp) dried oregano
×5ml (tsp) soft brown sugar
×5ml (tsp) salt
epper
bay leaf
₂×5ml (tsp) paprika*

METAL BLADE: Place the onion, cut into 2.5cm
1in) pieces, in the processing bowl. Pulse
n/off until finely chopped. Heat the oil in a

large pan and cook the onions until soft and transparent, but not browned. Place the garlic in the processor and pulse on/off until finely chopped. Add the tomatoes and liquid, tomato paste, herbs, sugar, salt and pepper. Process until smooth. Pour the mixture into the pan. Add the bay leaf and stir in the paprika. Cover and simmer for 1½ hours.

VARIATION: For spaghetti sauce consistency, add an extra 200g (7oz) can tomatoes to the sauce.

Preparation: 10 minutes
Cooking: 1½ hours

Pesto Sauce Over Pasta

Serves 6-8

This is an ideal dish to make if you have plenty of fresh basil in your garden. Increase the amount of oil by 2-3×15ml (tbsp) and the sauce will be thinner.

*1 quantity Rich Egg Noodles or Wholewheat Egg Noodles (see index) OR
255-325g (10-12oz) bought noodles
2×15ml (tbsp) oil
salt
150g (5oz) Parmesan cheese, at room temperature
4 teacups full of closely packed basil leaves
100-150ml (4-6fl oz) olive oil
2-4 large cloves garlic, crushed
50g (2oz) shelled pine nuts, optional*

Make the noodles according to directions. Cook after the sauce is prepared.

METAL BLADE: Place the Parmesan, cut into 2.5 cm (1in) pieces, in the processor bowl; process until finely chopped. Wash and thoroughly dry the basil leaves. Add half the basil to the cheese in the processing bowl. Turn the machine on and gradually add the remaining basil through the feed tube. Process until the mixture has the consistency of a purée. Add the garlic and, with the machine running, quickly pour in the oil. Add the pine nuts if used. Process until sauce is smooth.

Bring a large pan of water to the boil. Add 2×15ml (tbsp) oil and a pinch or two of salt. Cook the noodles until *al dente* in 4–7 minutes. Drain. Dried noodles will take a little longer to cook. Cook bought noodles as directed. Place the noodles in a large shallow dish, top with the sauce and toss to mix. Noodles may also be placed on individual dinner plates. Pass the sauce and let each person top and toss their own serving.

Preparation: 10 minutes
allow time to prepare the noodles
Protein g/s: 4 servings–20.5
6 servings–14

Lasagne with Aubergine-Mushroom Sauce

Serves 12

This is a convenient make-ahead dish. Make the sauce one or two days ahead. You do not need to reheat the sauce before assembling the dish.

125g (4oz) Parmesan cheese, at room temperature
325g (12oz) mozzarella cheese, well chilled
1 medium onion
2×15ml (tbsp) oil
1 aubergine, about 450g (1lb) unpeeled
350-450g (12-16) fresh mushrooms
1×300ml (10oz) jar tomato paste
1×400g (14oz) can whole tomatoes
1×5ml (tsp) dried basil
1×15ml(tbsp) dried oregano
pinch dried rosemary
1×5ml (tsp) soft brown sugar
salt and pepper
225g (8oz) bought wholewheat lasagne
675g (1½lb) curd cheese
2 eggs

METAL BLADE: Place the Parmesan cheese, cut into 2.5cm (1in) pieces, in the processing bowl. Process until finely chopped. Remove from the bowl and set aside.

SHREDDING DISC: Cut the mozzarella cheese to fit the feed tube; shred using light pressure. Remove from the bowl and set aside.

METAL BLADE: Place the onion, cut into 2.5cm (1in) pieces, in the processing bowl. Pulse on/off until finely chopped. In a 3-4l (6-8pt) saucepan heat the oil then add the onions and cook until soft in 3–5 minutes.

SLICING DISC: Quarter the aubergine lengthwise; cut into pieces to fit the feed tube vertically; slice. Wedge mushrooms in the feed tube; slice with firm pressure. Add to the onions and continue cooking for 2–3 minutes.

METAL BLADE: Place the tomatoes with the liquid, tomato paste, basil, oregano, rosemary and brown sugar in the processing bowl. Process until smooth. Pour into saucepan and stir to mix. Cover and simmer for about 1 hour or until thickened. Taste and adjust the seasoning.

While the sauce is cooking, cook the noodles according to directions until *al dente*. Drain and set aside. Preheat the oven to gas mark 4/180°C/350°F. In a small mixing bowl combine the curd cheese and eggs. Spread one third of the sauce over the bottom of an ungreased 23×33cm (9×13in) or similar sized baking dish. Layer half the noodles and spread over all the curd filling. Continue layering with half of the mozzarella cheese, one third of the sauce, remaining noodles, sauce and mozzarella cheese. Top with Parmesan cheese. Bake, covered, for 25–30 minutes or until hot and the cheese is bubbly. Allow to stand for 5 minutes, then cut into squares and serve.

Note: If planning to reheat to serve later, bake for only 15 minutes then cool and refrigerate. To reheat, bake in a preheated oven at gas mark 4/180°C/350°F for 30–40 minutes or until hot.

Preparation: 15–20 minutes
Cooking/Baking: 1 hour 45 minutes to 2 hours
Standing: 5 minutes
Protein g/s: 20.5

Cacciatore Sauce over Noodles

Serves 4-6

This has been a favourite with guests and family. When using a vegetable stock select one with a delicate vegetable flavour rather than a beefy one.

50-125g (2-4oz) Parmesan cheese, at room
temperature
2 medium or large onions
450g (1lb) carrots, peeled
350g (12oz) celery stalks, trimmed
4×15ml (tbsp) olive oil
½×5ml (tsp) salt
2 vegetable stock cubes
50ml (2fl oz) boiling water
4×15ml (tbsp) tomato paste
450-500ml (approx 1pt) dry sherry
salt and pepper
1 quantity Wholewheat Egg Noodles (see
index) OR
275-350g (10-12oz) bought wholewheat
tagliatelle OR
¾ quantity Rich Egg Noodles (freeze or dry
remainder for later use) OR
quantity Carrot Noodles
(freeze or dry remainder for later use)

METAL BLADE: Place the Parmesan, cut into 2.5cm (1in) pieces, in the processing bowl and process until finely chopped. Remove from the bowl and set aside. Place the onions, cut into 2.5cm (1in) pieces, in the processor and pulse on/off until fairly finely chopped.

SLICING DISC: Cut the carrots to fit the feed tube vertically; slice. Cut the celery to fit the feed tube vertically; slice.

Heat the oil in a 3-4l (6-8pt) saucepan. Add the onions and vegetables and cook until tender, in 5–8 minutes. Add ½×5ml (tsp) salt. Dissolve the stock cubes in boiling water and stir into the pan with the tomato paste and half the sherry. Cover and simmer for 15 minutes to allow the sauce to thicken. Add the remaining sherry and continue to simmer for 10 minutes. Stir in salt and pepper to taste. Meanwhile, bring a large pan of water to the boil, add 2×15ml (tbsp) oil and a pinch of salt. Boil the noodles until cooked *al dente*, about 4–7 minutes. Cook bought tagliatelle as directed. Drain. Serve the sauce over the hot noodles. Sprinkle 2×15ml (tbsp) Parmesan cheese over each serving.

Preparation: 10 minutes
Cooking: 35 minutes for the sauce
allow time to cook the noodles
Protein g/s: 4 servings–14
6 servings–11

Basic Marinara Sauce

Makes approx 3.5l (7pt)

This multi-purpose sauce is used in a number of our recipes. This recipe makes a large amount but it freezes well. Freeze in 250 or 500ml (½pt or 1pt) containers.

3-5 large onions
1 green pepper, halved and deseeded
4-5×15ml (tbsp) oil
4×400g (14oz) cans sieved tomatoes
1 ×300g (10oz) jar tomato paste
625ml (1pt) water
good pinch dried rosemary
good pinch dried oregano
1 bay leaf
½×5ml (tsp) dried thyme
½×5ml (tsp) dried marjoram
3 whole cloves
2×5ml (tsp) soft brown sugar
salt to taste
250ml (10fl oz) red wine (optional)

METAL BLADE: Place the onions, cut into 2.5cm (1in) pieces, in the processing bowl. Pulse on/off until chopped. Heat the oil in a large pan, add the onions and cook for 1–2 minutes. Meanwhile, place the green pepper, cut into 2.5cm (1in) pieces, in the processing bowl and pulse on/off until chopped fairly finely. Add the pepper to the onions and continue cooking until the onions are soft and transparent. Stir in the sieved tomatoes, tomato paste, water, rosemary, oregano, bay leaf, thyme, marjoram, cloves and brown sugar. Simmer, covered, for 1–2 hours. This can also be cooked in an electric slow cooker for about 4 hours. Add salt to taste, then add the wine and cook for a further 5–10 minutes to allow the flavours to blend.

Preparation: 10 minutes
Cooking: 1½–2 hours on the hob
         4 hours in a slow cooker

Gnocchi Verde

Serves 4-6, makes 20 dumplings

Topped with our Basic Marinara Sauce (see index), these spinach dumplings make an elegant main dish. Serve with slices of hot wholewheat French bread and a tossed green salad.

1×275g (10oz) packet frozen leaf spinach, defrosted and squeezed dry OR
450g (1lb) fresh spinach, cooked and squeezed dry
2×15ml (tbsp) butter or margarine
75g (3oz) curd cheese
pepper
½×5ml (tsp) nutmeg
2 eggs
75g (3oz) Parmesan cheese, at room temperature
50g (2oz) wholewheat flour
4×15ml (tbsp) freshly chopped basil
salt

Heat the butter in a large pan. Add the spinach and cook until all traces of moisture have evaporated, 4-6 minutes. Stir in the curd cheese, pepper and nutmeg. Continue cooking for 5 minutes, stirring constantly. Remove from the heat and allow to cool to room temperature, approximately 10 minutes.

METAL BLADE: Place the Parmesan cheese, cut into 2.5cm (1in) pieces, in the processing bowl. Process until finely chopped. With the machine off, add the spinach mixture, eggs, flour and basil. Pulse on/off until the spinach and basil are finely chopped and the ingredients are well mixed.

Season to taste with salt. Remove from the processor and place in a mixing bowl; cover and refrigerate for at least 1 hour. Bring a large pot of water to the boil and add a pinch of salt. For each gnocchi, shape about 1×5ml (tsp) spinach mixture into a ball. Flour and drop into the boiling water; stir once or twice to prevent sticking. Simmer for 8–10 minutes. Drain and serve.

Preparation: 20 minutes
Cooking: 20–25 minutes
Standing: 10 minutes
Chilling: 1 hour
Protein g/s: 4 servings–15.5
             6 servings–10.5

Baked Green Fettucine

Serves 6-8

We owe this garlic lover's delight to our friend, Ann Williams. When the noodles are made in advance, the dish is quick to prepare. The recipe can easily be halved. Freeze or dry the remaining noodles for later use.

1 quantity Spinach Noodles (see index), cut 5mm (¼in) wide OR
450g (1lb) bought green (spinach) noodles
325g (12oz) Parmesan cheese, at room temperature

3-4×15ml (tbsp) butter or margarine
4-8 large cloves garlic, crushed
2 sprigs parsley

METAL BLADE: Place the Parmesan cheese, cut into 2.5cm (1in) cubes, in the processing bowl and process until finely chopped. Remove and set aside. Wipe the processing bowl completely dry then prepare the noodles, if not made in advance.

Bring a large pan of water to the boil. Add 2×15ml (tbsp) oil and a pinch of salt. Boil the noodles until cooked *al dente*, about 4 minutes for fresh noodles, longer for dried. Drain. Cook bought pasta as directed.

Preheat the oven to gas mark 4/180°C/350°F. Layer ¼ of the noodles over the bottom of a large, greased baking dish. Dot with butter and garlic and sprinkle with ¼ of the Parmesan cheese. Repeat the layering, ending with a sprinkling of cheese.

METAL BLADE: Place the parsley in the processing bowl; pulse on/off until finely chopped. Set aside for garnish. Bake for about 20 minutes or until the aroma of garlic permeates the kitchen. Garnish with the parsley.

Preparation: 10 minutes, when the noodles are
    prepared in advance
Baking: 20 minutes
Protein g/s: 6 servings–28
    8 servings–21

Wholewheat Ravioli

Serves 6

Your pasta machine will roll sheets of dough thin enough for ravioli. With a great deal of elbow grease the dough can be rolled, by hand, to 1.5mm (1/16in) or thinner. When rolling by hand allow the dough to rest, covered, momentarily during the process to relax the gluten. Follow the directions at the beginning of this chapter.

1 quantity of Wholewheat Egg Noodles OR
Rich Egg Noodles (see index)
1×275g (10oz) packet frozen leaf spinach, defrosted
75g (3oz) Parmesan cheese, at room temperature
125g (4oz) curd cheese
ground nutmeg
2×15ml (tbsp) chopped fresh basil OR
1×15ml (tbsp) dried basil
2 eggs
1l (2pt) Basic Marinara Sauce (see index)
Additional Parmesan cheese for topping, optional

Make the noodle dough according to directions. Place in a plastic bag and allow to rest whilst making the filling. Wipe the processor bowl dry. Place defrosted spinach in a clean tea towel and squeeze out all the excess liquid. Set the spinach aside.

METAL BLADE: Place the Parmesan cheese, cut into 2.5cm (1in) pieces, in the processing bowl. Process until finely chopped. Add the spinach, curd cheese, nutmeg, basil and eggs. Pulse on/off until spinach is finely chopped.

Divide the dough into four pieces and place in a plastic bag to prevent drying. Remove one piece at a time and shape into a ball. Flour well, flatten and feed through the roller mechanism of your pasta machine as follows, flouring as necessary:

1st Setting: Pass through the rollers. Fold the dough into thirds and pass through two or more times, once horizontally and once vertically.

2nd Setting: Fold dough into thirds and pass through once, vertically.

3rd–4th Setting: Pass through each setting once without folding. Cut the dough in half, making two equally long wide pieces; flour.

5th Setting: Pass each piece through once without folding.

Take care not to allow the dough to dry during rolling or filling as dry dough does not seal well. The pieces will be very thin. Place one sheet on a floured board and dot with 1×5ml (tsp) of filling at 4cm (1½in) intervals, allowing a border around the edges. Place the second sheet of dough over the filling. With your fingertips press down between the filling mounds; cut into squares with a fluted pastry wheel. To be sure that the edges are well sealed trace again with the pastry wheel along the outer edge. Set ravioli aside on a floured surface until you are ready to cook.

Repeat with the remaining two sheets of dough. Bring a large pan of water to the boil. Add 2-3×15ml (tbsp) oil and a litle salt. Cook ravioli about 10–15 minutes. Heat marinara sauce. Drain the ravioli; place on serving plates and top with marinara sauce and a sprinkling of Parmesan.

Preparation: 2 hours, excluding marinara
sauce
Cooking: 15 minutes
Protein g/s: 17.5

Wheat Germ Noodles

Serves 4–8

This is a nutritious variation of our basic recipe.

175g (6oz) wholewheat flour
40g (1½oz) wheat germ
½×5ml (tsp) salt
2 eggs
5-9×15ml (tbsp) water, as required

METAL BLADE: Place the flour, wheat germ and salt in the processing bowl; pulse on/off to mix. Add the eggs and process until the mixture resembles crumbs, 3–4 seconds. With the machine running, slowly pour in the water by the 5ml (tsp) spoonful until the dough begins to gather into a ball. Stop adding the water and continue processing until the ball of dough is firm and elastic. Remove the dough from the processor and flour well. Proceed as in the basic instructions for making pasta at the beginning of this chapter.

Preparation: 45–55 minutes
Protein g/s: 4 servings–12.5
6 servings–8
8 servings–6

Parsley Noodles

Serves 4-6

Fresh parsley leaves are used in this simple recipe. To measure, pinch off the leaves, discard the stems and pack tightly into a teacup.

1 teacup parsley leaves, packed tightly
200g (7oz) wholewheat flour
½×5ml (tsp) salt
2 eggs
1-3×5ml (tsp) water

Wash and dry the parsley leaves.

METAL BLADE: Place the parsley in the processing bowl. Pulse on/off until the consistency is so fine that it is almost a purée. Stop the machine; add flour, salt and eggs. Pulse on/off until the mixture has the texture of crumbs. With the machine running, slowly pour in the water by the 5ml (tsp) spoonful until the dough begins to gather into a ball. Stop adding water and continue to process until the ball of dough is firm and elastic. Remove from the processor and flour well. Proceed as in the basic instructions for making pasta at the beginning of this chapter.

Preparation: 45–55 minutes
Protein g/s: 4 servings–10.5
6 servings–7

Spinach Lasagne

Serves 8

This version of our basic Lasagne (see index) has been popular with both family and friends.

ingredients as for Lasagne
1×275-325g (10-12oz) packet frozen leaf spinach or leaves from 325-425g (12-16oz) fresh spinach

Cook spinach in a small amount of water. Drain in a colander and allow to cool slightly. Place the spinach in a clean teatowel and squeeze to remove as much water as possible.

METAL BLADE: Place the curd cheese and spinach in the processing bowl. Process until the spinach is finely chopped. Stop the machine and scrape down the sides of the bowl as needed. The mixture should be smooth. Proceed as directed in Lasagne recipe.

Preparation: 10–15 minutes allow time to prepare the noodles
Cooking/Baking: 45–60 minutes
Protein g/s: 22

Aubergine or Courgette Parmesan

Serves 6-8

Whole grain bread and a tossed green salad make this a delightful meal.

2 aubergines, about 900-1125g (2-2½lb), unpeeled OR
900-1125g (2-2½lb) courgettes
2 eggs, beaten
50-75g (2-3oz) wholewheat flour
salt
oil for frying
40g (1½oz) Parmesan cheese, at room temperature
225g (8oz) mozzarella cheese, well chilled
400-500ml (15-20fl oz) Basic Marinara Sauce (see index) or similar sauce

With a sharp knife cut the aubergines or courgettes into 6mm (¼in) thick slices. Place the eggs and flour in two separate shallow dishes. Dip the aubergine into the beaten egg then into the flour. Salt the slices lightly. In a non-stick pan, heat 1-2×5ml (tsp) oil over a medium heat. Fry the aubergine until golden brown on both sides. As the slices are browned, place on paper towels to absorb the excess oil.

METAL BLADE: Place the Parmesan cheese, cut into 2.5cm (1in) pieces, in the processing bowl; process until finely chopped. Remove from the bowl and set aside.

SHREDDING DISC: Cut the mozzarella cheese to fit the feed tube; shred using light pressure. Preheat the oven to gas mark 5/190°C/375°F. Place overlapping slices of aubergine or courgette over the bottom of a greased 22×34cm (8½×13½in) or similar sized dish. Spoon on marinara sauce, top with mozzarella cheese and sprinkle on the Parmesan cheese. Bake, uncovered, for 20–30 minutes or until hot and the cheese is bubbly.

Preparation: 10 minutes
Cooking/Baking: 50 minutes
Protein g/s: 6 servings–15.5
　　　　　　 8 servings–11.5

Parmesan Courgette-Basil Sauce over Pasta

Serves 4

A quickly prepared sauce when you want a meal in a hurry. It is especially delicious over homemade pasta.

1 quantity Wholewheat Egg Noodles or Rich Egg Noodles (see index) OR
225-325g (8-12oz) bought wholewheat pasta
75g (3oz) Parmesan cheese, at room temperature
450g (1lb) courgettes, washed and trimmed
1×15ml (tbsp) oil
50g (2oz) butter or margarine
2×15ml (tbsp) oil
1×15ml (tbsp) wholewheat flour
250ml (10fl oz) skimmed milk
6-8 fresh basil leaves, chopped or 1×5ml (tsp) dried
salt

If making fresh noodles prepare them first. Do not cook them until the sauce is nearly ready. Bought pasta may be cooked in advance and kept warm.

METAL BLADE: Place the Parmesan cheese, cut into 2.5cm (1in) pieces, in the processing bowl. Process until finely grated. Remove from the bowl and set aside.

SLICING DISC: Cut the courgettes to fit the feed tube horizontally; slice. Remove the slices. Insert the pusher into the feed tube, leaving a space at the bottom. Hold the cover sideways and wedge a stack of sliced courgettes in horizontally with the cut sides at right angles to the cover. Slice again to produce julienne strips.

Heat 1×15ml (tbsp) oil in a 25cm (10in) frying pan. Cook the courgettes until golden brown, about 5 minutes. In a separate pan, heat the 2×15ml (tbsp) oil with the butter. Stir in the flour and cook for 1 minute. Gradually add the milk, stirring constantly with a wire whisk, until thickened. Stir in the courgettes, Parmesan, basil and salt to taste. Toss until the Parmesan is melted and the sauce is smooth. Serve immediately over hot cooked pasta.

Preparation: 15 minutes
Cooking: 10 minutes
Protein g/s: 18.5 using homemade noodles

Pasta Rustica

Serves 6

The beans, noodles and cheese are complementary in this hearty pasta dish with vegetables. Serve with a tossed green salad and hot whole grain bread.

1 quantity Wholewheat Egg Noodles (see index) OR
275-350g (10-12oz) bought wholewheat tagliatelle

1-2×15ml (tbsp) oil
salt
50g (2oz) Parmesan cheese, at room temperature
2 small carrots, peeled
1 small turnip, about 125g (4oz), peeled
1 large or 2 small leeks
2-3×15ml (tbsp) oil
3×15ml (tbsp) freshly chopped parsley
3×15ml (tbsp) fresh chopped basil or 1×5ml (tsp) dried basil
750ml (1½pt) Basic Marinara Sauce (see index)
225g (8oz) cabbage
3 small courgettes, washed
325g (12oz) cooked kidney beans, well drained (175g (6oz) dry)
salt and pepper

Bring a large pan of water to the boil, add 1-2×15ml (tbsp) oil and a little salt. Boil the noodles until cooked *al dente* in 4-7 minutes. Drain and set aside. When using bought noodles, cook as directed. Drain and set aside.

METAL BLADE: Place the Parmesan cheese, cut into 2.5cm (1in) pieces in the processing bowl; process until finely chopped. Remove from the bowl and set aside.

SLICING DISC: Cut the carrots to fit the feed tube vertically; slice. Remove from the bowl. Cut the turnip into 8 wedges. Place in the feed tube vertically; slice.

Wash leek(s) thoroughly to remove the grit collected between the leaves. Discard the tough, upper portions of the tops. With a sharp knife, cut into 6mm (¼in) pieces. In a 3-4l (6-8pt) saucepan, heat 2-3×15ml (tbsp) oil over a medium heat. Add the carrots, cook for 1-2 minutes; add the leeks and cook for 30 seconds; add the turnips and continue to cook for 3-4 minutes.

SLICING DISC: Cut the cabbage into wedges to fit the feed tube; slice. Cut the courgette to fit the feed tube vertically; slice. Stir into the marinara sauce. Continue cooking for 3-5 minutes or until the courgettes are just cooked.

Carefully stir in the noodles and beans. Cover and cook for 2 minutes to allow the flavours to blend. To serve, top individual portions with a sprinkling of Parmesan cheese.

Preparation: 15 minutes
Cooking: 20 minutes when noodles, beans and sauce are prepared ahead of time.
Protein g/s: 14

Hungarian Paprika Noodles

Serves 6

Homemade noodles are transformed into something special with this delightful sauce. While the taste is authentic, it's higher in protein and lower in fat than the traditional version. Rennetless cottage cheese, cultured with acidophilus, provides the taste, but not the fat, of sour cream. If it is not readily available, regular cottage cheese may be substituted. The final product will be a bit less flavourful but nonetheless acceptable.

1 quantity Wholewheat Noodles (see index) OR
noodles of your choice
4 medium onions
3-4×15ml (tbsp) oil
2-3×15ml (tbsp) paprika
2 vegetable stock cubes dissolved in 150ml (6fl oz) boiling water
450-575g (1-1¼lb) fresh mushrooms
1×5ml (tsp) Worcestershire sauce
1×5ml (tsp) salt
125ml (5fl oz) dry sherry
additional water, as required
575g (1¼lb) cottage cheese
3×15ml (tbsp) sour cream

METAL BLADE: Place the onions, cut into 2.5cm (1in) pieces, in the processing bowl; pulse on/off until finely chopped. Heat 3 × 15ml (tbsp) oil in a large saucepan, add the onions and cook until soft, 5–8 minutes. Stir in the paprika and cook for a further minute, stirring

to prevent the paprika from burning. Remove from the heat.

SLICING DISC: Wedge the mushrooms in the feed tube; slice. Heat the remaining oil in a pan, add the mushrooms and cook until they are tender and most of the liquid has evaporated. Add them to the onions and stir in the stock, Worcestershire sauce, sherry and salt. Return the pan to the heat and continue to simmer for 5 minutes to allow the flavours to blend. Add extra water only if the mixture begins to dry. Remove from heat.

METAL BLADE: Place the cottage cheese and sour cream in the processing bowl and process until just smooth in 30-60 seconds – do not overprocess. Stir the cottage cheese mixture into the saucepan. Place the sauce in a casserole dish and keep warm in the oven until ready to serve. Do not overheat after the cottage cheese has been added or the cheese will curdle. Cook the noodles according to directions, drain and serve topped with the sauce.

Preparation: 15 minutes
Cooking: 20 minutes plus time to cook the noodles
Protein g/s: 17

Cashew Noodle Crunch

Serves 8

Cashews make this dish a special treat.

175g (6oz) raw cashews, roasted at gas mark 4/180°C/350°F for 15-20 minutes
225g (8oz) Cheddar cheese, well chilled
1 medium onion
2 stalks celery, trimmed
1 medium green pepper, halved and deseeded
3-4×15ml (tbsp) oil
3 salad onions, cut into 2.5cm (1in) lengths
salt
3×15ml (tbsp) wholewheat flour

500ml (1pt) milk
1×5ml (tsp) Dijon mustard
1 quantity Wholewheat Egg Noodles (see index) OR *3/4 quantity Rich Egg Noodles (freeze or dry the remainder)* OR *275-325g (10-12oz) bought pasta shapes of your choice paprika*

SHREDDING DISC: Cut the Cheddar cheese to fit the feed tube; shred. Remove from the bowl and set aside.

METAL BLADE: Place the onions, cut into 2.5cm (1in) pieces, in the processing bowl; pulse on/off until chopped.

SLICING DISC: Cut the celery to fit the feed tube vertically: slice. Quarter each green pepper half, wedge into the feed tube vertically; slice.

Heat the oil in a saucepan, add the vegetables and cook until tender, 8–10 minutes. Add the salad onions and salt. Stir gently to mix. Sprinkle in the flour and toss to mix. Gradually stir in the milk and simmer until smooth and thickened. Add the mustard. Stir in the cheese and cook until it has melted and the sauce is smooth. Turn off the heat.

Bring a large pan of water to the boil, add 2×15ml (tbsp) oil and a pinch of salt. Boil the noodles for 4–7 minutes or until they are cooked *al dente*. Cook bought pasta as directed. Drain.

Preheat the oven to gas mark 4/180°C/350°F. Pour the noodles into a greased 23×33cm (9×13in) or similar baking dish. Pour in the sauce and toss to mix well. Top with the cashews and a generous sprinkle of paprika. Bake for 25–30 minutes or until hot and bubbly.

Preparation: 10 minutes
Cooking/Baking: 50–60 minutes
Protein g/s: 17

Pizzas and Turnovers

Mini Pitta Pizzas

Serves 1

Wholewheat pitta bread is used for the crust of this 'pizza'. Serve with a tossed green salad for a quick and simple dinner.

1 wholewheat pitta, homemade (see index) or bought
2×15ml (tbsp) Basic Marinara Sauce (see index)
pinch dried oregano
50g (2oz) mozzarella cheese, well chilled
1×15ml (tbsp) onion
25g (1oz) fresh mushrooms
¼ medium green pepper

Preheat the oven to gas mark 6/200°C/400°F. Spread the sauce on the pitta; sprinkle with oregano.

SHREDDING DISC: Cut the mozzarella cheese to fit the feed tube; using light pressure, shred. Sprinkle over the sauce.

METAL BLADE: Place the onion in the processor; pulse on/off to chop. Squeeze out any excess liquid then scatter the onion over the cheese.

SLICING DISC: Stack the mushrooms in the feed tube; slice. Cut the pepper into 4 pieces, stack in the feed tube vertically and slice. Place the mushrooms and green pepper evenly over the onions.
    Place the pitta pizza on a baking sheet; bake for 15–20 minutes or until the cheese is melted and bubbly.

Preparation: 10 minutes
Baking: 15–20 minutes
Protein g/s: 20.5

Cottage Cheese Oil Pizza Crust

Serves 8

This high protein baking powder crust is quick to prepare. The taste is surprisingly similar to a yeast-risen crust. It is based on a dough developed by the Dr Oetker test kitchens in Bielefeld, Germany.

225g (8oz) wholewheat flour
½×5ml (tsp) salt
2½×5ml (tsp) baking powder
150g (5oz) cottage cheese, well drained
4×15ml (tbsp) oil
3-5×15ml (tbsp) milk
additional flour for rolling out the dough

Preheat the oven to gas mark 6/200°C/400°F.

METAL BLADE: Place the flour, salt and baking powder in the processing bowl and pulse on/off to mix. Remove the cover of the processor and add the cottage cheese and oil.

Process until well mixed. With the machine running, add the milk by 15ml (tbsp) spoonfuls until the dough forms a soft ball. Stop the machine as soon as the ball has formed.

If the dough is sticky, sprinkle it with flour before placing on a floured board. Using a rolling pin, roll the dough to a circle measuring 36–38cm (14–15in) in diameter. If it is difficult to work the dough let it 'rest' for a few minutes and then continue shaping.

Place the dough on a well greased baking sheet or pizza pan. Pinch up the edges to form a slight ridge. Spread on your favourite sauce and toppings. Bake for 20–25 minutes.

Preparation: 6–8 minutes
Baking: 20–25 minutes
Protein g/s: Crust only–5.5

Onion Mushroom Pizza

Serves 8

A tossed green salad is perfect with this dish.

1 Cottage Cheese Oil Crust (see index)
300-375ml (12-15fl oz) Basic Marinara Sauce (see index)
½×5ml (tsp) dried oregano
1 medium onion
125g (4oz) fresh mushrooms
½ medium green pepper

Preheat the oven to gas mark 6/200°C/400°F. Spread the sauce over the pizza crust.

SHREDDING DISC: Cut the mozzarella cheese to fit the feed tube; shred using light pressure. Spread the cheese over the sauce. Sprinkle with the oregano.

METAL BLADE: Place the onion, cut into 8 wedges, in the processing bowl. Pulse on/off until roughly chopped. Remove any excess moisture by squeezing in paper towels. Arrange the onion in an even layer over the cheese.

SLICING DISC: Stack the mushrooms in the feed tube; slice. Cut green pepper into vertical strips, stack in the feed tube and slice. Top the pizza with sliced mushrooms and green pepper. Bake for 20–25 minutes or until the cheese is melted and bubbly.

Preparation: 10 minutes
Baking: 20–25 minutes
Protein g/s: 13.5

Sicilian Pizza

Serves 6

1×15ml (tbsp) easy-blend dried yeast
275g (10oz) wholewheat flour
¾×5ml (tsp) salt
250ml (10fl oz) water
2×15ml (tbsp) olive oil
50g (2oz) Parmesan cheese, at room temperature
225g (8oz) mozzarella cheese, well chilled
250ml (10fl oz) Two-in-One Tomato Sauce (see index)
choice of toppings; fresh sliced mushrooms, olives, green pepper, courgettes

METAL BLADE: Place the Parmesan, cut into 2.5cm (1in) pieces, in the processing bowl and process until finely chopped. Remove and set aside. Place the flour and salt in the processor with the easy-blend yeast. Pulse on/off to mix. With the machine running, gradually add the water until the ingredients form a soft ball of dough. You may not need all the water. Process the dough for 20 seconds. Pour in the olive oil and process for a further 10 seconds. Place the dough in a plastic bag and allow it to rest for 25 minutes.

SHREDDING DISC: Cut the mozzarella cheese to fit the feed tube; using light pressure, shred. Set aside.

SLICING DISC: Slice the toppings of your choice. Lightly grease a 25×36cm (10×14in) or similar size baking tin. Pat the dough to fit the tin. Cover with a plastic bag and set to rise in a warm place until almost doubled in bulk, in about 25 minutes. Preheat the oven to gas mark 6/200°C/400°F.Brush the top of the dough with olive oil. Bake in the preheated oven for 5 minutes or until a crust is just beginning to set. Remove from the oven and spread the sauce evenly over the crust. Top with the mozzarella and Parmesan cheeses and sliced toppings of your choice. Continue baking at gas mark 6/200°C/400°F for 20–25 minutes until the crust is golden brown and the cheese is bubbly.

Preparation: 15–20 minutes
Standing: allow 1–1½ hours for the dough to rise
Baking: 25–30 minutes
Protein g/s: 20

Quiches, Pies and Tarts

Wholewheat Quiche Shell

Makes 1

The egg white to glaze the shell is borrowed from the custard for the quiche. Return the unused portion to the custard.

125g (4oz) wholewheat flour
pinch salt
50g (2oz) butter, well chilled
1 egg
½×15ml (tbsp) lemon juice or water

METAL BLADE: Place the flour and salt in the processing bowl, pulse on/off to mix. Add the butter, cut into 2.5 (1in) pieces, pulse on/off until the mixture resembles crumbs. With the machine running, add the egg and lemon juice. Stop processing as soon as the dough begins to form a ball.

Flatten the dough into a 20cm (8in) circle and dust lightly with flour. Place between two sheets of waxed paper. Using a rolling pin, roll from the centre outward in all directions. Carefully peel off the top sheet of waxed paper to release dough, replace paper and turn over. Repeat on the second side. Continue rolling out dough, lifting off waxed paper and turning until a circle 28cm (11in) in diameter is formed.

Roll the dough over the lightly floured rolling pin and gently lift over a 23cm (9in) quiche tin with removable bottom. Unroll the dough into position and gently press into place. Trim excess away by rolling the pin across the top of the tin.

Prick the entire surface of the shell with a fork. To seal the dough against moisture and prevent it from becoming soggy, brush with lightly beaten egg white. Let the case dry uncovered in the refrigerator for about 1 hour. Glaze may also be set by placing the shell in a preheated oven at gas mark 8/250°C/450°F for 2–3 minutes. Remove to a rack and cool before filling.

Preparation: 5 minutes
Standing: allow 1 hour for egg white glaze to
             dry in refrigerator or for heated
             shell to cool
Protein g/s: 4

Wholewheat Filo Dough

Makes 16 sheets

Our fondness for spanakopita prompted us to develop this wholewheat version. While it is not as thin as machine-made filo sheets, it is a workable alternative for the nutrition-conscious cook. Good results are achieved using a food processor for the dough and an Italian pasta maker to obtain thin sheets. The only drawback is that the width of the dough is determined by the width of the pasta maker. For many uses it is not imperative to have large sheets.

225g (8oz) wholewheat flour
1 egg
2×5ml (tsp) oil, preferably olive
125ml (5fl oz) lukewarm water
1-5×15ml (tbsp) cornflour
additional cornflour

METAL BLADE: Place the flour, egg and oil in the processing bowl. Turn the machine on and slowly pour in the water. Continue processing until the dough forms a ball. This usually takes no more than 2–3 seconds after you have added the water. With the machine running add the cornflour, 1×15ml (tbsp) spoonful at a time. Usually 2–3 seconds are enough to make the dough smooth and elastic. The ball will break up and re-form each time you add cornflour. When sufficient has been added the dough will be silky smooth, moderately firm but still very elastic. Another sure sign is a clean work bowl when you remove the dough. Coat with cornflour.

Allow the dough to rest for about 10 minutes in a plastic bag. Divide into 8 pieces, kneading each one by hand for 30 seconds. Roll in cornflour. Keep the pieces in a plastic bag, removing them one at a time. Flatten the dough with the ball of your hand and insert into the roller mechanism as follows, flouring with cornflour as necessary.

1st Setting: Pass through once. Fold into thirds and pass through again lengthwise. By now the piece should measure roughly 5×15cm (2×6in) Fold into thirds and pass through again lengthwise.

2nd Setting: Fold into thirds and pass through horizontally. Stretch by hand to make the piece as nearly square as possible.

3rd–5th Setting: Pass through each setting vertically without folding. At this point the dough should measure roughly 13×38cm (5 × 15in). Cut into two 19cm (7½in) long pieces and flour well.

6th Setting: Pass each piece through once without folding. Now each piece should measure roughly 14×38cm (5½×15in).

Now do a little horizontal stretching with the tips of your fingers, working out from the centre to increase the width by 4–5cm (1½–2in). Flour well with cornflour and place between sheets of waxed paper until ready for use. Sheets should be used almost immediately because they dry out rapidly. They freeze well if layered between sheets of wax paper and sealed in a plastic bag.

Preparation: 40 minutes
Protein g/s: 4.5

Wholewheat Pâté Brisée Crust

Makes 1 shell

This is the wholewheat version of a recipe developed by Cuisinarts Inc. It makes an excellent shell for quiche or fruit pies because it does not absorb moisture easily. This pastry may be used immediately or chilled if desired. If chilled, allow to stand at room temperature to soften slightly.

175g (6oz) wholewheat flour
½×5ml (tsp) salt
125g (4oz) butter, well chilled
4×15ml (tbsp) ice water
1-2×15ml (tbsp) additional ice water if required

METAL BLADE: Place the flour and water in the processing bowl and pulse on/off to mix. Add the butter, cut into 2.5cm (1in) pieces, and pulse on/off until the mixture resembles crumbs. With the machine running, pour the ice water through the tube in a steady stream. Stop processing as soon as the pastry begins to form a ball. Only add extra water if required.

Flatten the pastry into a 20cm (8in) round circle and dust lightly with flour. Place between two sheets of waxed paper. Using a rolling pin, roll from the centre outwards in all directions. Carefully peel off the top sheet of paper to release the pastry, replace the paper and turn over. Repeat on the second side. Continue rolling out the dough, lifting off the waxed paper and turning until the circle is 3mm (⅛in) thick and 5cm (2in) larger than the pie tin.

Roll the pastry onto the rolling pin and gently lift over the tin then unroll into position. Press into place and trim the edges.

For a 27cm (10¾in) quiche tin trim the excess pastry by rolling the pin across the top of the tin.

For a 23cm (9in) springform tin, reserve one third of the pastry. Roll the remainder to a circle to fit the bottom of the tin. Divide the reserved pastry into 4 pieces. Roll each into a 15–16.5cm (6–6½in) strip. Press into the sides of the tin to form an edge about 2.5cm (1in) high. Join seams well.

Prick the entire surface of the shell evenly with a fork. Refrigerate the pastry for 10–15 minutes. Meanwhile, preheat the oven to gas mark 6/200°C/400°F. Bake for 12–15 minutes until golden. For a part-baked crust bake for 7–10 minutes.

Preparation: 10–15 minutes
Baking: 12–15 minutes
Chilling: 10–15 minutes
Protein g/s: 2.5

Mushroom Quiche

Serves 6

1×23cm (9in) Wholewheat Quiche Shell, glazed with egg white, cooled
25g (1oz) Parmesan cheese, at room temperature
3 salad onions
75g (3oz) butter or margarine
325g (12oz) mushrooms
1×15ml (tbsp) fresh lemon juice
2×15ml (tbsp) Madeira
salt
3 eggs
2×15ml (tbsp) dry white wine or vermouth
250ml (10fl oz) milk
salt and pepper
pinch nutmeg

METAL BLADE: Place the Parmesan cheese, cut into 2.5cm (1in) pieces, in the processing bowl. Process until finely chopped. Remove from the bowl and set aside. Place the onions,

cut into 5cm (2in) lengths, in the processing bowl and pulse on/off until finely minced. Scrape down the sides of the bowl as necessary. Heat the butter in a pan, add the onions and cook until soft, 3–5 minutes.

SLICING DISC: Stack the mushrooms sideways in the feed tube; slice with firm pressure. Add the mushrooms to the pan and cook for 2 minutes. Add the lemon juice, Madeira and salt. Cover the pan and cook for 5 minutes. Uncover, and cook until the liquid has evaporated. Stir the mushrooms occasionally to prevent them from sticking. Cook until the mushrooms are lightly browned. Preheat the oven to gas mark 5/190°C/375°F. Pour the wine into a measuring jug and add sufficient milk to make 250ml (10fl oz).

METAL BLADE: Place the eggs in the processing bowl. With the machine running, add the milk, salt, pepper and nutmeg. Process until blended. Sprinkle the Parmesan cheese evenly over the bottom of the quiche shell and top with the mushroom mixture. Place the shell on a baking sheet and carefully pour in the custard. Bake in the centre of the oven for 35–40 minutes or until the custard is set, puffy and lightly browned. Remove from the oven and slide onto a wire rack. Cool for 10 minutes, cut into wedges and serve.

Preparation: 15 minutes
Cooking/Baking: 45–50 minutes
Standing: 10 minutes
Protein g/s: 10

Courgette and Tomato Quiche

Serves 6

Start this quiche 1 hour before baking time. Courgettes can be drained the night before to shorten the preparation time.

1×23cm (9in) Wholewheat Quiche Shell, glazed with egg white, cooled

25g (1oz) Parmesan cheese, at room temperature
salt and pepper
pinch dried oregano
225g (8oz) courgettes, washed
1/2 small onion
1 clove garlic
1 1/2×5ml (tsp) oil
125g (4oz) Gruyere cheese, well chilled
25g (1oz) Cheddar cheese, well chilled
1 firm tomato
2 eggs
250ml (10fl oz) milk
dash cayenne pepper

METAL BLADE: Place the Parmesan, cut into small pieces, in the processing bowl; process until finely chopped. Add salt, oregano and a little pepper. Pulse on/off to mix. Remove from the processor and set aside.

SLICING DISC: Cut the courgettes to fit the feed tube vertically; slice. Transfer to a colander, sprinkle with 1 1/2×5ml (tsp) salt and allow to stand for 1 hour. Wash under cold water, drain and place in a clean teatowel and squeeze out any excess moisture.

METAL BLADE: Place the garlic and onion, cut into 2.5cm (1in) pieces, in the processing bowl. Pulse on/off until finely chopped. Heat the oil in a pan, add the onion and garlic and cook until soft, approx 2–3 minutes. Remove from the heat and allow to cool slightly. Preheat the oven to gas mark 5/190°C/ 375°F. Wipe the processor bowl dry with paper towel.

SHREDDING DISC: Cut the Gruyere to fit the feed tube; shred and set aside. Cut the Cheddar to fit the feed tube; shred. Remove and set aside.

SLICING DISC: Cut the tomato to fit the feed tube; slice using medium pressure.

METAL BLADE: Place the eggs and a dash of cayenne pepper in the processing bowl. With the machine running, pour in the milk. Process until blended.

Spread the Gruyere over the bottom of the pastry shell. Cover with courgette, tomato slices and onions. Sprinkle with the Parmesan mixture and top with Cheddar cheese. Place the pastry shell on a baking sheet and carefully pour in the custard mixture. Bake in the centre of the oven for 30–35 minutes or until the custard is set, puffy and lightly browned. Remove from the oven; slide onto a wire rack and cool for 10 minutes. Cut into wedges and serve.

Preparation: 10 minutes
Baking: 30–35 minutes
Standing: 1 hour to drain the courgettes
          10 minutes after baking
Protein g/s: 14

Cheese and Onion Quiche

Serves 6

Gruyere or Cheddar cheese may be used in this quiche. Try it both ways!

1×23cm (9in) Wholewheat Quiche Shell, glazed with egg white, cooled
175g (6oz) mature Cheddar or Gruyere, well chilled
225g (8oz) onions
salt and pepper
75g (3oz) butter or margarine
3 eggs
2×15ml (tbsp) white wine or vermouth
250ml (10fl oz) milk
salt and freshly ground pepper
pinch nutmeg

Preheat the oven to gas mark 6/200°C/400°F.

SHREDDING DISC: Cut the cheese to fit the feed tube; shred. Remove from the bowl and set aside.

SLICING DISC: Cut the onions to fit the feed tube; slice with light pressure. Heat the butter in a frying pan, add the onions and cook until soft and golden, 5–7 minutes. Add salt and pepper.

METAL BLADE: Place the eggs in the processing bowl. With the machine running, pour in the wine, milk, a little salt and pepper and a pinch of nutmeg. Process until blended.

Spread half the cheese mixture over the bottom of the pastry shell. Spread the onions over the cheese. Top with the remaining cheese. Place the pastry shell on a baking sheet and carefully pour in the custard. Bake in the centre of the oven for 5 minutes. Reduce the heat to gas mark 5/190°C/375°F and continue baking for 30–35 minutes or until the custard is set, puffy and lightly browned. Remove from the oven and slide onto a wire rack. Allow to cool for 10 minutes. Cut into wedges and serve.

Preparation: 10 minutes
Standing:, 10 minutes
Cooking/baking: 35–40 minutes
Protein g/s: 15.5

Pie Valasian

Serves 8

This double crust pie with a filling of Swiss cheese, leeks, potatoes and apples is an elegant company dish.

2 quantities Wholewheat Pâté Brisée Crust (see index), refrigerated until ready for use
4 medium potatoes
450g (1lb) Gruyere or Emmenthal cheese
450g (1lb) leeks
2-3×15ml (tbsp) oil
salt and pepper
paprika
18 large fresh basil leaves OR
1½×5ml (tsp) dried basil
2-3 tart apples, eg Granny Smiths
Glaze: 1 egg, beaten with 60ml (2½fl oz) water

Scrub the potatoes. Simmer in a pan of water until tender. Cool and peel.

SHREDDING DISC: Cut the cheese to fit the feed tube; shred. Remove from the bowl and set aside. Wash the leeks thoroughly and cut into 5cm (2in) lengths. Heat the oil in a pan. Add the leeks and cook until soft but not browned, 8–10 minutes. Season to taste with salt,

pepper and paprika. Remove from the heat and set aside.

Roll out two thirds of the pastry into a circle 3mm (⅛in) thick and 35.5–38cm (14–15in) in diameter. Fit into a well greased 24cm (9½in) springform tin. The edges will hang over the sides. Prick the bottom evenly with a fork and brush with oil. Slice the potatoes thinly and layer in the botttom of the tin. Sprinkle with salt, pepper and paprika.

METAL BLADE: Place the basil leaves in the processing bowl and pulse on/off until finely chopped. Sprinkle one third of the basil over the potatoes. Top with cheese, season lightly and add another third of the basil with some paprika. Peel, core and quarter the apples.

SLICING DISC: Place the apple quarters in the feed tube; slice. Arrange the slices over the cheese. Roll out the remaining pastry to cover the top of the pie. Trim and seal the edges of the pastry together. Pinch and flute to seal. Brush the pie with egg glaze. Prick the crust to allow steam to escape. Decorate with left-over pastry, if desired. Bake at gas mark 4/180°C/ 350°F for 30–40 minutes or until lightly browned.

Preparation: 30 minutes allow time to cook and cool the potatoes
Cooking/Baking: 1-1¼ hours
Protein g/s: 22

Sprout Quiche

Serves 6

1×23cm (9in) Wholewheat Quiche Shell, glazed with egg white, cooled
175g (6oz) mature Cheddar cheese, well chilled
1 small onion
1-2 stalks celery
225g (8oz) mung bean sprouts

2×5ml (tsp) dried thyme
1×15ml (tbsp) wholewheat flour
salt and pepper
3 eggs
250ml (10fl oz) milk
salt and freshly ground pepper
pinch nutmeg
1-2×15ml (tbsp) oil

Preheat the oven to gas mark 6/200°C/400°F.

SHREDDING DISC: Cut the cheese to fit the feed tube; shred. Remove from the bowl and spread over the bottom of the pastry case.

SLICING DISC: Cut the onions and celery to fit the feed tube vertically; slice. Heat the oil in a pan, add the onion and celery and cook until the onion is soft, 3–5 minutes. Add the bean sprouts and cook until just limp. Remove from the heat and drain off any excess liquid. Add a little salt and thyme. Sprinkle in the flour and toss to mix.

METAL BLADE: Place the eggs in the processing bowl. With the machine running, pour in the milk, some salt and pepper and the nutmeg. Process until blended. Place the pastry shell on a baking sheet. Spread the bean sprout mixture over the cheese and carefully pour in the custard.

Bake in the centre of the oven for 5 minutes. Reduce the heat to gas mark 5/190°C/375°F and continue cooking for 30–35 minutes or until the custard is set, puffy and lightly browned. Remove from the oven and slide onto a wire rack. Allow to cool for 10 minutes then cut into wedges and serve.

Preparation: 10 minutes
Cooking/Baking: 40–45 minutes
Standing: 10 minutes
Protein g/s: 16.5

Spanakopita

Serves 8

This is one of our most requested company dishes. We use Danish Feta because it is less salty. If you use Bulgarian or Greek Feta, add a little more curd cheese to reduce the salty taste.

2×275g (10oz) packets frozen spinach OR
900g (2lb) fresh spinach leaves, cooked and
squeezed dry
1 large onion
3×15ml (tbsp) olive oil
450g (1lb) Danish Feta cheese
450g (1lb) curd cheese or well drained cottage
cheese
4 eggs
pinch pepper
1×5ml (tsp) dried dill weed
175g (6oz) butter or margarine
450g (1lb) filo dough (see index)
1×5ml (tsp) anise seeds
additional butter

METAL BLADE: Place the onion, cut into 2.5cm (1in) pieces, in the processing bowl. Pulse on/off until finely chopped.

Heat the oil in a pan, add the onions and cook until soft and transparent. Do not let the onions brown. Remove from the heat and set aside. Rinse the Feta cheese under cold water to remove some of the salt. Pat dry with paper towel.

METAL BLADE: Place the Feta, broken into 5cm (2in) pieces, in the processing bowl with the curd or cottage cheese and process to break the Feta into small chunks. Add the eggs, pepper and dill. Process until blended. Remove to a large bowl. Place the spinach in the processing bowl. Pulse on/off until finely chopped but not puréed. Add the spinach and the onions to the cheese mixture. Stir to mix well. Cover and refrigerate.

Preheat the oven to gas mark 5/190°C/375°F. Melt the butter in a saucepan. Butter a 22×34cm (9×13in) Pyrex baking dish. Layer half the filo sheets in the bottom of the dish, brushing the top of each sheet with butter. Since the sheets will not fit the dish, overlap and alternate as necessary. Spoon on all the spinach mixture and continue layering until all the sheets are used. Generously butter the top filo layer. Sprinkle with anise seeds. Bake, uncovered, 25–35 minutes or until golden.

Preparation: 1 hour
Cooking/Baking: 25–35 minutes
Protein g/s: 25.5

Mushroom Cheese Tart

Serves 6

1 Wholewheat Pâté Brisée Crust, partially baked in a 24cm (9½in) springform tin (see index)
325g (12oz) mushrooms
50g (2oz) butter or margarine
450g (1lb) curd cheese
60ml (2½fl oz) sour cream
60ml (2½fl oz) yogurt
2 eggs
pinch nutmeg
salt and pepper

Preheat the oven to gas mark 4/180°C/350°F.

SLICING DISC: Wipe the mushrooms with a damp paper towel. Stack sideways into the feed tube; slice using firm pressure. Heat the butter in a pan, add the mushrooms and cook until soft and the liquid has evaporated. Remove from the heat and allow to cool slightly.

METAL BLADE: Place the curd cheese, sour cream, yogurt, eggs, salt and pepper in the processing bowl. Combine with 2–3 on/off pulses. Stop the machine and scrape down the sides of the bowl. Continue to process until smooth and well blended.

Reserve a few mushrooms for garnish. Combine the remaining mushrooms and the cheese mixture in a large bowl. Spoon into the pastry shell. Top with the reserved mushrooms. Place on a baking sheet and bake

for 30–40 minutes, or until the custard is set, puffy and lightly browned. Remove the tart from the oven and slide onto a wire rack. Allow to cool for 10 minutes then cut into wedges and serve.

Preparation: 15 minutes
Cooking/Baking: 40–50 minutes
Standing: 10 minutes
Protein g/s: 12.5

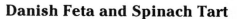

Danish Feta and Spinach Tart

Serves 6

We use Danish Feta as it is less salty than the Bulgarian or Greek variety.

1 Wholewheat Pâté Brisée Crust, partially baked in a 24cm (9½in) springform tin (see index)
75g (3oz) Cheddar cheese, well chilled
1 medium onion
2×15ml (tbsp) oil
225g (8oz) Danish Feta cheese, rinsed in cold water
275g (10oz) cottage cheese
2 eggs
1×275g (10oz) packet frozen leaf spinach OR leaves from 450g (1lb) fresh spinach, cooked and squeezed dry
5×15ml (tbsp) soured cream (optional)
paprika

SHREDDING DISC: Cut the Cheddar cheese to fit the feed tube; shred. Remove from the bowl and set aside.

METAL BLADE: Place the onion, cut into 2.5cm (1in) pieces, in the processing bowl and pulse on/off until finely chopped. Heat the oil in a pan, add the onions and cook until soft and transparent. Remove from the heat and allow to cool. Preheat the oven to gas mark 4/180°C/350°F. Place the Feta, cottage cheese and eggs in the processing bowl. Process until smooth. Add the spinach. Pulse on/off until just mixed. Do not overprocess and purée the spinach.

Carefully remove the metal blade from the work bowl. Add the onions and mix with a wooden spoon. Spoon into the pastry shell. Dot with the soured cream, if used. Sprinkle generously with paprika and top with Cheddar cheese. Bake in the centre of the oven for 30–35 minutes or until the filling is set.

Remove from the oven; slide onto a wire rack and allow to cool for 10 minutes. Cut into wedges and serve.

Preparation: 10 minutes
Cooking/Baking: 35–40 minutes
Standing: 10 minutes
Protein g/s: 19.5

Wholewheat Oil Crust

1 shell, serves 8

If you are cutting down on your intake of butter, this is a good crust to substitute for our wholewheat quiche shell. It is a pliable dough and easy to work.

150g (5oz) wholewheat flour
½×5ml (tsp) salt
75ml (3fl oz) oil
6×15ml (tbsp) cold milk

Pour the oil and milk into a cup, do not stir.

METAL BLADE: Place the flour and salt in the processing bowl, pulse on/off to mix. With the machine running, pour in the liquids. Stop the machine as soon as all the liquid has been added. The dough will be crumbly and will not form into a ball. Carefully remove the metal blade. Gather the crumbs of dough into a ball and flatten into a 15cm (6in) circle. Place between two sheets of waxed paper and allow to rest for 5 minutes.

With a rolling pin, roll from the centre outwards in all directions to form a 30.5cm (12in) circle. Peel off top sheet of paper. Fold pastry in half and unfold carefully into a

25.5cm (10in) quiche dish. Trim excess dough by rolling the pin across the top of the tin. Prick the entire surface of the pie crust evenly with a fork to prevent puffing.

Baked crust: Refrigerate crust while preheating the oven to gas mark 6/200°C/400°F. Bake for 12–15 minutes or until just browned. Remove to a rack and allow to cool.

Partially baked crust: Refrigerate crust while preheating the oven to gas mark 6/200°C/400°F. Bake for 8–10 minutes. Remove to a rack and allow to cool.

Glazed crust, unbaked: Brush surface of crust with slightly beaten egg white. Allow to dry uncovered in the refrigerator for about 1 hour. Glaze may also be set by placing the crust in a preheated oven at gas mark 8/250°C/450°F for 2–3 minutes. Remove to rack and allow to cool.

Preparation: 10 minutes
Standing: 5 minutes
Baking: 8–15 minutes
Chilling: 15 minutes while preheating the oven
Protein g/s: 3

Harvest Vegetable Quiche

Serves 6

1×23cm (9in) Wholewheat Quiche Shell, glazed with egg white, cooled
125g (4oz) Gruyere cheese, well chilled
1 clove garlic
1 small onion
1 small courgette, washed
1 small carrot
225g (8oz) mushrooms
1×15ml (tbsp) oil
25g (1oz) butter
3 eggs
250ml (10fl oz) milk
½×5ml (tsp) salt
½×5ml (tsp) dried thyme
pepper

Preheat the oven to gas mark 5/190°C/375°F.

SHREDDING DISC: Cut the chese to fit the feed tube; shred using light pressure. Spread the cheese evenly over the bottom of the pastry shell.

METAL BLADE: Place the garlic and onion, cut into 2.5cm (1in) pieces, in the processor bowl; pulse on/off until finely chopped. Heat the oil in a large frying pan, add the garlic and onions and cook until soft, 4–6 minutes.

SHREDDING DISC (or 6mm (¼in) square julienne disc): Cut the courgette and carrot to fit the feed tube horizontally; shred using moderate to firm pressure. Add the vegetables to the pan and cook for 3–5 minutes. Remove to a small bowl and set aside.

SLICING DISC: Stack the mushrooms sideways in the feed tube; slice with firm pressure. In the same frying pan melt the butter. Cook the mushrooms for 5 minutes or until soft and the liquid has all evaporated.

METAL BLADE: Place the eggs, salt, thyme and pepper in the processing bowl. With the machine running pour in the milk and process until blended. Spread the onion, courgette and carrot mixture over the cheese and top with the mushrooms. Place the pastry shell on a baking sheet and carefully add the custard. Bake in the centre of the oven for 35–40 minutes or until the custard is set, puffy and lightly browned. Remove from the oven; slide onto a wire rack and allow to cool for 10 minutes. Cut into wedges and serve.

Preparation: 5–8 minutes
Cooking/Baking: 50–55 minutes
Standing: 10 minutes
Protein g/s: 14

Mozzarella Cheese Quiche

Serves 6

No cooking is required to prepare the filling for this quiche. It's simple and fast!

1×23cm (9in) Wholewheat Quiche Shell, glazed with egg white, cooled
65g (2½oz) Parmesan cheese, at room temperature
2 sprigs fresh parsley
225g (8oz) mozzarella cheese, well chilled
salt and pepper
3 eggs
250ml (10fl oz) milk
pinch nutmeg

Preheat the oven to gas mark 5/190°C/375°F.

METAL BLADE: Place the Parmesan, cut into 2.5cm (1in) pieces, in the processing bowl. Process until finely chopped. Add the parsley and process until finely chopped.

SHREDDING DISC: Cut the mozzarella to fit the feed tube; shred with light pressure. Remove the mozzarella, parsley and Parmesan and set aside. Season the cheeses with salt and pepper and toss to mix.

METAL BLADE: Place the eggs in the processing bowl. With the machine running, add the milk, a little salt and pepper and nutmeg: process until well blended.

Spread the cheese mixture over the bottom of the pastry case. Place the quiche on a baking sheet and carefully pour in the custard. Bake in the centre of the oven for 30–35 minutes, or until the custard is set, puffy and lightly browned. Remove from the oven; slide onto a wire rack and allow to cool for 10 minutes. Cut into wedges and serve.

Preparation: 10 minutes
Standing: 10 minutes
Cooking/Baking: 30–35 minutes
Protein g/s: 19

Courgette and Green Chilli Quiche

Serves 6

This quiche can be easily assembled and put into the oven if the courgettes are drained the night before or earlier in the day.

1×23cm (9in) Wholewheat Quiche Shell,
glazed with egg white, cooled
325g (12oz) courgettes, washed
175g (6oz) Cheddar cheese, well chilled
½ small onion
2 canned whole green chillies, rinsed and
deseeded
1×15ml (tbsp) wholewheat flour
1×15ml (tbsp) oil
3 eggs
250ml (10fl oz) milk
salt and pepper

SHREDDING DISC: Cut the courgettes to fit the feed tube vertically; shred. Remove to a colander, sprinkle with ½×15ml (tbsp) salt and leave for 30 minutes. Rinse well in cold water, place in a clean teatowel and squeeze out any excess moisture. Wipe the processing bowl dry with paper towels. Cut the cheese to fit the feed tube; shred using light pressure. Remove to a small bowl and set aside.

SLICING DISC: Cut the onion to fit the feed tube; slice using light pressure. Heat the oil in a pan, add the onions and cook until soft in 3–5 minutes. Add the courgettes and cook for 2–3 minutes then stir in the flour. Remove the pan from the heat. Preheat the oven to gas mark 6/200°C/400°F.

METAL BLADE: Dry the chillies on paper towels and place in the processing bowl. Pulse on/off until roughly chopped. Spread half the cheese over the bottom of the pastry shell. Top with the courgette and onion mixture. Add the chillies and the remaining cheese. Place the eggs in the processing bowl. With the machine running, pour in the milk with a little salt and pepper. Process until blended.

   Place the pastry shell on a baking sheet and carefully pour in the custard. Bake in the centre of the oven for 15 minutes. Reduce the heat to gas mark 4/180°C/350°F and continue baking for 20 minutes or until the custard is set, puffy and lightly browned. Remove from the oven and slide onto a wire rack. Allow to cool for 10 minutes then cut into wedges and serve.

Preparation: 15 minutes
Cooking/Baking: 40–45 minutes
Standing: 30 minutes for the courgettes
                 10 minutes to cool
Protein g/s: 16

Pepper Olive Quiche

Serves 6

1×23cm (9in) Wholewheat Quiche Shell,
glazed with egg white, cooled
1 medium green pepper, halved and deseeded
1×5ml (tsp) oil
175g (6oz) mature Cheddar cheese, well
chilled
2 canned whole green chillies, rinsed and
deseeded
1×400g (14oz) can black olives, drained and
pitted
3 eggs
250ml (10fl oz) milk
salt and pepper
pinch of nutmeg

SLICING DISC: Wedge the green pepper into the feed tube; slice. Heat the oil in a pan, add the green pepper and cook until soft, about 5 minutes. Remove from heat and allow to cool slightly. Preheat the oven to gas mark 5/190°C/375°F.

SHREDDING DISC: Cut the Cheddar to fit the feed tube; slice. Remove from the bowl and set aside.

METAL BLADE: Pat the chillies dry with kitchen paper then place in the processing bowl. Pulse on/off until coarsely chopped.

SLICING DISC: Place the drained olives in the feed tube; slice. Spread half the Cheddar over the bottom of the pastry shell. Top with chopped chillies, olives, green peppers and remaining cheese.

METAL BLADE: Place the eggs, salt and pepper and a pinch of nutmeg in the processing bowl. With the machine running pour in the milk and process until blended. Place the pastry shell on a baking sheet and carefully add the custard. Bake in the centre of the oven for 30–35 minutes or until the custard is set, puffy and lightly browned. Remove from the oven and slide onto a wire rack. Cool for 10 minutes then cut into wedges and serve.

Preparation: 10 minutes
Cooking/Baking: 35–40 minutes
Standing: 10 minutes
Protein g/s: 16

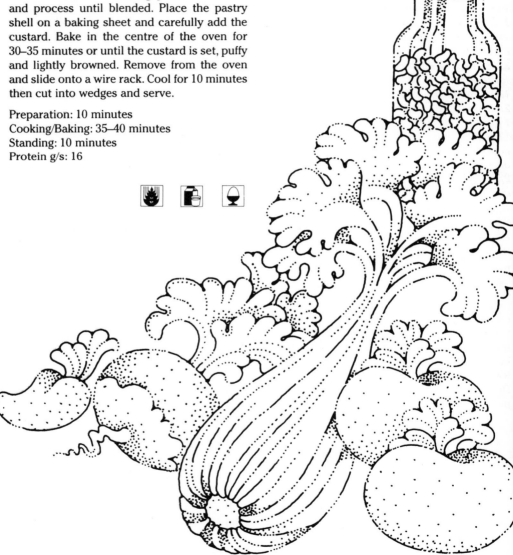

Bean and Chilli Cheese Pie

Serves 8

The filling can be prepared ahead of time. Spoon into the crust just before baking.

1 Wholewheat Oil Crust, unbaked; fit into a 23cm (9in) pie plate. Refrigerate crust while making filling
1 medium onion
1 small green pepper
1×125g (4oz) can whole green chillies, rinsed and deseeded
275g (10oz) cooked kidney beans, cold (about 150g (5oz) dry)
150g (5oz) sweetcorn kernels
2×5ml (tsp) dried oregano
1×5ml (tsp) ground cumin
¾×5ml (tsp) chilli powder
good pinch salt
dash cayenne pepper
275g (10oz) mature Cheddar cheese, well chilled
1 egg
60ml (2½fl oz) milk
1 medium tomato, sliced thinly
oil for cooking vegetables

Preheat the oven to gas mark 4/180°C/350°F.

METAL BLADE: Place the onion, cut into 2.5cm (1in) pieces, in the processing bowl. Pulse on/off until finely chopped. Remove from the processor and set aside. Place the pepper, cut into 2.5cm (1in) pieces, in the processing bowl; pulse on/off until finely chopped. Remove from the bowl and add to the onions. Dry the chillies on paper towels; add to the processor bowl; pulse on/off until roughly chopped. Add to the vegetables.

Heat the oil in a 2–3l (4-6pt) saucepan. Add the onions, pepper and chillies and cook until soft, 3–4 minutes. Stir in the oregano, cumin and chilli powder and a little salt and pepper. Remove from the heat.

METAL BLADE: Place the kidney beans in the processing bowl. Pulse on/off until roughly chopped. Add the beans and sweetcorn to the cooked vegetables and stir gently to mix.

SHREDDING DISC: Cut the cheese to fit the feed tube; shred. Remove from the processing bowl and set aside. Toss to mix.

METAL BLADE: Place the egg in the processing bowl. With the machine running, pour in the milk. Stop the processor as soon as all the milk has been added. Stir into the bean mixture with one third of the cheese. Spread one third of the cheese over the bottom of the crust. Spoon in the filling and press down gently. Arrange the sliced tomatoes over the top and sprinkle with the remaining cheese. Bake, uncovered, for 35–40 minutes or until the filling is set and the top is lightly browned. Remove from the oven and slide onto a wire rack. Allow to cool for 10 minutes then cut into wedges and serve.

Preparation: 10 minutes
Cooking/Baking: 40–45 minutes
   allow time to cook and cool the beans
Standing: 10 minutes
Protein g/s: 15.5

Crêpes and Enchiladas

Wholewheat Crêpes

Makes 9 crêpes

Crêpe batters may be made the night before and refrigerated, covered. Should the batter become too thick add a little extra milk. We bake the crêpes in a well-seasoned 18–20cm (7–8in) crêpe pan or in a SilverStone lined non-stick pan.

375ml (15fl oz) skimmed milk
2×15ml (tbsp) oil
½×5ml (tsp) salt
2 eggs
125g (4oz) fine wholewheat flour
addtional oil for baking

In a large jug combine the milk, oil, salt and eggs.

METAL BLADE: Place the flour in the processing bowl. With the machine running, pour in the liquid in a slow steady stream. Process until well blended. Pour the batter into a mixing bowl, cover and refrigerate for at least 1 hour so that the milk and flour will be well combined.

Pour about 1×15ml (tbsp) oil into the pan and heat until hot. Tip out the oil. Return the pan to a moderately high heat. Pour about 3×15ml (tbsp) batter into the pan and roll it around quickly until the bottom of the pan is completely covered. Tip out excess crêpe batter. The crêpe should be as thin as possible. When the batter appears dull and the edges begin to brown, flip it onto the other side. Continue to cook until the second side is lightly browned. Remove the crêpe from the pan and discard. The first crêpe absorbs the oil from the pan.

It is not necessary to add any more oil to the pan after the first crêpe is made. The oil in the batter will prevent the crêpe from sticking. As each crêpe is cooked, stack on a clean teatowel. The first side of the crêpe to be cooked is presented as the outside as it has the more attractive appearance of the two sides.

Preparation: 5 minutes
Standing: 1 hour
Cooking: 20–30 minutes
Protein g/s: 4.5

Wholewheat Sesame Crêpes

Makes 9-10 crêpes

Sesame seeds, ground into a fine flour, add a slightly nutty flavour to these crêpes. Directions are given for a 18–20cm (7–8in) pan.

125g (4oz) fine wholewheat flour
60g (2½oz) hulled white sesame seeds
330ml (13fl oz) skimmed milk
½×5ml (tsp) salt
2 eggs
2×15ml (tbsp) oil
additional oil for baking

In a large measuring jug combine the milk, salt, eggs and oil.

METAL BLADE: Place the flour and sesame seeds in the processing bowl; process until the sesame seeds are finely ground, 2–3 minutes. With the machine running, pour in the liquid in a steady stream. Process until well blended. Pour the batter into the mixing bowl, cover and refrigerate for at least 1 hour so that the milk and the flour will be well combined.

Pour 1×15ml (tbsp) oil into the pan and heat until hot. Tip out the oil. Return the pan to a moderately high heat. Pour about 3×15ml (tbsp) batter into the pan and roll it around quickly until the bottom of the pan is completely covered. Tip out excess batter. The crêpes should be as thin as possible. When the batter appears dull and the edges begin to brown, flip it onto the other side. Continue to cook until the second side is lightly browned. Remove the crêpe from the pan and discard. The first crêpe absorbs the oil from the pan.

It is not necessary to add any more oil to the pan after the first crêpe is made. The oil in the batter will prevent the crêpe from sticking. As each crêpe is cooked, stack on a clean teatowel. The first side of the crêpe to be cooked is presented as the outside as it has the more attractive appearance of the two sides.

Preparation: 5 minutes
Standing: 1 hour
Cooking: 20–30 minutes
Protein g/s: 9 crêpes–6
10 crêpes–5.5

Feta Spinach Crêpes

Makes 8 crêpes

1 quantity Wholewheat Crêpes OR
Wholewheat Sesame Crêpes (see index)
1 medium onion
2×15ml (tbsp) oil
225g (8oz) curd cheese or cottage cheese, well drained

125g (4oz) Danish Feta cheese, well rinsed
2 eggs
1×275g (10oz) package frozen leaf spinach, cooked, cooled, squeezed dry
½×5ml (tsp) dried dill weed
pinch nutmeg
salt
yogurt and paprika to garnish

METAL BLADE: Place the onion, cut into 2.5cm (1in) pieces, in the processing bowl. Pulse on/off until roughly chopped. Heat the oil in a pan, add the onion and cook until soft and transparent, 3–5 minutes. Remove from heat and set aside. Place the Feta cheese, cut into small chunks, curd cheese, and eggs in the processing bowl. Process until smooth. Stop the machine, add spinach, onions, dill, nutmeg and salt. Pulse on/off until spinach is finely chopped.

Divide the filling between the crêpes. Roll the crêpes and place in a well greased or buttered 21.5×34cm (8½×13½in) or similar size baking dish or tin. Cover with foil. With a sharp knife carefully make about 12 slits in the foil to allow some of the steam to escape. Bake at gas mark 4/180°C/ 350°F for 15–20 minutes. Garnish with yogurt and paprika.

Preparation: 10–15 minutes
Cooking/Baking: 35 minutes
Protein g/s: 12.5

Fresh Corn Enchiladas

Serves 6

High in protein and tasty – a winning combination. Experience with chillis will allow you to determine how many you wish to use.

225g (8oz) sweetcorn kernels, cooked and drained
1½-2 medium onions

2-4 canned whole green chillies, rinsed and deseeded
salt and pepper
$1/2 \times 5ml$ (tsp) ground cumin
$1/2 \times 5ml$ (tsp) chilli powder
pinch cayenne pepper
325g (12oz) mild Cheddar cheese, well chilled
275g (10oz) cottage cheese
325ml (12fl oz) Enchilada Sauce (see index)
OR *from a packet mix*
12 corn tortillas, homemade or purchased
oil for frying tortillas
3 sprigs fresh coriander (optional)

METAL BLADE: Place the onion, cut into 2.5cm (1in) pieces, in the processing bowl. Pulse on/off until chopped. Heat the oil in a pan, add the onions and cook until soft and transparent, 3–5 minutes. Dry the chillies with paper towels. Cut the chillies into thirds and place in the processing bowl. Pulse on/off until roughly chopped. Add the chillies and sweetcorn to the pan, cook for 1–2 minutes. Stir in the cumin, chilli powder, cayenne and salt and pepper to taste. Remove from the heat.

SHREDDING DISC: Cut the cheese to fit the feed tube; shred. Remove about half the cheese and set aside for the topping.

METAL BLADE: Place the cottage cheese in the processing bowl and process with the remaining Cheddar until smooth. In a large bowl, combine the cheese and corn mixtures. Pour the enchilada sauce into a shallow dish. Preheat the oven to gas mark 4/180°C/350°F.

Heat 3mm ($1/8$in) of oil in a frying pan over a medium heat. Fry the tortillas for a few seconds until just soft. Do not overcook or they will be difficult to roll. Rest the fried tortillas briefly on paper towel to absorb any excess oil. Dip the tortillas in the enchilada sauce. Fill each tortilla with a little of the filling, roll up and arrange in a single layer in a long, well greased baking dish or tin. Spoon on the remaining sauce, taking care to cover the edges of the tortillas. Top with the reserved cheese. Bake, uncovered, 15–20 minutes, or until hot. Garnish with fresh coriander.

Preparation: 20 minutes
Cooking/Baking: 25–30 minutes
Protein g/s: 23

Bean and Raisin Enchiladas

Serves 6

Serve these slightly sweet and sour enchiladas with rice and a tossed green salad with avocados.

125g (4oz) raisins
2 medium onions
$1/2$ large pepper, deseeded
2 canned whole green chillies, rinsed and deseeded
2-3 × 15ml (tbsp) oil
450g (1lb) cooked pinto beans (about 225g (8oz) dry)
salt
1 × 200g (7oz) can chopped tomatoes, sieved
$1 1/2 \times 5ml$ (tsp) chilli powder (or more to taste)
good pinch ground cumin
3-4 × 15ml (tbsp) distilled malt vinegar
330ml (13fl oz) Enchilada Sauce (see index)
OR *from a packet mix*
12 Corn Tortillas, homemade or purchased
oil for frying tortillas
125-175g (4-6oz) Cheddar cheese, well chilled

Plump the raisins by boiling for 1–2 minutes, in water to cover, over a high heat. Drain and set aside.

METAL BLADE: Place the onions, cut into 2.5cm (1in) pieces, in the processing bowl. Pulse on/off until roughly chopped. Add the pepper, cut into 2.5cm (1in) pieces; pulse on/off until roughly chopped. Dry the chillies with paper towels, cut into thirds; add to the processing bowl. Pulse on/off until roughly chopped.

Heat the oil in a 3–4l (6-8pt) saucepan. Add the onions and cook until soft and transparent, 4–5 minutes. Stir in the beans, salt, tomatoes, chilli powder, cumin, vinegar and raisins. Cover and simmer for 3–4

minutes, stirring occasionally. Pour the
enchillada sauce into a shallow dish. Preheat
the oven to gas mark 4/180°C/350°F.

Heat 3mm (⅛in) oil in a frying pan over
medium heat. Fry tortillas for a few seconds to
soften – do not overcook or they will become
brittle and difficult to roll. Rest the fried
tortillas briefly on paper towels to absorb the
excess oil. Dip the tortillas into the enchillada
sauce. Divide the filling between the tortillas,
roll up and arrange in a single layer in a long,
well greased baking dish. Spoon on the
remaining sauce, taking care to cover the
edges of the tortillas.

SHREDDING DISC: Cut the cheese to fit the feed
tube; shred. Sprinkle the cheese evenly
over the enchiladas. Bake, uncovered, 15–20
minutes or until hot.

Preparation: 15 minutes
Cooking/Baking: 30 minutes
Protein g/s: 17

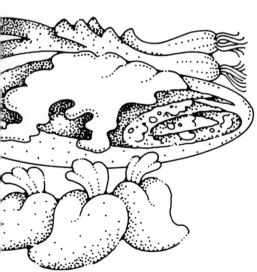

Enchiladas Coloradas

Serves 6

Tortillas surround a low-fat filling of cottage
cheese and Cheddar cheese, flavoured with
olives and salad onions.

8-10 salad onions, about 175g (6oz)
2×15ml (tbsp) oil
275g (10oz) cottage cheese
225g (8oz) Cheddar cheese, well chilled
1×400g (14oz) can black olives, drained and
pitted
330ml (13fl oz) Enchilada Sauce (see index)
OR *from a packet mix*
1×200g (7oz) can chopped tomatoes, sieved
12 corn tortillas, homemade or purchased
oil for frying tortillas

METAL BLADE: Place the salad onions, cut into
2.5cm (1in) pieces, in the processing bowl.
Pulse on/off until finely chopped; scrape down
the sides of the bowl as necessary. Heat the oil
in a 2–3l (4–6pt) pan. Add the onions and cook
until just beginning to soften, 30–60 seconds.
Remove from the heat. Place the cottage
cheese in the processing bowl; process until
smooth. Carefully remove the metal blade and
insert the shredding disc.

SHREDDING DISC: Cut the Cheddar cheese to fit
the feed tube; shred into the cottage cheese.

SLICING DISC: Wedge the olives into the feed
tube; slice. Reserve a few sliced olives for
garnish. Combine the cheese-olive mixture
with the onions in the pan. Stir gently to mix
well. In a shallow dish, stir together the
enchilada sauce and the sieved tomatoes.
Preheat the oven to gas mark 4/180°C/350°F.

Heat 3mm (⅛in) of oil in a frying pan over a
medium heat. Fry the tortillas for only a few
seconds to soften – do not overcook to
become brittle otherwise the tortillas will not
roll. Rest the fried tortillas briefly on kitchen
paper to drain any excess oil. Dip the tortillas
in the enchilada sauce. Divide the filling
between the tortillas and roll up, arranging in
a single layer in the bottom of a long, well
greased baking dish or tin. Spoon the

remaining sauce over, taking care to cover the edges of the tortillas. Bake, uncovered, 15–20 minutes or until hot. Garnish with reserved olives.

Preparation: 15 minutes
Cooking/Baking: 25–30 minutes
Protein g/s: 17

Enchilada Sauce

Makes approx 3l (6pt)

In Mexico, this red chilli sauce is made without tomato sauce. In our vegetarian version, tomato sauce provides added flavour. We suggest that you taste the chillies before proceeding with the recipe to make sure that they are mild enough. Unless you like your sauce really hot, remove all the seeds from the chillies. The capsaicin that makes peppers hot is concentrated in and near the seeds.

125g (4oz) dried mild red chillies
2l (4pt) hot water
1×400g (14oz) can sieved tomatoes
2×15ml (tbsp) tomato paste
2-3 large cloves garlic, crushed
pinch ground cumin
1×5ml (tsp) salt
1×5ml (tsp) dried oregano
cayenne pepper to taste, optional

Preheat the oven to gas mark 5/190°C/375°. Place the chillies on a baking sheet and toas for 3–5 minutes. Make sure that the chillies d not burn – you will not like the flavou Remove them from the oven and allow to coo Remove and discard the stems, seeds an pulp.

METAL BLADE: Place the chillies, torn into sma pieces, in the processing bowl. Process unt ground to a rough powder. With the machin running, pour in part of the water: 250n (10fl oz) for small machines, 375–500n (15–20fl oz) for larger capacity machine. Process until the mixture is thick. Pour in th tomatoes, tomato paste, garlic, cumin, sa and oregano. Process until mixed.

Carefully remove the processing bowl an pour the mixture into a large mixing bowl; st in the remaining water. Taste the sauce an add cayenne pepper, a pinch or two at a time until the required heat is reached. Freeze i containers of approx 375ml (15fl oz) of sauc. Makes enough sauce for 4–5 enchilad recipes.

Preparation: 15 minutes

Tofu

Scrambled Tofu

Serves 4

Our friend Donna Howard, a public health nutritionist, contributes this versatile dish. It is ideal for breakfast or brunch. When served with rice and a tossed salad, it is a quick supper dish.

25g (1oz) Parmesan cheese, at room temperature
2×15ml (tbsp) oil
1 medium onion
225g (8oz) mushrooms
1×5ml (tsp) ground turmeric
1×5ml (tsp) ground cumin
1×15ml (tbsp) Madras curry powder
1 block tofu, 575-625g (20-22oz), drained
1×15ml (tbsp) tamari sauce
salt
1 tomato, diced

METAL BLADE: Place the Parmesan cheese, cut into small pieces, in the processing bowl; process until finely chopped. Remove and set aside.

SLICING DISC: Quarter the onion and insert vertically into the feed tube; slice using light pressure. Heat the oil in a large pan, add the onions and cook for 2–3 minutes. Stir in the turmeric, cumin and curry powder. Continue cooking 1 minute to bring out the flavour of the spices.

Stack the mushrooms in the feed tube; slice. Add to the pan and cook until soft. Break the tofu into large chunks and add to the pan. Stir in the tamari and salt to taste. Cook for 1–2 minutes, stirring and breaking into smaller chunks. Add the diced tomato and cook until they are soft and all the ingredients are hot. Sprinkle in the Parmesan and toss to mix.

Preparation: 5–8 minutes
Cooking: 10 minutes
Protein g/s: 12

Tofu with Fresh Mushrooms

Serves 4

Serve with a grain or milk product to complement the protein in the tofu. This is especially nice with Chinese Style Fried Rice (see index).

2×15ml (tbsp) oil
2 medium carrots, peeled
225g (8oz) mushrooms
1 small piece fresh ginger
1 large clove garlic, crushed
1 block tofu, drained, 575-625g (20-22oz) cut into 2.5cm (1in) cubes
1-2×15ml (tbsp) soy sauce
4 salad onions, cut into 2.5cm (1in) lengths
salt to taste

SLICING DISC: Cut the carrots to fit the feed tube vertically; slice. Heat the oil in a large frying pan, add the carrots and cook for 40–45 minutes. Stack the mushrooms sideways into the feed tube; slice with firm pressure. Add to the carrots and mix. Cook for 3–4 minutes or until the mushrooms are tender.

METAL BLADE: Cut the ginger into small pieces. With the machine running, drop in the ginger pieces and process until finely chopped. Stir the garlic and the ginger into the vegetable mixture. Gently stir in the tofu cubes and soy sauce. Cook for 2–3 minutes to heat the tofu. Add the salad onions and toss gently to mix.

Preparation: 10 minutes
Cooking: 10 minutes
Protein g/s: 10

Vegetable Tofu Curry

Serves 4

This spicy dish is delicious served over brown rice. When using Madras or Indian curry powder, decrease the amount slightly as this mixture tends to be a bit more spicy. DO NOT use the food processor to grind your own curry powder. The turmeric stains the bowl bright yellow and the hard spices produce deep scratches.

2 cloves garlic
1 small onion
2×15ml (tbsp) oil
50g (2oz) butter
2×15ml (tbsp) curry powder* OR
bought curry powder
225g (8oz) green beans
1 small cauliflower, broken into florets
450g (1lb) broccoli, trimmed and broken into florets
3 carrots, peeled
2 courgettes, washed
1 block tofu, drained, 575-625g (20-22oz) cut into 2.5cm (1in) squares
½×5ml (tsp) salt
1×5ml (tsp) soft brown sugar
250ml (10fl oz) yogurt

METAL BLADE: Place the garlic and the onion, cut into 2.5 cm (1in) pieces, in the processor bowl. Pulse on/off until finely chopped. Heat the butter and oil in a 5–6l (10–12pt) saucepan. Add the garlic and onion and cook until clear but not brown, in 3–4 minutes. Stir in the curry powder, reduce the heat to low

and cook for 15 minutes, stirring frequently to avoid burning and sticking. Pour in 125ml (5fl oz) water, cover and continue cooking for 15 minutes. Meanwhile, prepare and steam each vegetable separately to maintain individual textures. Do not overcook, vegetables should be crisp but cooked.

SLICING BLADE: Cut the carrots to fit the feed tube vertically; slice. Remove from the bowl. Cut the courgette to fit the feed tube vertically and slice; remove from the bowl. Place the broccoli stalks in the feed tube vertically slice. Snap the green beans into 2.5-5cm (1–2in) lengths. Add the cooked vegetables, tofu, salt, sugar and yogurt to the spice mixture. Mix gently, cover and simmer for about 10 minutes.

*To make your own curry powder, in a heavy-duty blender or electric spice grinder grind:

2×5ml (tsp) ground turmeric
½×5ml (tsp) ground ginger
3 whole cloves
2 cardamom seeds
½ stick cinnamon, broken into small pieces
¼–½×5ml (tsp) crushed dried red chilli
½×5ml (tsp) peppercorns
½×5ml (tsp) whole mustard seed
½×5ml (tsp) cumin seed
2×5ml (tsp) whole coriander seed

Preparation: 5–10 minutes
Cooking: 40 minutes
Protein g/s: 12

Sweet and Sour Tofu

Serves 4

The surprise ingredients in the sauce are tomato, honey and lemon. Serve with brown rice topped with toasted sesame seeds.

×15ml (tbsp) oil
large onions
large carrots, peeled
stalks celery, trimmed
large green pepper, quartered and deseeded
×400g (14oz) can sieved tomatoes
25ml (5fl oz) water
-5×15ml (tbsp) honey, or to taste
×15ml (tbsp) lemon juice, or to taste
block tofu, 575-625g (20-22oz), drained

Preparation: 10 minutes
Cooking: 15–20 minutes
Protein g/s: 10

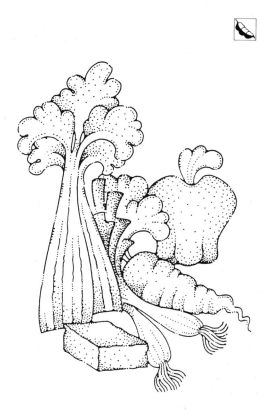

Heat the oil in a large pan. As the vegetables
are chopped and sliced, add them to the pan.

METAL BLADE: Place the onions, cut into 2.5cm
(1in) pieces, in the processing bowl; pulse
on/off until chopped. Place in the pan and
start cooking.

SLICING DISC OR THIN SLICING DISC: Cut the carrots
to fit the feed tube vertically; slice using light
pressure. Add to the onions. Cut the celery to
fit the tube vertically; slice; add to the pan.
Wedge the pepper quarters in the feed tube
vertically; slice, add to the pan. Continue
cooking until the vegetables are just cooked
but crisp. Stir in the tomatoes, water, honey
and lemon juice. Simmer until the sauce is
thick, about 10 minutes. Cut the tofu into
2.5cm (1in) cubes and add to the sauce. Cover
and cook for 1–2 minutes or until the tofu is
heated. Do not allow the tofu to boil
vigorously or the cubes will break up. Stir
gently to mix.

Side Dishes

Vegetables

Mangetout with Bamboo Shoots

Serves 2-3

Mangetout are flavoured with brown bean sauce or 'mein see'. The sauce is now widely available in supermarkets. The unused portion will store for several months in the refrigerator.

1×15ml (tbsp) oil
1 small onion
1 can bamboo shoots, 240g (8½oz) drained weight
225g (8oz) mangetout
125ml (5fl oz) water
2×5ml (tsp) sherry
1×15ml (tbsp) brown bean sauce
1×5ml (tsp) cornflour
oil

SLICING DISC: Cut the onion in half, stack in the feed tube and slice. Heat 1×15ml (tbsp) oil in a pan over a medium heat, add the onions and stir fry for 3–4 minutes until the onions are soft. Cut the drained bamboo shoots to fit the feed tube, slice. Add to the onions and cook for a further 1–2 minutes. Add the mangetout, stir. Mix together the water, sherry, brown bean sauce and cornflour. Pour into the vegetables and stir gently to mix. Reduce the heat to low, cover the pan and cook for 2–3 minutes until the mangetout are just cooked but still crisp. Do not overcook. Add a few drops of oil and serve immediately.

Preparation: 5 minutes
Cooking: 6–8 minutes

Ratatouille

Serves 6-8

A version of the popular vegetable dish. Serve hot or at room temperature. For a picnic treat stuff halved pitta bread with ratatouille and top with shredded lettuce or beansprouts.

2 large cloves garlic
2 green peppers, halved and deseeded
2 salad onions
450g (1lb) aubergines, unpeeled
2 courgettes, washed
2 firm tomatoes
½×5ml (tsp) dried basil
½×5ml (tsp) dried thyme
½×5ml (tsp) dried oregano
pinch marjoram
pinch rosemary
salt and pepper
6×15ml (tbsp) tomato paste
60ml (2½fl oz) olive oil

METAL BLADE: Place the garlic in the processing bowl; pulse on/off until finely minced. Remove from the bowl and set aside. Place the salad onions, cut into 5cm (2in) lengths in the processor; pulse on/off until finely chopped. Remove from the bowl and set aside.

SLICING DISC: Stack the green peppers in the feed tube, slice. In a 5l (10pt) saucepan, heat the olive oil over a moderate heat. Add the garlic and cook, stirring constantly, until soft but not brown. Add the salad onions and green peppers and cook for a further 3 minutes. Cut the aubergine and courgettes to fit the feed tube vertically; slice. (Use a thick slicing disc if available.) Cut the tomatoes in half, stack in the feed tube and slice.

Add the vegetables to the pan and stir gently to mix. Reduce the heat to medium and cook for 5 minutes, stirring occasionally. Add all the seasonings and the tomato paste. Stir to mix. Cover and simmer until the vegetables are cooked to your liking. Stir occasionally. The vegetables should have some texture and not be mushy. To evaporate excess liquid, remove the cover, increase the heat and cook quickly. Watch carefully to ensure that the bottom does not burn.

Preparation: 10 minutes
Cooking: 20 minutes

Red Cabbage with Apples

Serves 8

We like to serve this with German Potato Pancakes or noodles (see index).

1 large head red cabbage, 1350g (3lb)
2×15ml (tbsp) oil
2 large cooking apples
½–1×5ml (tsp) salt
125ml (5fl oz) water
4×15ml (tbsp) distilled malt vinegar
3×15ml (tbsp) soft brown sugar

SLICING DISC: Trim the cabbage, core and cut into wedges to fit the feed tube; slice. Heat the oil and butter in a large pan over a moderate heat. Add the cabbage and cook for 5 minutes. Add salt. Peel, core and quarter the apples. Stack in the feed tube vertically and slice. Add to the cabbage. Stir well to mix and continue cooking for 5 minutes. Add the water, cover and cook until just cooked but still crisp, about 20 minutes. Stir occasionally. Add the vinegar and brown sugar. Taste and adjust the seasoning.

Preparation: 5 minutes
Cooking: 20–25 minutes

Chinese Stir-Fried Vegetables with Cashews

Serves 4

A good accompaniment to Fried Rice (see index). Reduce the amount of nuts when serving as a side dish. As part of a main course, serve with a grain product and a milk or soy product, such as Chinese Style Stir-Fry Noodles (see index). The texture of the individual vegetables is maintained by slicing and cooking each separately.

1×5ml (tsp) cornflour
1×15ml (tbsp) dry sherry
1-2×15ml (tbsp) soy sauce
175g (6oz) raw cashew nuts
1 medium or large onion
2 large carrots, peeled
1 medium courgette, washed
1 medium green pepper, halved and deseeded
1 small piece fresh ginger
1 clove garlic
oil
fresh coriander for garnish

In a jug stir together the cornflour, sherry and soy sauce. Set aside. Spread the cashews on a baking sheet and bake in a preheated oven at gas mark 4/180°C/350°F for 10–15 minutes or until lightly browned. Set aside.

SLICING DISC: Cut the onion in half, stack in the feed tube and slice. Remove and set aside. Cut carrots to fit the feed tube vertically; slice. Remove and set aside. Cut the courgettes to fit the feed tube vertically; slice. Remove and set aside. Stack the green pepper in the feed tube; slice. Remove and set aside. Heat 1×5ml (tsp) oil in a large frying pan or wok over a medium-high heat. Stir fry each vegetable until tender but crisp. As each vegetable is cooked, remove to a large mixing bowl.

METAL BLADE: Cut the ginger into small pieces. With the machine running, drop in the pieces and process until finely chopped. Add the garlic, pulse on/off until finely chopped. Heat about 1×5ml (tsp) oil in the frying pan or wok over a medium-high heat for 20 seconds. Add the ginger and garlic and stir-fry for 15-20 seconds. Add the vegetables and toss gently to mix. Stir the sauce mixture and add to the pan. Stir to mix and cook until the liquid has thickened. Remove to serving platter and top with cashews and coriander.

Preparation: 10 minutes
Cooking: 20 minutes
Protein g/s: 7.5

Courgette Pancakes

Makes 10 pancakes

Add brown rice and a tossed green salad for a quick meal.

2 medium courgettes, 325g (12oz), washed
1 small onion
4 eggs
2×5ml (tsp) soy sauce
dash pepper

SHREDDING DISC: Cut the courgettes into lengths to fit the feed tube horizontally; shred. Cut the onions to fit the feed tube; shred. Remove to a mixing bowl.

METAL BLADE: Place the eggs, soy sauce and pepper in the processing bowl. Process until well mixed. Pour into the courgette mixture and stir. Heat 1×15ml (tbsp) oil in a pan over a moderate heat. Add 3×15ml (tbsp) of the mixture to the hot pan. Flatten to form a 8–10cm (3–4in) pancake. Cook until lightly browned, about 2 minutes. Turn and cook the other side. Keep warm until all the pancakes are cooked.

Preparation: 5 minutes
Cooking: 10–15 minutes
Protein g/s: 8.5 per 3 pancakes

Grains and Pulses

Chinese Style Fried Rice

Serves 6

Traditionally, fried rice is prepared with cold left-over rice. Cook the rice the night before or earlier in the day. Add variety to this dish by adding your choice of 'extras' – fresh chopped chives, chopped water chestnuts, shredded carrots or sliced bamboo shoots.

3-4×15ml (tbsp) oil
3 eggs, beaten, to make an egg pancake
3-4 salad onions
1 large onion
150-175g (5-6oz) fresh mushrooms
75g (3oz) frozen peas, thawed but not cooked
1350g (3lb) cold cooked brown rice (about 275g (10oz) raw)
1-2×15ml (tbsp) soy sauce

To make the egg pancake, heat a 20-30.5cm (10-12in) frying pan over a moderate heat for about 30 seconds. Brush the bottom of the pan with about 1×5 ml (tsp) oil. Pour in the beaten eggs. Reduce the heat to low and, working quickly, tip the pan from side to side until a thin round pancake forms. Cook over a low heat until firm. Flip over and cook briefly, about 15–20 seconds. Fold into thirds and remove from the pan. When cool enough to handle, cut cross-wise into 6mm (¼in) shreds. Set aside.

METAL BLADE: Place the salad onions, cut into 2.5 cm (1in) lengths, in the processing bowl. Pulse on/off until finely chopped. Remove from bowl and set aside. Place the onion, cut into 2.5cm (1in) pieces, in the processing bowl; pulse on/off until quite finely chopped. Heat 1×15ml (tbsp) oil in a 4-5l (8-10pt) saucepan over a medium high heat. Add the chopped onions and cook until soft and transparent, 3–5 minutes. Remove to a bowl and set aside.

SLICING DISC: Stack the mushrooms in the feed tube sideways; slice with firm pressure. In the same pan heat a further 15ml (tbsp) oil over a medium heat. Add the mushrooms and cook until soft. Add to the cooked onions. Cook the peas until hot and add to the mushrooms. Heat about 15ml (tbsp) oil in the same pan. Add the rice and stir-fry until the rice begins to warm. Add the salad onions, cooked vegetables, egg shreds and soy sauce. Toss gently to mix and stir fry for 2–3 minutes until ingredients are mixed and the rice is hot. Taste and adjust the seasoning

Preparation: 10 minutes
Cooking: 10 minutes
     allow time to cook the rice in advance
Protein g/s: 6

Yellow Rice Pilaf

Serves 4-6

As saffron is so expensive we developed this variation using turmeric. A good accompaniment to our curry dishes and dals.

1 medium onion
3×15ml (tbsp) oil
1 large clove garlic, crushed
ground black pepper
6 whole cloves
6 whole cardamoms
1 cinnamon stick
¼×5ml (tsp) ground allspice
¼×5ml (tsp) ground turmeric
225g (8oz) long grain brown rice
700ml (28fl oz) boiling water
½×5ml (tsp) salt
75g (3oz) raisins
1×5ml (tsp) demerara sugar
50g (2oz) unroasted pistachio nuts OR *roasted cashew nuts*

METAL BLADE: Place the onion, cut into 2.5cm (1in) pieces, in the processing bowl; pulse on/off until chopped finely. Heat the oil over a medium heat in a frying pan that has a tightly fitting lid. Add the onions and cook until transparent, 3–5 minutes. Stir in the garlic, pepper, cloves, cardamom, cinnamon, allspice and turmeric. Continue cooking, stirring constantly, for 1–2 minutes. Add the rice and stir until coated with spices. Pour in the water and bring to the boil, reduce heat, cover and simmer for 30 minutes. Remove the lid, stir in the salt, raisins, sugar and nuts. Cover and continue cooking for 10–15 minutes or until the rice is tender and the liquid absorbed. Pick out the whole spices before serving.

Preparation: 5 minutes
Cooking: 45–50 minutes
Protein g/s: 4 servings–5.5
           6 servings–3.5

Hummus Bi Tahini

Serves 4-6

This tasty purée is a nutritious main dish when served as a filling for Wholewheat Pitta Bread (see index) or an excellent appetiser when served with raw vegetables.

1 clove garlic
325g (12oz) well-cooked chick peas
juice of 1 lemon
3-4×15ml (tbsp) cold water
60ml (2½fl oz) sesame tahini, homemade or purchased
½×5ml (tsp) salt
1×15ml (tbsp) olive oil
dash cayenne pepper, optional
fresh coriander for garnish

METAL BLADE: Place the garlic in the processing bowl and process until finely chopped. Add the chick peas, lemon juice, water, tahini and salt. Process until smooth, scraping down the sides of the bowl with a spatula as needed. Taste and adjust the seasoning. Spread the hummus in a shallow dish. Trickle on the olive oil and garnish with coriander.

Preparation: 5 minutes
Protein g/s: 4 servings–13
           6 servings–9

Buckwheat Mushroom Pilaf

Serves 4-6

This dish is best served with beans, peas or lentils. Buckwheat cooks in 7–12 minutes.

2×15ml (tbsp) oil
3 sprigs parsley
1 large onion
1 large stalk celery, trimmed
1 medium green pepper, halved and deseeded
225g (8oz) mushrooms
25g (1oz) fresh chives
225g (8oz) buckwheat kernels
3 vegetable stock cubes
450ml (18fl oz) boiling water
½-¾×5ml (tsp) dried thyme
½×5ml (tsp) dried summer savory (optional)
1-2 large cloves garlic, crushed
salt

Select a frying pan with a tightly fitting lid. Heat the oil in it over a moderate heat and cook the vegetables as they are prepared.

METAL BLADE: Place the parsley in the processing bowl; pulse on/off until finely chopped. Add to the frying pan and cook. Place the onions, cut into 2.5cm (1in) pieces, in the processing bowl; pulse on/off until finely chopped. Stir into the parsley.

SLICING DISC: Cut the celery to fit the feed tube vertically; slice using medium pressure. Quarter each green pepper half. Stack into the feed tube vertically and slice. Add to the frying pan. Wedge the mushrooms in the feed tube sideways; slice with firm pressure. Stir into frying pan. Wipe the processing bowl dry.

METAL BLADE: Place the chives, cut into 2.5cm (1in) lengths, in the processing bowl; pulse on/off until finely chopped. Add to the vegetables and cook until the vegetables are tender and all the liquid has evaporated, in 5–6 minutes. Add the buckwheat kernels and stir until well mixed. Dissolve the stock cubes in the water and add to the pan. Stir in the thyme, summer savory and garlic. Bring the liquid to the boil; reduce the heat to low, cover and simmer for 10 minutes. Remove the lid; the water should be absorbed and the kernels tender. If not, continue cooking for 2–3 minutes. Taste and adjust the seasonings. Fluff with a fork and serve.

Preparation: 5 minutes
Cooking: 15–20 minutes
Protein g/s: 4 servings–5
　　　　　　6 servings–3

Breads

Supplying several of the B vitamins, iron, protein, fibre and food energy – whole grain breads are the staff of life in a vegetarian diet. We have enhanced the protein power of many of our breads with the addition of dried milk, wheatgerm, nuts, seeds, cheeses and non-wheat whole grains or flours – buckwheat, corn, oat, dark rye and soy.

Friends often ask how we find time to bake yeast breads regularly. We explain that bread making, contrary to popular belief, is not a time-consuming chore. The entire process from mixing the dough to eating the first slice does take about 2½–3 hours, but the actual time spent tending the dough is about 20 minutes – 10 minutes to mix and knead and another 10 minutes to shape. The remainder of the time, the bread is left to take care of itself – rising and baking. Meanwhile, relax with a book you've been wanting to read, prune and fertilise your plants, do some shopping, or put on your running shoes and go for a run around the block.

We started as only occasional weekend bakers. With thoughts of mixing and kneading that sticky glob of dough until our arms ached and of scraping the worktop clean afterwards, we usually found something else to do.

But now, the food processor has so simplified bread making that tasty and nutritious wholegrain breads are an essential part of our diets and baking schedules. Flours and liquid are quickly mixed and transformed into an elastic ball of dough in the processing bowl, eliminating lengthy manual mixing and kneading and greatly reducing the clearing up time.

Most machines on the market will process yeast dough from recipes using up to 325g (12oz) flour. However, some machines have a greater than average capacity for mixing yeast doughs. Check your instruction manual for flour capacity before you try the recipes. Experience will allow you to adjust the recipes to your machine's capabilities.

Baking Ingredients

Grains, Flours and Cereals

Wholewheat flour is milled from the whole kernel and contains the the bran and wheat germ which provides protein, all the B vitamins, iron and other nutrients naturally present in wheat. The volume of breads made with wholewheat flour is slightly lower and the texture coarser than those of bread made with unbleached white flour.

Wheat flour contains a substance called gluten, an elastic protein. When wheat flour is mixed and kneaded with liquid, gluten forms an elastic framework that traps the bubbles of gas produced during the rising. The bread rises and achieves a light texture. Without gluten, a leavened bread cannot be produced.

Wheat flakes are made from whole wheat, steamed and rolled to form flakes. The flakes may be substituted for rolled oats in yeast breads and muffins.

Cracked wheat or *bulgur wheat* is wheat that is cracked or cut rather than ground. It is usually softened in hot water before use and adds a nice chewy texture.

Bran, miller's bran, or *unprocessed bran*

flakes are the skin of wheat. A number of our recipes include bran for extra fibre. When bran is called for in this book it is the unprocessed bran flakes. You may increase the amount of bran, but do so slowly as the resulting product will be more compact. Try adding about 15g (½oz) to your favourite recipes. You can increase the amount as long as the product is acceptable.

Wheat germ is the part of the wheat that germinates when the kernel is planted. It is rich in B and E vitamins and contains protein, iron and fat. Store wheat germ in an airtight container in the refrigerator.

Buckwheat flour is milled in much the same way as wheat flour but is a herb rather than a true grain. It has rather a strong flavour, has no gluten power and is generally combined with a large proportion of wheat flour.

Cornmeal or *maizemeal* is ground corn. When water-ground or stone-ground, it retains the germ. Cornmeal does not contain gluten, so is not used alone for making most breads, but small amounts added to recipes give a nice crunch. When sprinkled on the baking sheet or in the bottom of a loaf tin it prevents the bread from sticking.

Rolled oats, old fashioned oats or *oatmeal* are made from whole oat groats softened by steam and crushed between rollers. Unless otherwise noted, we do not use instant or quick cooking oatmeal. Oats have the highest protein content of any cereal grain, and breads containing oats are tender, moist, and chewy.

Oat flour is easily made in your processor. For 125g (4oz) flour, process 125-175g (4-6oz) uncooked rolled oats with the metal blade for about one minute. Store in a tightly covered container in a cool dry place. Oat flour has no gluten strength.

Dark rye flour is milled from whole rye and contains all of the grain. Rye flour is usually mixed with wheat flour because the rye flour gluten provides stickiness but lacks elasticity. Breads made with a large proportion of rye flour are moist and compact.

Rye flakes are made by rolling the grain and are similar to rolled oats.

Soy flour is made by grinding whole raw soy beans. This flour has a slightly sweet flavour and is high in protein. Breads and cakes containing soy flour tend to brown more quickly, so watch carefully.

Triticale flour is milled from a hybrid plant, a cross between rye and wheat. It is reported to have a slightly better amino acid balance than wheat alone.

Leavening or Rising Agents
Light breads, muffins and cakes are the result of the action of leavening. Leavening agents include yeast, baking powder, baking soda, buttermilk, air and steam.

Yeast feeds on sugars in the flour and forms carbon dioxide gas. These gas bubbles raise the dough. Yeast needs a warm temperature for growth; too low a temperature inhibits growth; too high a temperature kills the yeast.

As *easy-blend yeast* is now readily available it is included in our recipes. This yeast requires no frothing before use. It also stores well, being packed in small foil packets.

Baking powder is a combination of baking soda and an acid ingredient that reacts in the batter to form gas bubbles.

Bicarbonate of Soda is used when the batter contains acid ingredients such as buttermilk, honey, molasses or fruit juice. Gas bubbles form in the same way as when baking powder is used, but the action is immediate. The product must be baked as soon as it is mixed.

Air in beaten egg whites is a leavening agent. Be sure that the bowl and beater are free from oil. Allow the whites to come to room temperature to achieve maximum volume.

Steam leavens the mixture in some quick breads such as popovers.

Fat
Margarine, vegetable oil or *butter* makes bread more tender, adds flavour and prevents rapid spoiling. Small amounts are used to prevent interference with the formation of gluten in the dough. Some breads, such as French bread, contain no fat.

Eggs

Eggs add flavour and nutritive value to baked products. The proteins in eggs coagulate when heated, strengthening the framework of batters and doughs.

Sweeteners

Honey, maple syrup, molasses and *brown sugar* flavour baked goods and increase tenderness, volume and keeping qualities. These sweeteners also help to brown crusts. In yeast-raised breads, the sweetener is food for the yeast.

Liquids

Water, fruit juice, liquid buttermilk and *liquid skimmed milk* are among the liquids used to blend dry ingredients in making doughs and batters. It is the amount of liquid in a mixture that determines its bulk – whether it is a dough or a batter. A dough is any mixture thick enough to be rolled or kneaded. A batter is thin enough to pour or drop from a spoon.

Water makes crusty breads. Bread made with milk has higher protein value. The crust is softer and browner and the crumb is tender. Most of the recipes in this book call for milk powder which is added to the flour along with other dry ingredients, eliminating the step of heating fresh milk. Unheated fresh milk often contains an ingredient that produces a soft dough. This dough lacks the strength to hold the gas bubbles during rising and causes the loaf to collapse during baking.

Salt

A small amount of salt flavours the bread but, more importantly, inhibits and regulates the growth of yeast. Yeast dough without salt rises dramatically. A word of caution – if you eliminate the salt from the recipes do not allow the dough to rise above the level of the tin as it may collapse.

Processor Bread Baking Basics

Measuring Ingredients

Though precise measurements of flours and liquids for yeast doughs are not critical, accuracy is important for other baked goods. Using the right utensil and method will ensure a perfect product each time.

Flours: when spoon measures are given they are flat not rounded spoonfuls.

Liquids: place the measuring jug on a flat surface to check measures.

Brown sugar: when brown sugar is called for by the spoonful, it is a flat not mounded spoonful.

Baking powder, spices, bicarbonate of soda, etc: these are measured by the level not mounded spoonful.

Honey, molasses, maple syrup: a little oil on the measuring spoon will help the sweeteners to drop from the spoon.

Mixing

Methods of mixing vary for different types of baked goods. In the preparation of yeast bread dough, easy-blend yeast is added to the flour before the liquid. The mixture is then vigorously mixed and kneaded to develop the gluten in the wheat flour. The elasticity of the gluten allows the dough to rise as carbon dioxide is produced by the yeast. In yeast-raised breads, gluten must be developed to give volume to the loaf.

Muffins are processed with a few on/off pulses until the dry ingredients are just moistened. Overmixing results in poor texture with large holes and tunnels.

Mixing batter for breads leavened by bicarbonate of soda, baking powder or other means requires a light touch. You do not want the gluten to develop, or the product will be tough. The flour is added last and combined with a few quick on/off pulses until barely moist.

Step-By-Step Method

Experienced and first-time bread makers will benefit from reading through this simplified lesson in the preparation of yeast dough using the food processor. The first loaf that you make may take more time than subsequent loaves, as is the case when learning any new technique. Be sure to check the instructions that are included with your processor.

Basic Bread Recipe

Have all ingredients at room temperature.

easy-blend yeast
oil
honey
wholewheat flour
milk powder
salt
warm water as needed to form a ball of dough

Adding the Liquid to the Flour Mixture

With the proper blade in a dry processing bowl, add the flour, milk powder, salt and easy-blend yeast. Pulse on/off to mix.

With the processor on, add the yeast mixture. Pour in the remaining liquid in a steady stream, only as fast as the flour will absorb it. All the liquid may not be needed. When the flour and liquid proportion is correct, the dough will form into a ball. With experience, you will know just when to stop adding the liquid.

If too much liquid is added, the motor slows. You will hear this; do not worry, add 1-2×15ml (tbsp) of flour and then the speed should pick up. Sometimes the dough will be very sticky – did you pour in too much liquid too fast? Stop the machine, scrape the dough from the sides of the bowl with a spatula, sprinkle with 1-2×15ml (tbsp) flour then continue processing.

Due to the varying moisture content of flours, you may need more liquid. Dribble the additional amount in slowly, stopping as soon as the dough forms into a ball.

Kneading

Process the ball of dough for 20 seconds. Stop the machine and feel the dough. It should be elastic, sticky and wet. If not, process 10 seconds longer. Sprinkle the dough with an additional 1-2×15ml (tbsp) flour, pulse machine on/off to coat the dough for easy removal from the processing bowl.

The food processor method of preparing yeast doughs differs from the traditional method in that the consistency of the dough is controlled by the amount of liquid added rather than by the addition of flour.

Preparing the Bowl for Rising

Place about 1×15ml (tbsp) oil in a ceramic bowl and swirl to coat the bottom. Place the ball of dough in the bowl and turn the bottom to the top so the entire surface is oiled. Cover with a plastic bag or damp cloth to to prevent the dough from drying out. Plastic bags, unlike plastic wrap, have their own film of oil that prevents the dough from sticking.

First Rising, Creating a Warm Place

Let rise in a warm place (30°C/80-85°F), free from draughts until doubled in bulk. There are several ways to create a 'warm place':
* Fill a large bowl with steaming hot water and place it on the bottom shelf of an unheated oven. Then put the bowl of dough, covered with a damp towel to keep it moist, on the shelf above. This method does not work in a gas oven.
* Fill a bowl with steaming water, top it with a wire rack and place the bowl of dough on the rack. Leave on the worktop to rise.
* The dough can be placed in a fan oven, following the cooker manufacturer's instructions.
* Yeast doughs can rise in a microwave oven. Check your instruction manual for directions.
* The dough may also be placed, covered, in the airing cupboard.

The first rising will take about an hour. Whole grain breads take longer to rise. When you think that the dough has doubled in size, test it by poking two fingers into the dough to the depth of 1cm (½in). Chose a point half way between the edge and the centre of the bowl. Quickly pull your fingers out. The dough is ready if the imprint remains. If the hole begins to fill, give the dough a little longer to rise.

Knocking Back

When the dough has doubled in bulk you are ready to knock back. Sink your fist down into the centre of the bowl. Pull the dough from the edge of the bowl towards the imprint and remove the dough from the bowl.

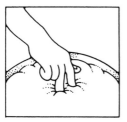 

Lightly flour the worktop or a pastry board. Knead the dough for 30 seconds as follows: Pat dough out to 2.5cm (1in) thick; lift one half and fold over the other. Press the dough down with the heels of your hands and push the dough away. Give the dough a quarter turn and repeat the kneading process. This breaks up the large bubbles of air that form during the rising into smaller bubbles, thus giving the dough a more even grain. When making two loaves, divide the dough into two pieces.

Cover the dough and allow it to rest on the worktop for about 5 minutes. During this time the gluten relaxes, making the dough easier to roll and shape.

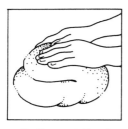 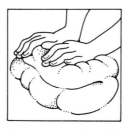

Roll or pat the dough into a rectangle with the short side as long as the bread tin you are

using. When using a 21.5×11.5cm (8½ ×4½ in) loaf pan, roll out a rectangle approximately 20.5×31cm (8×12in). Starting at the 20.5cm (8in) end, tightly roll the dough like a Swiss roll.

Stop after each full turn to press the edge of the roll firmly into the flat sheet of dough to seal. Press with fingertips. Pinch seam to seal. Hold the roll with the seam underneath. Press the ends of the loaf down with the edges of your hands. Tuck the flattened ends under and pinch gently to seal.

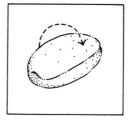 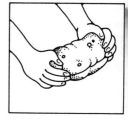

Alternatively, you can press the ball of dough into a flat oval, about the length of the baking tin. Fold the oval in half and pinch the seam tightly to seal. Turn the roll so that the seam is underneath and press the ends of the loaf down with the edges of your hands. Tuck the flattened ends under and pinch gently to seal.

Placing the Dough in the Tins

Place the shaped loaf in a greased 21.5×11.5cm (8½ ×4½ in) loaf tin, seam side down. Gently press the loaf into the tin so that both ends touch the edge of the tin.

Second Rising

Cover and allow to rise again in a warm place, free from draughts, until doubled in size – about 45 minutes. The centre of the dough will rise about 2.5cm (1in) above the level of the tin. To test, press finger gently into a corner. The loaf is ready to bake if the imprint remains.

Baking

Preheat the oven. If using the oven to prove the dough remember to remove the water and dough before preheating. Place the bread in the centre of the middle shelf of the oven. Do not let the tins touch each other or the sides of the oven.

Before baking you may brush the bread with a beaten egg for a shiny crust or milk or butter for a soft crust. Most of our breads go into the oven without a glaze. We keep the crusts soft by covering the loaf with a cloth while it cools.

Bake the loaves for the specified period of time. Resist the temptation to open the oven door during the first 20 minutes of baking, or the loaf may collapse. Open the door gently and quickly. If the tops are browning too quickly, cover with foil.

If using a fan oven, follow the manufacturer's instructions for baking.

Testing the Loaf

Remove the loaf from its baking tin and tap the bottom crust. It will sound hard and hollow when cooked. If it is soft, return the bread to the oven, out of the tin, for an additional 5-10 minutes. Test again.

Cooling and Storing

Remove bread from the tins immediately to avoid soggy crusts. Place on a wire rack to cool.

It is important to allow the bread to cool completely before storing as condensation can cause mould to form rapidly. When cooled, place the bread in a plastic bag and seal with a wire twist. Store at room temperature if it is to be eaten in a few days.

For longer storage, slice the loaf, wrap and freeze. Remove individual slices as required. Whole loaves may also be frozen unsliced. Place in a plastic bag and freeze. Thaw the wrapped loaf at room temperature. Remove the plastic, wrap in foil and reheat for 15 minutes at gas mark 4/180°C/350°F.

Slicing

A serrated bread knife, kept razor-sharp, is an indispensable piece of equipment. Use your bread knife only for slicing bread and it will last for years. Even a hot loaf of bread can be sliced when using the right knife. For even slices, place the loaf on its side and slice with a gently sawing motion.

Create Your Own Dough

Puréed vegetables (potatoes, pumpkin, carrots), fruits (apple sauce), grated and shredded cheese, seeds, nuts, raisins, dates and other chopped dried fruits are some of the 'extras' that we have put into our breads for flavour, texture and increased food value.

It is easy to master bread baking using the food processor method. Soon you will be creating your own breads or making variations of the recipes that we offer. How about adding raisins to the honey wheat loaf or substituting rye flakes for oat flakes? Be creative! The combinations are endless.

Do not let loaf tins limit the shape of your loaves. Any decorative mould that can be placed in the oven can be used. Terracotta bread bakers are widely available for round loaves and old fashioned flower pots may also be used.

Almost any yeast bread can be baked as rolls. This is a time saver, as rolls take less time to rise and bake.

Here are a few tips to remember when creating your own dough:

* 325g (12oz) flour makes a 675g (1½ lb) loaf
* 325g (12oz) flour will absorb about 250ml (10fl oz) liquid
* 1 large (size 2) egg is approximately 60ml (2½fl oz)
* Use 1×15ml (tbsp) easy-blend yeast, ½×15ml (tbsp) salt, 2×15ml (tbsp) oil and 2-4×15ml (tbsp) sweetener for a loaf made from 325g (12oz) flour.
* Substitute no more than one third of the total amount of wholewheat flour with a cereal or non-wheat flour. In a 325g (12oz) flour recipe you might substitute a third of the wholewheat flour with some oat flour, soy flour or cornmeal. Remember, gluten found in wholewheat flour is essential for the bread to rise.

Tins

The type of tin you use affects the final baking results. Shiny tins reflect heat; their use results in pale, soft crusts. Dull, dark-coloured, very heavy gauge pans absorb the heat, which result in dark thick crusts. Glass (Pyrex) and Corning Ware absorb heat exceptionally well and produce a golden crust. Reduce the oven temperature by 1 gas mark, 10°C/25°F when using glass or Corning Ware. A teflon-coated or other non-stick surface eliminates greasing and is easy to clean.

Using the tin size specified in the recipes will give you the best results. If you must substitute remember that a larger pan will cause the batter or dough to spread out and bake faster. Breads baked in smaller tins will take longer. Quick bread batter should fill no more than half the tin or it may overflow before it has set. A tin two thirds full with yeast dough produces a high loaf.

Evenly baked goods result when the air is allowed to circulate around the food as it cooks. Try to allow at least 5cm (2in) between each tin, the sides and back of the oven and the door. Place the oven shelf so that the food not the shelf is in the centre of the oven. When using two shelves, stagger the tins so that they are not directly above each other.

Timing

A change in plans can sometimes interrupt the usual sequence of yeast bread baking, but you need not be a slave to your bread. Should the loaf expand to more than double its bulk because you did not get home in time to check, simply knock it back, reshape and allow to rise again. The dough is ready to bake but you are not? Refrigerate the loaf, covered with a plastic bag. Allow it to come to room temperature while preheating the oven then bake as usual.

No time to wait for the bread to rise? Bake the bread after one rising, starting in a cold oven. The texture of the loaf will be coarser than if allowed to rise twice but the flavour is not affected.

You may like to try the 'Coolrise Method' of proving. Double the amount of yeast is required and the loaves tend to be more compact but still delicious!

After kneading the ball of dough for 20 seconds, remove from the processor and place on a board or the worktop. Cover with a plastic bag or inverted bowl and leave for 20 minutes. Knock back the dough, shape and

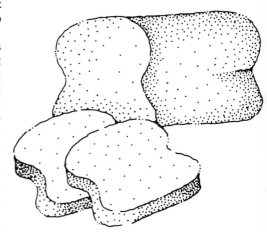

place with the seam downwards in a greased baking tin. Brush the top of the loaf with cooking oil. Cover loosely with plastic to allow for a rise to 2.5-5cm (1-2in) above the sides of the tin. Refrigerate for 2-24 hours. Loaves may be removed and baked whenever convenient during that time. Remove the loaf from the refrigerator and take off the plastic. Leave to stand, uncovered, for 15 minutes while preheating the oven to gas mark 6/200°C/400°F. Bake for 35-40 minutes or until the loaves are golden brown and sound hollow when tapped on the bottom crust. Remove to a wire rack to cool completely before storing.

What Went Wrong?

Heavy compact texture, dry crumb	too much flour, under-rising	Pale crust	oven temperature too low, drying of dough during rising
Coarse texture	under-kneading, too little flour, over-rising	Yeasty flavour, fallen centre	dough allowed to rise too long
Uneven shape	too much dough for the tin, bad shaping	Cracks and bulging crust	dough too stiff, uneven heat in oven
Porous bread	over-rising	Holes in the centre	air bubbles not knocked out before shaping, over-rising
Small flat loaf	ingredients too warm, old yeast, under-rising		

Yeast Breads

Complementary Bread

1 small loaf, 15 slices; 1 medium loaf, 16 slices

A moist high-protein, all-purpose bread. Double the recipe for two small loaves if your machine is able to process 625g (22oz) flour.

1 loaf, 20×10cm (8×4in)

1×15ml (tbsp) easy-blend dried yeast
1½×15ml (tbsp) oil
2×15ml (tbsp) honey
300g (11oz) wholewheat flour
50g (2oz) + 3×15ml (tbsp) soy flour
good pinch salt
250ml (10fl oz) water

1 loaf, 21.5×11.5cm (8½×4½in)

1×15ml (tbsp) easy-blend dried yeast
2×15ml (tbsp) oil
3×15ml (tbsp) honey
400g (14oz) wholewheat flour
75g (3oz) + 2×15ml (tbsp) soy flour
1×5ml (tsp) salt
300ml (12fl oz) water

METAL BLADE OR PLASTIC DOUGH BLADE: Place the flours, salt and yeast in the processing bowl; pulse on/off to mix. Add the oil and honey then, with the machine running, pour in the water in a steady stream, only as fast as the flour can absorb it. Not all the water may be required to form a ball of dough. Process the ball of dough for 20 seconds. Stop the machine and feel the dough – it should be elastic, sticky and wet. If not, process for an additional 10 seconds. Sprinkle the dough with the extra soy flour and pulse the machine on/off to coat the dough for easy removal from the processing bowl.

Transfer the dough to an oiled bowl and turn so that the entire surface is oiled. Cover with a plastic bag or a damp cloth and put to rise in a warm place, free from draughts, until it doubles in size in about 1 hour. Knock back the dough and knead for about 30 seconds to press out the bubbles. Divide in half if making two loaves. Shape the dough into a ball and allow to rest for 5 minutes, covered. Shape into a loaf and place in a greased loaf tin. Cover and leave to rise in a warm place, until doubled in size, about 45 minutes.

Preheat the oven to gas mark 5/ 190°C/375°F. Bake the bread in the centre of the oven for 35-40 minutes or until the bottom crust has a hollow sound when tapped. Remove from the loaf tin immediately and allow to cool on a wire rack.

Note: when doubling the recipe for two small loaves with 625g (22oz) wholewheat flour, the machine may not be able to process the ball of dough easily. If this is the case, remove a portion of the dough and set aside. Continue processing the remainder until it is elastic and sticky. Remove from the bowl and then process the remaining portion. Knead the two portions together and then proceed as directed.

Preparation: 10 minutes
Standing: allow 2–2½ hours for the dough to rise
Baking: 35–40 minutes
Protein g/s: small loaf–4
medium loaf–5

Bran Bread

1 loaf, 15 slices

A light, moist bread that provides extra fibre.

1×15ml (tbsp) easy-blend dried yeast
2×15ml (tbsp) oil
2×15ml (tbsp) honey
300g (11oz) wholewheat flour
25g (1oz) bran
½×5ml (tsp) salt
250ml (10fl oz) water

METAL BLADE: Place the flour, bran, yeast and salt in the processing bowl and pulse on/off to mix. Add the oil and honey. With the machine running, pour in the water in a steady stream, only as fast as the flour can absorb the liquid. All the water may not be required to form a ball of dough. Process the ball of dough for 20 seconds then stop the machine and feel the dough. It should be elastic, sticky and wet. If not, process for 10 seconds longer. Sprinkle the dough with an additional 1-2×15ml (tbsp) flour. Pulse on/off to coat the dough for easy removal from the processing bowl.

Transfer the dough to an oiled bowl and turn so that the entire surface is coated. Cover with a plastic bag or damp cloth and leave in a warm place, free from draughts, to rise until doubled in bulk, about 1 hour. Knock back the dough and knead lightly to press out the air bubbles. Cover and allow to rest for 5 minutes. Shape into a loaf and place in a greased 20×10cm (8×4in) loaf tin. Cover and leave in a warm place to rise until doubled in bulk, about 45 minutes.

Preheat the oven to gas mark 5/190°C/375°F. Bake the loaf in the centre of the oven for 30-35 minutes or until the bottom crust sounds hollow when tapped. Remove from the tin immediately and allow to cool on a wire rack.

Preparation: 10 minutes
Standing: allow 2 hours for the dough to rise
Baking: 30–35 minutes
Protein g/s: 3.5

Carrot Wholewheat Bread

2 loaves, 16 slices per loaf

For machines with smaller capacities, halve the recipe and make 1 loaf. Speckled with shredded carrots, this loaf makes excellent sandwiches.

2×15ml (tbsp) easy-blend dried yeast
2×15ml (tbsp) oil
6×15ml (tbsp) honey
3 medium carrots, peeled
675g (1½lb) wholewheat flour
25g (1oz) dried milk powder
2×5ml (tsp) salt
200-250ml (8-10fl oz) water

SHREDDING DISC: Cut the carrots to fit the feed tube vertically; shred. Remove the shredding disc and insert the metal blade or plastic dough blade.

METAL BLADE OR PLASTIC DOUGH BLADE: Add the flour, salt, yeast and milk powder to the carrots in the processing bowl and pulse on/off to mix. Add the oil and honey. With the machine running, pour in enough water in a steady stream, only as fast as the flour can absorb the liquid, to form a ball of dough. Process the ball of dough for 20 seconds. Stop the machine and feel the dough – it should be elastic, sticky and wet. If not process for 10 seconds longer. Sprinkle the dough with an additional 1-2×15ml (tbsp) flour and pulse on/off to coat, to make it easier to remove the dough from the processing bowl.

Transfer the dough to an oiled bowl and turn so that the entire surface is coated. Cover with a plastic bag or damp cloth and leave in a warm place to rise until doubled in bulk, about 1 hour. Knock back the dough and knead lightly to press out the air bubbles. Divide the dough into two pieces. Shape into balls and allow to rest for 5 minutes, covered. Shape each ball into a loaf and place in a greased loaf tin, 21.5×11.5 (8½×4½in). Cover and leave in a warm place to rise until doubled in bulk, about 45 minutes.

Preheat the oven to gas mark 5/190°C/375°F. Bake the loaves in the centre of the oven for

35-40 minutes, or until the bottom crust sounds hollow when tapped. Remove from the loaf tin immediately and allow to cool on a wire rack.

Preparation: 10 minutes
Standing: allow 2–2½ hours for the dough to rise
Baking: 35–40 minutes
Protein g/s: 3.5

Double Cheese Bread

1 loaf, 16 slices

The combination of Cheddar and cottage cheeses makes this moist loaf a tasty treat.

1×15ml (tbsp) easy-blend dried yeast
1×15ml (tbsp) oil
2×15ml (tbsp) honey
125g (4oz) Cheddar cheese, well chilled
325g (12oz) wholewheat flour
1×5ml (tsp) salt
2×5ml (tsp) dill weed
275g (10oz) cottage cheese
250ml (10fl oz) water

SHREDDING DISC: Place the Cheddar cheese in the feed tube; shred. Remove the shredding disc.

METAL BLADE: Add the flour, salt, cottage cheese, dill weed and yeast to the processing bowl. Pulse on/off to mix. Add the oil and honey. With the machine running add the water, pouring in a steady stream, only as fast as the flour can absorb the liquid. All the water may not be required for the dough to form a ball. Process the ball for 20 seconds. Stop the machine and feel the dough – it should be elastic, sticky and wet. If not, process for a further 10 seconds. Sprinkle the dough with an additional 1-2×15ml (tbsp) flour and pulse on/off to coat the dough for easy removal from the processing bowl.

Transfer the dough to an oiled bowl and turn to coat the entire surface. Cover with a plastic bag or a damp cloth and leave in a warm place until doubled in size, about 1 hour. Knock back the dough and knead lightly for 30 seconds to press out any air bubbles. Shape into a ball and allow to rest for 5 minutes, covered. Shape into a loaf and place in a greased loaf tin, 21.5×11.5cm (8½×4½in). Cover and leave in a warm place to rise until doubled in size, about 45 minutes.

Preheat the oven to gas mark 5/190°C/375°F. Bake the loaf in the centre of the oven for 30 minutes or until the bottom crust sounds hollow when tapped. Remove from the tin immediately and allow to cool on a wire rack.

Preparation: 10 minutes
Standing: allow 2–2½ hours for the dough to rise
Baking: 30–35 minutes
Protein g/s: 6.5

Honey Wheat Bread

1 small loaf, 15 slices; 1 medium loaf, 16 slices

An all-purpose sandwich bread sweetened with honey. Double the recipe for 2 small loaves if your machine can process 675g (1½lb) flour.

1 loaf, 20×10cm (8×4in)

1×15ml (tbsp) easy-blend dried yeast
2×15ml (tbsp) oil
2×15ml (tbsp) honey
325g (12oz) wholewheat flour
15g (½oz) dried milk powder
½×5ml (tsp) salt
250ml (10fl oz) water

1 loaf, 21.5×11.5cm (8½×4½in)

1×15ml (tbsp) easy-blend dried yeast
2×15ml (tbsp) oil
3×15ml (tbsp) honey
425g (15oz) wholewheat flour
15g (½oz) dried milk powder
½×5ml (tsp) salt
300ml (12fl oz) water

METAL BLADE OR PLASTIC DOUGH BLADE: Place the flour, milk powder, yeast and salt in the processing bowl; pulse on/off to mix. Add the oil and honey. With the machine running gradually add the water in a steady stream, only as fast as the flour can absorb the liquid. You may not require all the water to make the dough form a ball. Process the ball for 20 seconds. Stop the machine and feel the dough – it should be elastic, sticky and wet. If not, process for an additional 10 seconds. Sprinkle the dough with an additional 1-2×15ml (tbsp) flour and pulse on/off to coat to make removal from the processing bowl easier.

Transfer the dough to an oiled bowl and turn to coat the entire surface. Cover with a plastic bag or a damp cloth and leave in a warm place to rise until doubled in size, about 1 hour. Knock back and knead lightly for 30 seconds to press out any air bubbles. Divide the dough into two if making two loaves. Shape the dough into a ball and allow to rest, covered, for 5 minutes. Shape into a loaf and place in a greased loaf tin. Cover and leave in a warm place to rise until doubled in size, about 45 minutes.

Preheat the oven to gas mark 5/190°C/375°F. Bake the loaf in the centre of the oven for 30–35 minutes or until the bottom crust sounds hollow when tapped. Remove from the tin immediately and allow to cool on a wire rack.

Preparation: 10 minutes
Standing: allow 2–2½ hours for the dough to rise
Baking: 30–35 minutes
Protein g/s: small loaf–4
           medium loaf–4.5

Oat Bran Bread

1 loaf, 16 slices

Try this bread once you have made a few loaves following the procedure at the beginning of this chapter, and when you are familiar with your machine. The method for making this light, moist loaf with a slightly chewy texture from the oats, is slightly different to the standard method.

40g (1½oz) rolled oats
25g (1oz) bran
1×15ml (tbsp) oil
2×15ml (tbsp) molasses
250ml (10fl oz) boiling water
1×15ml (tbsp) easy-blend dried yeast
300g (11oz) wholewheat flour
1×5ml (tsp) salt
125ml (5fl oz) water, as needed

In a medium bowl combine the oats, bran, oil and molasses. Pour in the boiling water. Stir and allow to cool until luke-warm, about 30 minutes. To hasten the cooling, place the bowl in a cold water bath. When at the right temperature, you should be able to hold your little finger in the mixture without it feeling hot or cold.

METAL BLADE OR PLASTIC DOUGH BLADE: Place the flour, salt and yeast in the processing bowl; pulse on/off to mix. Remove the cover and pour in the oat/bran mixture all at once. Use a spatula to mix. Turn on the machine and process to make a ball of dough. Gradually add the remaining water if needed. Do not add too much water at a time – it takes a little time for the flour to absorb the oat/bran mixture. It may be necessary to stop the machine and push the dough to loosen the ball to help distribute the liquid. Process the ball of dough for 20 seconds. Stop the machine and feel the dough – it should be elastic, sticky and wet – if not, process for a further 10 seconds. Sprinkle the dough with an additional 1-2×15ml (tbsp) of flour and pulse on/off to coat the dough in order to make it easier to remove from the processing bowl.

Transfer the dough to an oiled bowl and turn so that the entire surface is coated. Cover with a plastic bag or a damp cloth and leave in a warm place to rise until doubled in size, about 1 hour. Knock back the dough and knead for 30 seconds to press out the air bubbles. Shape into a ball and allow to rest, covered, for 5 minutes. Shape into a loaf and place in a greased 21.5×11.5cm (8½×4½in) loaf tin. Cover and leave in a warm place to rise until doubled in size, about 45 minutes.

Preheat the oven to gas mark 4/180°C/350°F. Bake the loaf in the centre of the oven for 40–45 minutes, or until the bottom crust sounds hollow when tapped. Remove from the tin immediately and allow to cool on a wire rack.

Preparation: 10 minutes
Standing: 30 minutes for the oat/bran mixture
        to cool
        2 hours for the dough to rise
Baking: 40–45 minutes
Protein g/s: 4.5

Irish Oatmeal Loaf

1 loaf, 15 slices

One of our all-time favourites. The rolled oats are added last to keep the texture.

1×15ml (tbsp) easy-blend dried yeast
1×15ml (tbsp) oil
2×15ml (tbsp) honey
1 egg, beaten
250g (9oz) wholewheat flour
3×15ml (tbsp) dried milk powder
½×5ml (tsp) salt
60g (2½oz) rolled oats
150ml (6fl oz) water
75g (3oz) raisins or currants
Glaze: 1 egg, beaten

METAL BLADE: Place the flour, salt, milk powder and yeast in the processing bowl; pulse on/off to blend. Add the oil, honey and beaten egg. With the machine running add the water in a steady stream. Stop the machine when all the water has been added. Add the rolled oats and continue processing until a ball of dough is formed; add extra water if necessary. Process the ball of dough for 20 seconds. Stop the machine and feel the dough – it should be elastic, sticky and wet. If not, process for an additional 10 seconds. Sprinkle the dough with an additional 1-2×15ml (tbsp) flour and pulse on/off to coat the dough for easy removal from the processing bowl.

Transfer the dough to an oiled bowl and turn to coat the entire surface. Cover with a plastic bag or a damp towel and leave in a warm place to rise until doubled in size, about 1 hour. Knock back the dough and knead lightly for 30 seconds, adding and evenly distributing the raisins and pressing out any air bubbles. Shape into a ball and allow to rest, covered, for 5 minutes. Shape into a high rounded loaf, about 16.5cm (6½in) across. Place on a well greased baking sheet. Cover and leave in a warm place to rise until doubled in size, about 45 minutes.

Preheat the oven to gas mark 4/180°C/350°F. Brush the top of the loaf with egg glaze and bake in the centre of the oven for 35–45 minutes or until the lower crust sounds hollow when tapped. Remove to a wire rack and allow to cool.

Preparation: 10 minutes
Standing: allow 2–2½ hours for the dough to
        rise
Baking: 35–45 minutes
Protein g/s: 4

Sunflower Seed Bread

1 loaf, 15 slices

Sunflower seeds add the crunch to this delicious loaf. A good all-round sandwich loaf.

1×15ml (tbsp) easy-blend dried yeast
1×15ml (tbsp) oil
2×15ml (tbsp) honey
300g (11oz) wholewheat flour
½×5ml (tsp) salt
50g (2oz) sunflower seeds
250ml (10fl oz) water

METAL BLADE: Place the flour, yeast and salt in the processing bowl; pulse on/off to mix. Add the oil and honey. With the machine running add the water in a steady stream, pouring only as fast as the flour can absorb the liquid. Add only as much water as required to form a ball. Process the ball of dough for 20 seconds. Stop the machine and feel the dough – it should be elastic, sticky and wet. If not, process for a further 10 seconds. With the machine running, gradually add the sunflower seeds and process until just mixed. Sprinkle the dough with an extra 1-2×15ml (tbsp) flour, pulse on/off to coat the dough to make it easier to remove from the processing bowl.

Transfer the dough to an oiled bowl and turn the dough over to cover the entire surface. Cover the bowl and leave in a warm place to rise until the dough is doubled in size, about 1 hour. Knock back and knead lightly for 30 seconds to press out the air bubbles. Shape into a ball and allow to stand for 5 minutes, covered. Shape into a loaf and place in a greased 21.5×11.5cm (8½×4½in) loaf tin. Cover and leave in a warm place until the dough has doubled in size, about 45 minutes.

Preheat the oven to gas mark 4/180°C/350°F. Bake in the centre of the oven for 35–40 minutes or until the bottom crust sounds hollow when tapped. Remove from the tin immediately and allow to cool on a wire rack

Preparation: 10 minutes
Standing: allow about 2 hours for the dough to rise
Baking: 35–40 minutes
Protein g/s: 3.5

Rye Bread

1 loaf, 16 slices

A small amount of gluten flour enhances the rising power, producing a bread with a light texture. For a more compact but equally delicious and moist loaf, omit the gluten flour and increase the wholewheat flour to 175g (6oz). We use dark rye flour for its higher protein value. If you prefer a less sweet loaf, use the smaller amount of honey.

1×15ml (tbsp) easy-blend dried yeast
1×15ml (tbsp) oil
1-2×15ml (tbsp) honey
150g (5oz) wholewheat flour
150g (5oz) rye flour
25g (1oz) gluten flour
½×5ml (tsp) salt
200-250ml (8-10fl oz) water
2×5ml (tsp) caraway seeds
additional caraway seeds for topping
Glaze: 1 egg, beaten with 2×15ml (tbsp) water

METAL BLADE: Place the flours, salt and yeast in the processing bowl and pulse on/off to mix. Add the oil and honey. With the machine running, add the water in a steady stream, only as fast as the flour can absorb the liquid. All the water may not be required to form the dough into a ball. Process the ball for 20 seconds. Stop the machine and feel the dough – it should be elastic, sticky and wet. Rye doughs are characteristically stickier and less elastic than those made with wholewheat flour. Process for a further 10 seconds if required. With the machine running, slowly add the caraway seeds, processing until just mixed. Sprinkle the dough with 1-2×15ml (tbsp) extra flour and pulse on/off until the dough is coated, making it easier to remove from the bowl.

Transfer the dough to an oiled bowl and turn so that the entire surface is coated. Cover the bowl and leave in a warm place to rise until doubled in size, about 1 hour to 1 hour 15 minutes. Knock back the dough and knead lightly for 30 seconds to press out the air bubbles. Shape into a ball and allow to rest for 5 minutes, covered. On a lightly floured surface, roll the dough to form a rectangle measuring 20×30.5cm (8×12in). Starting at the 30.5cm (12in) end tightly roll the dough as for a Swiss roll, pinch the seam and seal. Turn the roll so that the seam is underneath and pinch the end of the loaf down with the edges of your hands. Tuck the flattened ends under and pinch gently to seal. Place the loaf on a well greased baking sheet, with the seam underneath. Cover and leave to rise in a warm place until doubled in size, about 40 minutes.

Preheat the oven to gas mark 4/180°C/350°F. With a sharp knife, slash the loaf with 3-4 diagonal cuts. Brush the top with egg glaze and sprinkle on additional caraway seeds. Bake the loaf in the preheated oven for 35–40 minutes or until the bottom crust sounds hollow when tapped. Remove from the sheet and allow to cool on a wire rack.

Preparation: 10 minutes
Standing: allow 2 hours for the dough to rise
Baking: 35–40 minutes
Protein g/s: 3.5

Wholewheat French Bread

1 loaf, 12 slices

A delightful bread with the characteristic crunch and chewiness of the original but with the added goodness of wholegrain and buttermilk. This recipe makes one long loaf. If you have a double French bread tin, you can quickly process the recipe twice.

1×15ml (tbsp) easy-blend dried yeast
325g (12oz) wholewheat flour
1×5ml (tsp) salt
250ml (10fl oz) buttermilk, at room temperature
125-250ml (5-10fl oz) water
maizemeal for dusting the tin

METAL BLADE: Place the flour and salt with the yeast in the processing bowl. With the machine running, add the buttermilk then sufficient water to bring the dough into a ball. Process the ball of dough for 20 seconds. Stop the machine and feel the dough – it should be elastic, sticky and wet. If not, process for a further 10 seconds. Sprinkle the dough with an extra 1-2×15ml (tbsp) flour, pulse on/off to coat the dough to make it easier to remove from the processing bowl.

Transfer the dough to an oiled bowl and turn the dough over to cover the entire surface. Cover the bowl and leave in a warm place to rise until the dough is doubled in size, about 1 hour. Knock back and knead lightly for 30 seconds to press out the air bubbles. Shape into a ball and allow to rest for 5 minutes, covered.

On a floured surface, roll the dough into a rectangle approximately 38×25.5cm (15×10in). Starting with the 38cm (15in) side roll up the dough as a Swiss roll. Pinch the seam to seal. Turn the roll so that the seam is underneath, press the ends of the loaf down with the edges of your hands. Tuck the flattened ends under and pinch gently to seal. Place on a greased baking sheet or a French bread tin sprinkled with maizemeal. Cover and leave in a warm place until doubled in size, about 45 minutes.

Preheat the oven to gas mark 6/200°C/400°F approximately 15 minutes before the dough will be ready to be baked. Prepare the oven by placing a shallow roasting tin on the lowest shelf. Five minutes before baking, pour about 375ml (15fl oz) water from the hot tap into the pan. Brush or spray the loaf with cold water. With a sharp knife, slash the loaf with diagonal cuts. Bake in the centre of the oven for 35–45 minutes, or until the bottom crust sounds hollow when tapped. Remove from the baking sheet or tin immediately and place on a wire rack to cool.

Preparation: 10 minutes
Standing: allow 2 hours for the dough to rise
Baking: 35–45 minutes
Protein g/s: 4.5

Malted Milk Bread

1 loaf, 15 slices

The gluten flour may be omitted, producing a more compact but delicious, moist loaf. Increase the wholewheat flour to 325g (12oz).

1×15ml (tbsp) easy-blend dried yeast
1×15ml (tbsp) oil
300g (11oz) wholewheat flour

25g (1oz) gluten flour (optional)
25g (1oz) malted milk powder
½×5ml (tsp) salt
250ml (10fl oz) water

METAL BLADE: Place the flours, malted milk powder, salt and yeast in the processing bowl; pulse on/off to mix. Add the oil. With the machine running pour the water into the flour in a steady stream, only as fast as the flour can absorb the liquid. You may not require all the water to form a ball of dough. Process for 20 seconds. Stop the machine and feel the dough – it should be elastic, sticky and wet. If it is not, process for an additional 10 seconds. Sprinkle an extra 1-2×15ml (tbsp) flour over the dough; pulse to coat the dough to make removal from the processing bowl easier.

Transfer the dough to an oiled bowl and turn to coat the entire surface. Cover with a plastic bag or a damp cloth and leave in a warm place to rise until doubled in size, about 45–60 minutes. Knock back the dough and knead lightly for 30 seconds to press out the air bubbles. Shape into a ball, cover and allow to rest for 5 minutes. Shape into a loaf and place in a greased tin 21.5×11.5cm (8½×4½in), cover and leave in a warm place to rise until doubled in size, about 45 minutes.

Preheat the oven to gas mark 4/180°C/350°F. Bake in the centre of the oven for 45–55 minutes or until the bottom crust sounds hollow when tapped. Remove immediately from the tin and allow to cool on a wire rack.

Preparation: 10 minutes
Standing: allow 2 hours for the dough to rise
Baking: 45–55 minutes
Protein g/s: 4

Tofu Wheat Bread

1 loaf, 15 slices

This is a heavy moist bread. The dough has a consistency much like rye bread.

1×15ml (tbsp) easy-blend dried yeast
250g (9oz) firm tofu, drained and broken into pieces
2×15ml (tbsp) oil
2×15ml (tbsp) honey
325g (12oz) wholewheat flour
15g (½oz) dried milk powder
½×5ml (tsp) salt
100ml (4fl oz) water

METAL BLADE: Place the tofu, honey and oil in the processing bowl. Process until smooth. Turn the machine off and add the flour, milk powder, salt and yeast. Process to form a ball of dough, adding extra water as required. Process the ball of dough for 20 seconds. Stop the machine and feel the dough – it should be elastic, sticky and wet. If not, process for a further 10 seconds. Sprinkle the dough with an extra 1-2×15ml (tbsp) flour and pulse on/off to coat the dough to make it easier to remove from the processing bowl.

Transfer the dough to an oiled bowl and turn so that the entire surface is coated. Cover with a plastic bag or damp cloth and leave in a warm place to rise until doubled in size, about 1¼ hours. Knock back the dough and knead lightly for 30 seconds to press out any air bubbles. Shape into a ball, allow to rest, covered, for 5 minutes. Shape into a loaf and place in a greased loaf tin, 20×10cm (8×4in). Leave in a warm place to rise until doubled in size, about 45–60 minutes.

Preheat the oven to gas mark 5/190°C/375°F. Bake in the centre of the oven for 35–40 minutes or until the lower crust sounds hollow when tapped. Remove from the loaf tin immediately and cool on a wire rack.

Preparation: 10 minutes
Standing: allow 2½–3 hours for the dough to rise
Baking: 35–40 minutes
Protein g/s: 5

Wholewheat Christmas Stollen

1 stollen, 16 slices

You do not have to wait until Christmas to bake this tender festive loaf filled with fruits – not the usual sweet candied type – nuts and spices. Vary the amount of flavourings to suit your taste.

1×15ml (tbsp) easy-blend dried yeast
125ml (5fl oz) milk, scalded and cooled to lukewarm
1 egg, beaten
300g (11oz) wholewheat flour
pinch salt
50g (2oz) soft brown sugar
125g (4oz) butter, well chilled, cut into 2.5cm (1in) pieces
1×5ml (tsp) lemon juice
1×5ml (tsp) almond essence
grated rind 1 lemon
1½-2×5ml (tsp) vanilla essence
75g (3oz) raisins
40g (1½oz) blanched almonds
125g (4oz) dried apricots
125g (4oz) glacé pineapple
sugar for sprinkling

METAL BLADE: Place the flour, salt, brown sugar and yeast in the processing bowl. Pulse on/off to mix. Add the butter and process until the mixture resembles crumbs. Add the lemon juice, almond and vanilla essences and grated lemon rind. Add the egg. With the machine running add the cooled milk in a steady stream, only as fast as the flour will absorb the liquid. Add sufficient liquid to bring the dough to a ball then process the ball for 20 seconds. Turn the machine off and feel the dough – it should be elastic, sticky and wet. If not, process for a further 10 seconds. Sprinkle the dough with an extra 1-2×15ml (tbsp) flour, pulse on/off to coat the dough to make it easier to remove from the processing bowl.

Transfer the dough to an oiled bowl and turn the dough over to cover the entire surface. Cover the bowl and leave in a warm place to rise until the dough is doubled in size, about 1-1½ hours. While the dough is rising, process the fruits and nuts.

METAL BLADE: To retain the texture of each ingredient, process them separately. Coarsely chop the nuts, apricots and pineapple, removing each ingredient to a bowl as processed. Add a little flour to the fruits during processing to prevent the pieces sticking together. Knock back the dough on a lightly floured board, and knead in the nuts and fruits until evenly distributed throughout the dough.

SHAPING: Roll the dough into a square about 28×28cm (11×11in). Fold one side over to overlap two thirds of the dough. Press the centre of the loaf upwards between your hands to form the characteristic stollen 'hump', as illustrated.

Place the stollen on a buttered baking sheet. Cover and leave in a warm place to rise until doubled in size, about 1 hours. Preheat the oven to gas mark 3/160°C/325°F. Bake in the centre of the oven for 30 minutes. Carefully remove from the tin and allow to cool on a wire rack.

Preparation: 15–20 minutes
Standing: allow 3–3½ hours for the dough to rise
Baking: 30 minutes
Protein g/s: 4

Poppy Seed Milk Rolls

12 rolls

Milk powder enhances the protein quality of these delicious dinner rolls, which also make good sandwich buns.

1×15ml (tbsp) easy-blend dried yeast
2×15ml (tbsp) oil
2×15ml (tbsp) honey
300g (11oz) wholewheat flour
25g (1oz) dried milk powder
pinch salt
250ml (10fl oz) water, as required
poppy seeds for decoration
Glaze: 1 egg, beaten with 50ml (2fl oz) water

METAL BLADE: Place the flour, milk powder, salt and yeast in the processing bowl; pulse on/off to mix. Add the oil and honey. With the machine running, add the water in a steady stream , only as fast as the flour can absorb the liquid, until the dough forms a ball. Process the ball for 20 seconds. Stop the machine and feel the dough – it should be elastic, sticky and wet. If not, process for a further 10 seconds. Sprinkle the dough with an

extra 1-2×15ml (tbsp) flour, pulse on/off to coat the dough to make it easier to remove from the processing bowl.

Transfer the dough to an oiled bowl and turn the dough over to cover the entire surface. Cover the bowl and leave in a warm place to rise until the dough is doubled in size, about 1 hour. Knock back and knead lightly for 30 seconds to press out the air bubbles. Divide the dough into 12 pieces, then allow to stand for 5 minutes, covered. Shape each piece into a ball and place on a greased baking sheet. Cover and leave in a warm place until doubled in size, about 45 minutes.

Preheat the oven to gas mark 4/180°C/350°F. Bake in the centre of the oven for 15–20 minutes or until the rolls sound hollow when tapped. Remove from the baking sheet immediately and allow to cool on a wire rack.

Preparation: 15–20 minutes
Standing: allow about 2 hours for the dough to
        rise
Baking: 15–20 minutes
Protein g/s: 3.5

Herb Buttermilk Bread

1 loaf, 14 slices

A hint of herbs will make this the star at the dinner table. Double the recipe and make 2 loaves if your machine has a large capacity.

1×15ml (tbsp) easy-blend dried yeast
2×15ml (tbsp) oil
1×15ml (tbsp) honey
275g (10oz) wholewheat flour
½×5ml (tsp) salt
1½×15ml (tbsp) dried mixed herbs
250ml (10fl oz) warm buttermilk

METAL BLADE: Place the flour, salt, herbs and yeast in the processing bowl and pulse on/off to mix. Add the oil and honey. With the machine running add the buttermilk, pouring in a steady stream, only as fast as the flour can absorb the liquid. Not all the milk may be needed to form a ball of dough. Process the ball of dough for 20 seconds then stop the machine and feel the dough. It should be elastic, wet and sticky. If it is not, process for a further 10 seconds. Sprinkle the dough with 1-2×15ml (tbsp) extra flour and pulse on/off to coat the dough and to make it easier to remove from the processor.

Transfer the dough to an oiled bowl and turn to coat the entire surface. Cover with a plastic bag or a damp cloth. Leave in a warm place to rise until doubled in bulk, about 1 hour. Knock back the dough and knead lightly for 30 seconds to press out any air bubbles. Divide the dough into halves if making 2 loaves. Divide each portion into three and shape into balls then allow to rest, covered, for 5 minutes.

TO SHAPE PLAIT: Roll each ball into a strand about 30.5cm (12in) long. Place three strands together and pinch the tops, plait. Tuck both ends under and pinch well to seal. Place each plait on a greased baking sheet and cover. Leave in a warm place until doubled in bulk, about 45–60 minutes.

Preheat the oven to gas mark 4/180°C/350°F. Bake the plait in the centre of the oven for 30–35 minutes or until the bottom crust sounds hollow when tapped. Transfer the plait immediately to a wire rack to cool.

Preparation: 15 minutes
Standing: allow 2 –3 hours for the dough to rise and to shape the plait.
Baking: 30–35 minutes
Protein g/s: 3.5

Apple Sauce Cinnamon Wholewheat Bread

2 loaves, 16 slices per loaf

Delicious breakfast toast or serve with Cheddar cheese. The recipe may be halved to make 1 loaf.

2×15ml (tbsp) easy-blend dried yeast
2×15ml (tbsp) oil
2×15ml (tbsp) honey
500ml (1pt) applesauce, at room temperature
675g (1½lb) wholewheat flour
2×5ml (tsp) salt
1×15ml (tbsp) ground cinnamon
175g (6oz) raisins
50ml (2fl oz) water

METAL BLADE OR PLASTIC DOUGH BLADE: Place the flour, yeast, salt and cinnamon in the processing bowl; pulse on/off to mix. Add the oil and honey. With the machine running, pour in the apple sauce and enough water to form a ball of dough. It may be necessary to stop the machine and scrape down the sides of the bowl. Process the ball of dough for 20 seconds then stop the machine and feel the dough. It should be elastic, sticky and wet. If not, process for an additional 10 seconds. Sprinkle the dough with an additional 1-2×15ml (tbsp) flour and pulse on/off to coat the dough for easy removal from the processing bowl.

Place the dough on a lightly floured surface and knead in the raisins. Transfer the dough to an oiled bowl and turn so that the entire surface is coated. Cover with a plastic bag or damp cloth and leave to rise in a warm place, free from draughts, until doubled in size, about 1–1½ hours. Knock back the dough and knead lightly to press out the air bubbles. Divide the dough into two and allow to rest for 5 minutes, covered. Shape each ball into a loaf and place in a greased 21.5×11.5cm (8½×4½in) loaf tin. Cover and leave in a warm place to rise until doubled in bulk, about 1 hour.

Preheat the oven to gas mark 5/190°C/375°F. Bake the loaves in the centre of the oven for 30–35 minutes, or until the bottom crust sounds hollow when tapped. Remove from the tins immediately and cool on a wire rack.

Preparation: 10 minutes
Standing: allow 2 hours for the dough to rise
Baking: 30–35 minutes
Protein g/s: 3

Potato Loaf

1 loaf, 16 slices

Fresh mashed potatoes make this loaf moist and chewy. Slices thinly with ease. Double the recipe to make 2 loaves.

150g (5oz) potatoes
2×15ml (tbsp) water
1½×15ml (tbsp) oil
1½×15ml (tbsp) honey
1×15ml (tbsp) easy-blend dried yeast
300g (11oz) wholewheat flour
1×5ml (tsp) salt
2×15ml (tbsp) dried milk powder
1 egg, slightly beaten

Boil the potatoes in water until tender. While hot, peel and mash. Add the cold water, oil and honey.

METAL BLADE: Place the flour, salt, milk powder and yeast in the processing bowl; pulse on/off to mix. Add the potato mixture. With the machine running, add the egg and sufficient water to bring the dough into a ball. Add extra water or flour to bring the dough to a ball as required. Knead the dough for 20 seconds. Stop the machine and feel the dough – it should be elastic, sticky and wet. If not, process for a further 10 seconds. Sprinkle the dough with 1-2×15ml (tbsp) flour and pulse on/off to coat the dough to make it easier to remove from the processing bowl.

Transfer the dough to an oiled bowl and turn the dough so that the entire surface is coated. Cover the bowl with a plastic bag or damp cloth and leave in a warm place to rise until doubled in size, about 1 hour. Knock back the dough and knead lightly for 30 seconds to press out any air bubbles. Shape into a ball and allow to rest, covered, for 5 minutes. Shape into a loaf and place in a well greased 21.5×11.5cm (8½×4½in) loaf tin. Cover and leave to rise in a warm place until doubled in size, about 45–60 minutes.

Preheat the oven to gas mark 5/190°C/375°F. Bake the loaf in the centre of the oven for 30–35 minutes, or until the bottom crust sounds

hollow when tapped. Remove from the tin immediately and allow to cool on a wire rack.

Preparation: 10 minutes
Standing: 2–2½ hours for the dough to rise
Cooking/Baking: 30–35 minutes to bake
        20–25 minutes to cook the potatoes
Protein g/s: 3.5

Swiss and Rye Bread

1 loaf, 15 slices

Double the recipe if your processor can manage the larger amount of dough. This is a close grained bread, moist and solid.

125g (4oz) Gruyere cheese, well chilled
1×15ml (tbsp) easy-blend yeast
1×15ml (tbsp) honey
250g (9oz) wholewheat flour
75g (3oz) rye flour
½×5ml (tsp) salt
15g (½oz) dried milk powder
250ml (10fl oz) water

SHREDDING DISC: Place the Gruyere in the feed tube; shred. Remove the shredding disc and insert the metal blade.

METAL BLADE: Add the flours, salt, milk powder and yeast to the cheese; pulse on/off to mix. Add the honey. With the machine running, add the water in a steady stream, not faster than the flour can absorb the liquid. Add only sufficient water to bring the dough into a ball. Process the ball of dough for 20 seconds. Stop the machine and feel the dough – it should be elastic, sticky and wet. If not, process for a further 10 seconds. Sprinkle the dough with an extra 1-2×15ml (tbsp) flour, pulse on/off to coat the dough to make it easier to remove from the processing bowl.

Transfer the dough to an oiled bowl and turn the dough over to cover the entire surface. Cover the bowl and leave in a warm place to rise until the dough is doubled in size, about 1 hour. Knock back and knead lightly for

30 seconds to press out the air bubbles. Shape into a ball and allow to stand for 5 minutes, covered. Shape into a loaf and place in a greased 20×10cm (8×4in) loaf tin. Cover and leave in a warm place until the dough has doubled in size, about 30–35 minutes.

Preheat the oven to gas mark 5/190°C/375°F. Bake in the centre of the oven for 35–40 minutes or until the bottom crust sounds hollow when tapped. Remove from the tin immediately and allow to cool on a wire rack.

Preparation: 10 minutes
Standing: allow 2½ hours for the dough to rise
Baking: 35–40 minutes
Protein g/s: 5.5

Cottage Wheat Loaf

1 loaf, 16 slices

Cottage cheese and milk powder give this tangy loaf 'extra' protein.

1×15ml (tbsp) easy-blend dried yeast
2×15ml (tbsp) oil
2×15ml (tbsp) honey
150g (5oz) small curd cottage cheese
300g (11oz) wholewheat flour
25g (1oz) rye flour
2×15ml (tbsp) bran
1×5ml (tsp) salt
15g (½oz) dried milk powder
about 200ml (8fl oz) water

METAL BLADE: Place the wheat and rye flours, yeast, bran, milk powder and salt in the processing bowl. Pulse on/off to mix. Add the oil, honey and cottage cheese. With the machine running pour in the water in a steady stream, only as fast as the flour can absorb the liquid. Add sufficient water to form a ball of dough. Process the ball for 20 seconds. Stop the machine and feel the dough – it should be elastic, sticky and wet. If not, process for an additional 10 seconds. Sprinkle the dough with an additional 1-2×15ml (tbsp) flour and pulse on/off to coat the dough and make it easier to remove from the processing bowl.

Transfer the dough to an oiled bowl and turn so that the entire surface is coated. Cover with a plastic bag or a damp cloth and leave in a warm place to rise until doubled in bulk, about 1 hour. Knock back the dough and knead lightly to press out the air bubbles. Shape into a ball and allow to rest for 5 minutes, covered. Shape into a loaf and place in a greased loaf tin, 20×10cm (8×4in). Cover and leave in a warm place to rise until doubled in bulk, about 1 hour.

Preheat the oven to gas mark 5/190°C/375°F. Bake the loaf in the centre of the oven for 30–35 minutes or until the bottom crust sounds hollow when tapped. Remove from the tin immediately and allow to cool on a wire rack.

Preparation: 10 minutes
Standing: allow 2–2½ hours for the dough to rise
Baking: 35 minutes
Protein g/s: 4.5

Nut Butter Bread

1 loaf, 16 slices

This moist, close-grained loaf slices easily. Try it with sliced apples topped with Cheddar cheese.

1×15ml (tbsp) easy-blend dried yeast
2×15ml (tbsp) honey
175g (6oz) crunchy, unsalted peanut butter, or nut butter of your choice
275g (10oz) wholewheat flour
15g (½oz) dried milk powder
½×5ml (tsp) salt
250ml (10fl oz) water, approximately

METAL BLADE OR PLASTIC DOUGH BLADE: Place the flour, milk powder, salt and yeast in the processing bowl. Pulse on/off to mix. Add the honey and the peanut butter. With the machine running, pour in sufficient water to bring the dough to a ball – add the water in a steady stream, only as fast as the flour can absorb it. Process the ball of dough for 20 seconds. Stop the machine and feel the dough – it should feel elastic, sticky and wet. If not, process for a further 10 seconds. Sprinkle the dough with an additional 1-2×15ml (tbsp) flour and pulse on/off to coat the dough to make it easier to remove from the processing bowl.

Transfer the dough to an oiled bowl and turn to coat the entire surface. Cover with a plastic bag or damp cloth and leave in a warm place to rise until doubled in size, about 1 hour. Knock back the dough and knead gently for 30 seconds to press out the air bubbles. Shape into a ball and allow to rest for 5 minutes, covered. Shape into a loaf and place in a greased 21.5×11.5cm (8½×4½in) loaf tin. Cover and leave in a warm place to rise until doubled in size, about 1 hour.

Preheat the oven to gas mark 5/190°C/375°F. Bake the loaf in the centre of the oven for 30–35 minutes or until the bottom crust sounds hollow when tapped. Remove from the tin immediately and allow to cool on a wire rack.

Preparation: 10 minutes
Standing: allow 2–2½ hours for the dough to rise
Baking: 30–35 minutes
Protein g/s: 6.5

Buckwheat Bread

1 loaf, 17 slices

This makes a large loaf. For small machines, cut the ingredients roughly in half and bake in a small loaf tin, 20×10cm (8×4in).

1×15ml (tbsp) easy-blend dried yeast
2×15ml (tbsp) oil
2×15ml (tbsp) honey
450g (1lb) wholewheat flour
50g (2oz) rye flour
40g (1½oz) buckwheat flour
3×15ml (tbsp) maizemeal
½×15ml (tbsp) salt
500ml (1pt) water, approximately

METAL BLADE OR PLASTIC DOUGH BLADE: Place the flours, maizemeal, salt and yeast in the processing bowl; pulse on/off to mix. Add the oil and honey. With the machine running, pour in sufficient water to bring the dough into a ball, pouring in a steady stream only as fast as the flour can absorb the liquid. Process the ball of dough for 20 seconds. Stop the machine and feel the dough – it should be elastic, sticky and wet. If not, process for a further 10 seconds. Sprinkle the dough with an extra 1-2×15ml (tbsp) flour, pulse on/off to coat the dough to make it easier to remove from the processing bowl.

Transfer the dough to an oiled bowl and turn the dough over to cover the entire surface. Cover the bowl and leave in a warm place to rise until the dough is doubled in size, about 1 hour. Knock back and knead lightly for 30 seconds to press out the air bubbles. Shape into a ball and allow to stand for 5 minutes, covered. Shape into a loaf and place in a greased 22.5×12.5cm (9×5in) loaf tin. Cover and leave in a warm place until the dough has doubled in size, about 45 minutes.

Preheat the oven to gas mark 5/190°C/375°F. Bake in the centre of the oven for 45–50 minutes or until the bottom crust sounds hollow when tapped. Remove from the tin immediately and allow to cool on a wire rack.

Preparation: 10 minutes
Standing: allow about 2 hours for the dough to rise
Baking: 45–50 minutes
Protein g/s: 4

Yogurt Bran Bread

1 loaf, 16 slices

Double the recipe for 2 loaves.

1×15ml (tbsp) easy-blend dried yeast
1×15ml (tbsp) oil
2×15ml (tbsp) honey
1 egg, beaten

125ml (5fl oz) yogurt
325g (12oz) wholewheat flour
2×15ml (tbsp) dried milk powder
2×15ml (tbsp) sesame seeds
1×5ml (tsp) salt
25g (1oz) bran
200ml (8fl oz) water

METAL BLADE: Place the flour, milk powder, sesame seeds, salt, bran and yeast in the bowl; pulse on/off to mix. Add the egg, oil, honey and yogurt. With the machine running, gradually add sufficient water to bring the dough to a ball. Add the water in a steady stream, only as fast the flour can absorb the liquid. Process the ball for 20 seconds. Stop the machine and feel the dough – it should be elastic, sticky and wet. If not, process for a further 10 seconds. Sprinkle the dough with an extra 1-2×15ml (tbsp) flour, pulse on/off to coat the dough to make it easier to remove from the processing bowl.

Transfer the dough to an oiled bowl and turn the dough over to cover the entire surface. Cover the bowl and leave in a warm place to rise until the dough is doubled in size, about 1 hour. Knock back and knead lightly for 30 seconds to press out the air bubbles. Divide into two if making two loaves. Shape each piece into a ball and allow to stand for 5 minutes, covered. Shape into a loaf and place in a greased 21.5×11.5cm (8½×4½in) loaf tin. Cover and leave in a warm place until the dough has doubled in size, about 45 minutes.

Preheat the oven to gas mark 5/190°C/375°F. Bake in the centre of the oven for 30–35 minutes or until the bottom crust sounds hollow when tapped. Remove from the tin immediately and allow to cool on a wire rack.

Preparation: 10 minutes
Standing: allow about 2 hours for the dough to rise
Baking: 30–35 minutes
Protein g/s: 4.5

Molasses Wheat Bread

1 loaf, 16 slices

This is a good, all-round sandwich bread, not too sweet.

1×15ml (tbsp) easy-blend dried yeast
2×15ml (tbsp) oil
1½×15ml (tbsp) molasses
450g (1lb) wholewheat flour
½×5ml (tsp) salt
15g (½oz) dried milk powder
250ml (10fl oz) water

METAL BLADE OR PLASTIC DOUGH BLADE: Place the flour, salt, milk powder and yeast in the processor bowl; pulse on/off to mix. Add the oil and molasses. With the machine running, pour in the water in a steady stream, only as fast as the flour can absorb it. All the water may not be required to form a ball of dough. Process the ball of dough for 20 seconds. Stop the machine and feel the dough – it should be elastic, wet and sticky. If not, process for a further 10 seconds. Sprinkle an extra 1-2×15ml (tbsp) flour over the dough and pulse on/off to coat to make the removal of the dough from the processing bowl easier.

Transfer the dough to an oiled bowl and turn so that the entire surface is coated. Cover the bowl with a plastic bag or damp cloth and leave in a warm place to rise until doubled in size, about 1 hour. Knock back the dough and knead lightly for about 30 seconds to press out the air bubbles. Shape into a ball and allow to rest for 5 minutes, covered. Shape into a loaf and place in a greased 21.5×11.5cm (8½×4½in) loaf tin. Cover and leave to rise in a warm place until doubled in size, about 1 hour.

Preheat the oven to gas mark 5/190°C/375°F. Bake the loaf in the centre of the oven for 30–35 minutes or until the bottom crust sounds hollow when tapped. Remove from the tin immediately and allow to cool on a wire rack.

Preparation: 10 minutes
Standing: allow 2–2½ hours for the dough to rise

aking: 30–35 minutes
rotein g/s: 4.5

Wholewheat Pitta Bread

erves 8

nce you have eaten wholewheat pittas,
traight from the oven, you probably will
ever buy any more! The tricks for getting
hem to puff are: a very hot oven, kneading
ach portion of dough before shaping and an
bsolutely grease-free baking tin. After you
ave tried wholewheat pittas, try adding the
uttermilk and bran variations.

Wholewheat Pitta

×15ml (tbsp) easy-blend dried yeast
25g (12oz) wholewheat flour
₂×5ml (tsp) salt
50ml (10fl oz) water, as required

Buttermilk Pitta

×15ml (tbsp) easy-blend dried yeast
25g (12oz) wholewheat flour
₂×5ml (tsp) salt
25ml (5fl oz) buttermilk, at room temperature
25ml (5fl oz) water, as required

Bran Pitta

×15ml (tbsp) easy-blend dried yeast
00g (11oz) wholewheat flour
5g (½oz) bran
₂×5ml (tsp) salt
50ml (10fl oz) water, as required

ETAL BLADE: Place the flour, salt, yeast and
ran (if used) in the processing bowl; pulse
n/off to mix. With the machine running add
he liquid in a steady stream, only as fast as
he flour can absorb it, until the dough forms a
all. If using buttermilk, add that first and then
add water as required. Process the ball of
dough for 20 seconds. Stop the machine and
feel the dough – it should be elastic, sticky and
wet. If not, process for a further 10 seconds.
Sprinkle the dough with an extra 1-2×15ml
(tbsp) flour, pulse on/off to coat the dough to
make it easier to remove from the processing
bowl.

Transfer the dough to an oiled bowl and
turn the dough over to cover the entire
surface. Cover the bowl and leave in a warm
place to rise until the dough is doubled in size,
about 1 hour to 1 hour 15 minutes. Knock back
and knead lightly for 30 seconds to press out
the air bubbles. Divide into 8 and shape each
piece into a ball, kneading for about 30
seconds. Cover the balls with plastic and
allow to stand for 30 minutes. After 20
minutes, preheat the oven to the highest
possible setting, gas mark 9/250°C/500°F, and
place the oven shelf in the lowest possible
position.

When the oven is hot, use a rolling pin to
roll each ball into a circle about 6mm (¼in
thick). Flour well on the underside and place
on an ungreased baking sheet. Place the filled
sheet immediately into the oven. Bake for
about 4 minutes or until the pittas puff. Turn
over and bake for a further 4 minutes. Remove
from the oven and serve at once. Pittas may
also be kept warm by wrapping in a clean tea
towel until ready to serve. If not serving the
pittas immediately, remove to a wire rack to
cool.

DO NOT ALLOW THE CIRCLES TO RISE
AGAIN. They may not puff. Shape only as many
circles as can be baked at one time.

Preparation: 20 minutes
Standing: allow 1 hour 30 minutes to 1 hour 45
minutes for rising
Baking: 16 minutes (in two batches)
Protein g/s: with buttermilk–6.5
with water–6

 or

Quick Breads

Banana Walnut Bran Muffins

12 muffins

One 15ml tablespoon of baking powder is needed to produce a light muffin from the heavy bran batter. A delicious snack or accompaniment to any meal.

75g (3oz) walnuts
150g (5oz) whole wheat flour
2×15ml (tbsp) dried milk powder
1×15ml (tbsp) baking powder
½×5ml (tsp) bicarbonate of soda
½×5ml (tsp) salt
40g (1½oz) bran
2 medium bananas, ripe
125ml (5fl oz) milk
1 egg
2×15ml (tbsp) oil
2×15ml (tbsp) honey
1×5ml (tsp) vanilla essence

Preheat oven to gas mark 6/200°C/400°F

METAL BLADE: Place walnuts in processing bowl. Pulse on/off to coarsely chop. Remove to medium mixing bowl. Set aside. Place flour, milk powder, baking powder, bicarbonate of soda, salt and bran in processing bowl. Pulse on/off to mix. Add to bowl with nuts, toss to mix. Place bananas, cut into pieces, in the processor. Process until smooth. Add milk, egg, oil, honey and vanilla essence. Pulse on/off 2–3 times until flour is just moistened. Do not overprocess. Spoon batter into 12 well-greased muffin tins, filling each two-thirds full. Bake 16–18 minutes or until skewer inserted in centre comes out clean. Remove from muffin tins and serve hot or place on metal rack to cool.

Preparation: 5 minutes
Baking: 16–18 minutes
Protein g/s: 4.5

Apple Bran Muffins

6-9 muffins

Your processor will quickly chop the apple for these moist muffins.

80ml (3½fl oz) skimmed milk
1 egg
3×15ml (tbsp) oil
1×15ml (tbsp) honey
1 small Golden Delicious apple, unpeeled, cored, quartered
75g (3oz) whole wheat flour
25g (1oz) bran
1×5ml (tsp) heaped baking powder
pinch bicarbonate of soda
pinch of salt
½×5ml (tsp) ground cinnamon

Preheat oven to gas mark 6/200°C/400°F. In a measuring jug, stir together skimmed milk, egg, oil and honey. Set aside.

METAL BLADE: Place the flour and apple quarters in the processing bowl. Pulse on/off to coarsely chop apple. Add bran, baking powder, bicarbonate of soda, salt and cinnamon. Pulse on/off to mix.

Stop machine, remove cover and pour in

liquid mixture all at once. Pulse on/off 3–4 times until flour is just moistened. Spoon batter into greased muffin tins, filling each two-thirds full. Bake 18-22 minutes or until a skewer inserted in centre comes out clean. Remove from muffin tins and serve hot or place on wire rack to cool.

Preparation: 5 minutes
Baking: 18–22 minutes
Protein g/s: 6 muffins–4.5
         9 muffins–3

Apricot Yogurt Bran Muffins

12 muffins

250ml (10fl oz) yogurt
1 egg
60ml (2¹/₂fl oz) oil
2×15ml (tbsp) honey
2×15ml (tbsp) molasses
125g (4oz) wholewheat flour
75g (3oz) dried apricot halves
40g (1¹/₂oz) bran
¹/₄×5ml (tsp) heaped bicarbonate of soda
¹/₄×5ml (tsp) salt

Preheat oven to gas mark 7/220°C/425°F. In a measuring jug, stir together yogurt, egg, oil, honey and molasses. Set aside.

METAL BLADE: Place wholewheat flour and apricot halves in the processor bowl. Pulse on/off to coarsely chop apricots. Add bran, bicarbonate of soda and salt. Pulse on/off 3–4 times until flour is just moistened. Spoon batter into greased muffin tins, filling each two-thirds full. Bake 20–25 minutes or until a skewer inserted in centre comes out clean. Remove from muffin tins and serve hot or place on metal rack to cool.

Preparation: 5 minutes
Baking: 20–25 minutes
Protein g/s: 3

Sunny Prune Muffins

8-10 muffins

Sunflower seeds and prunes add crunch and moistness to these tasty muffins.

125ml (5fl oz) milk
1 egg
3×15ml (tbsp) oil
3×15ml (tbsp) honey
12 pitted prunes
75g (3oz) wholewheat flour
1×5ml (tsp) baking powder
pinch bicarbonate of soda
good pinch salt
good pinch ground cinnamon
25g (1oz) sunflower seeds

Preheat oven to gas mark 6/200°C/400°F. In a measuring jug, stir together milk, egg, oil, and honey. Set aside.

METAL BLADE: Place wholewheat flour and prunes in processor bowl. Pulse on/off to mix. Stop machine, remove cover and pour in liquid mixture all at once. Pulse on/off 3–4 times until flour is just moistened. Spoon batter into greased muffin tins, filling each two-thirds full. Bake 16–18 minutes or until a skewer inserted in centre comes out clean. Remove from muffin tins and serve hot or place on metal rack to cool.

Preparation: 6 minutes
Baking: 16–18 minutes
Protein g/s: 8 muffins–4
         10 muffins–3.5

Oat Raisin Muffins

12 muffins

This is sure to be one of your favourites.

75g (3oz) rolled oats
250ml (10fl oz) warm water
60ml (2½fl oz) oil
6×15ml (tbsp) honey
1 egg
125g (4oz) wholewheat flour
1×15ml (tbsp) baking powder
1×5ml (tsp) ground cinnamon
pinch salt
15g (½oz) dried milk powder
75g (3oz) raisins

Preheat oven to gas mark 6/200°C/400°F. In a large measuring jug stir together rolled oats and warm water. Allow to stand for 15 minutes. Stir in oil, honey and egg. Set aside.

METAL BLADE OR PLASTIC MIXING BLADE: Place flour, baking powder, cinnamon, salt, milk powder and raisins in the processing bowl. Pulse on/off to mix. Stop machine, remove cover and pour in liquid mixture all at once. Pulse on/off 2–3 times until flour is just moistened. Batter will be lumpy. Spoon batter into greased muffin tins, filling each two-thirds full. Bake 20–22 minutes or until a skewer inserted in centre comes out clean. Remove from muffin tins and serve hot or place on metal rack to cool.

Preparation: 5 minutes
Standing: allow 15 minutes to soften rolled oats
Baking: 20–22 minutes
Protein g/s: 3.5

Banana Nut Bread

1 loaf, 15 slices

Slice for slice, most banana nut breads contain too much sugar and oil. We have cut down on these two ingredients and have come up with a bread that is sure to be one of your favourites.

175g (6oz) wholewheat flour
½×5ml (tsp) salt
½×5ml (tsp) bicarbonate of soda
1×5ml (tsp) baking powder
50g (2oz) walnuts
2 medium ripe bananas
75-125g (3-4oz) brown sugar
80ml (3½fl oz) oil
2 eggs
1×5ml (tsp) vanilla essence

Preheat oven to gas mark 4/180°C/350°F

METAL BLADE: Place flour, salt, bicarbonate of soda, baking powder and walnuts in processing bowl. Pulse on/off to coarsely chop nuts. Remove and set aside. Add bananas, cut into pieces, brown sugar, oil, eggs and vanilla extract to processor. Process until well-blended and bananas are smooth. Remove work processor cover, scrape down sides and add all dry ingredients at once. Combine with 4–5 on/off pulses only until batter is mixed. Before last on/off, scrape down sides of processor bowl. Do not over-process.

Grease bottom and sides of a 21.5×11.5 cm (8½×4½in) loaf tin. Line bottom with wax paper. Pour batter into the tin. Bake 40–50 minutes or until a skewer inserted into the centre comes out clean. Cool for 10 minutes; remove bread from tin and allow to cool completely on a wire rack.

Preparation: 10 minutes
Baking: 40–50 minutes
Protein g/s: 3

Raisin Spice Bread

1 loaf, 15 slices

A slice of this moist bread will spice up any lunch.

125g (4oz) wholewheat flour
½×5ml (tsp) bicarbonate of soda
1×5ml (tsp) ground cinnamon
pinch salt
pinch ground cloves
pinch ground nutmeg
1 egg
80ml (3½fl oz) yogurt
60ml (2½fl oz) oil
8×15ml (tbsp) honey
75g (3oz) raisins

Preheat oven to gas mark 4/180°C/350°F.

METAL BLADE OR PLASTIC MIXING BLADE: Place flour, bicarbonate of soda, cinnamon, salt, cloves, and nutmeg in processing bowl. Pulse on/off to mix. Remove and set aside. Place egg in the processing bowl and process 30 seconds. Scrape down the sides of the processing bowl. Add yogurt, oil and honey. Mix with on/off pulses until well-blended. Remove the processing bowl cover, scrape down sides and add all dry ingredients at once. Add raisins. Combine with 5 on/off pulses only until batter is mixed. Before last on/off, scrape down sides of work bowl. Do not overprocess.

Grease bottom and sides of a small loaf tin, 20×10cm (8×4in). Line bottom with wax paper. Pour in batter. Bake 30–35 minutes or until a skewer inserted in the centre comes out clean. Cool in tin 10 minutes. Carefully turn out to wire rack. Serve warm or cold.

Preparation time: 8 minutes
Baking: 30–35 minutes
Protein g/s: 1.5

Pineapple Bran Bread

1 loaf, 15 slices

Pineapple and honey flavour this moist, high-fibre bread. Allow the loaf to age for at least one day.

125g (4oz) walnuts
200g (7oz) wholewheat flour
1×5ml (tsp) salt
1×5ml (tsp) ground cinnamon
2×5ml (tsp) baking powder
25g (1oz) bran
3×15ml (tbsp) oil
12×15ml (tbsp) honey
1 egg
250ml (10fl oz) pineapple juice

Preheat the oven to gas mark 4/180°C/350°F. In a mixing bowl combine the flour, salt, cinnamon, baking powder and bran. Set aside.

METAL BLADE: Place the walnuts in the processing bowl. Pulse on/off until coarsely chopped. Remove to bowl with flour. Place the oil, honey and egg in the processor bowl. Process for 15 seconds. With the machine running, pour in the pineapple juice. Stop the machine as soon as all the juice is added. Remove the processing bowl cover and add the flour mixture all at once. Combine with 3–4 on/off pulses until the flour is just moistened.

Grease a 23×13cm (9×5in) tin, line the bottom with waxed paper. Pour batter into the tin and bake for 1–1¼ hours or until browned and a skewer inserted into the centre comes out clean and dry. Cover the loaf with a tent of foil during the last 10-15 minutes of baking to prevent the top from overbrowning. Allow to cool in the tin for 10 minutes before removing to a wire rack to cool completely.

Preparation: 10 minutes
Baking: 60–75 minutes
Protein g/s: 3

Cheese and Chilli Corn Bread

Serves 6-9

This moist, mildly spicy bread is almost a meal in itself. Serve with a steamed vegetable and fresh fruit salad.

1×125g (4oz) can whole green chillies, rinsed and drained
125g (4oz) mature Cheddar cheese, well chilled
small onion
150g (5oz) sweetcorn
150g (5oz) maizemeal
40g (1½oz) wholewheat flour
1×15ml (tbsp) soft brown sugar
1×5ml (tsp) salt
2×5ml (tsp) bicarbonate of soda
15g (½oz) dried milk powder
2 eggs
180ml (7½fl oz) warm water
60ml (2½fl oz) oil

Preheat the oven to gas mark 7/225°C/425°F.

METAL BLADE: Dry the chillies on a paper towel and add to the processor bowl. Pulse on/off until roughly chopped. Remove the metal blade and insert the shredding disc.

SHREDDING DISC: Cut the cheese to fit the feed tube; shred. Cut the onion into small wedges, stack in the feed tube and shred. Remove the chillies, cheese and onion to a mixing bowl. Add sweetcorn and toss to mix. Set aside.

METAL BLADE: Place the maizemeal, wholewheat flour, sugar, salt, bicarbonate of soda and dried milk in the processing bowl. Pulse on/off to mix. In a measuring jug, stir together eggs, warm water and oil. With the machine running, pour the liquid through the tube in a steady stream. Stop the machine as soon as all the liquid has been added. Remove the processing bowl cover and scrape down the sides of the bowl. Add the cheese and corn mixture all at once. Combine with 2–3 on/off pulses. Do not over-process. The sweetcorn should remain whole.

Pour into a well greased 22.5×22.5cm (9×9in) baking tin. Bake for 25–30 minutes, or until a skewer inserted into the centre comes out clean. Place on a wire rack and allow to cool for 5 minutes before cutting. Serve warm.

Preparation: 10 minutes
Baking: 25–30 minutes
Standing: 5 minutes
Protein g/s: 6 servings–13
          9 servings–8.5

Banana Yogurt Nut Bread

1 loaf, 15 slices

Yogurt gives this spicy moist bread a tang!

175g (6oz) wholewheat flour
½×5ml (tsp) bicarbonate of soda
¼×5ml (tsp) baking powder
good pinch salt
good pinch ground cinnamon
50g (2oz) walnuts
1 egg
60ml (2½fl oz) yogurt
60ml (2½fl oz) oil
8×15ml (tbsp) honey
1 large ripe banana

Preheat oven to gas mark 4/180°C/350°F

METAL BLADE: Place flour, bicarbonate of soda, baking powder, salt, cinnamon and walnuts in the processing bowl. Pulse on/off to coarsely chop nuts. Remove and set aside. Add egg, process 30 seconds. Scrape down sides of processing bowl. Add yogurt, oil, honey and banana (cut into small pieces). Pulse on/off until well mixed and banana is puréed. Remove processing bowl cover, scrape down sides and add all dry ingredients at once. Combine with 5 on/off pulses only until batter is mixed. Before last on/off, scrape down sides of work bowl. Do not over-process.

Grease bottom and sides of a small foil tin 20×10cm (8×4in). Line bottom with wax paper. Spoon batter into the tin. Bake 45–50 minutes or until a skewer inserted into the centre comes out clean. Cool for 15 minutes; remove bread from tin and allow to cool completely on a wire rack.

Preparation: 10 minutes
Baking: 40–45 minutes
Protein g/s: 3

Carrot Sesame Bread

1 loaf, 8-10 slices

A tender extra moist quick bread. Sesame seeds give this loaf an interesting texture. Serve warm or cold.

3 medium carrots peeled
75g (3oz) wholewheat flour
50g (2oz) soy flour
1×5ml (tsp) baking powder
1×5ml (tsp) bicarbonate of soda
1×5ml (tsp) ground cinnamon
good pinch salt
75g (3oz) raisins
25g (1oz) sesame seeds
2 eggs
125ml (5fl oz) oil
12×15ml (tbsp) honey

Preheat oven to gas mark 4/180°C/350°F.

SHREDDING DISC: Cut carrots to fit feed tube vertically; shred. Remove shredding disc; replace with metal blade.

METAL BLADE: Add to the processor bowl with shredded carrots, the wholewheat flour, soy flour, bicarbonate of soda, cinnamon and salt. Pulse on/off to mix. Remove to medium mixing bowl, add raisins and sesame seeds. Toss to mix and set aside. Add eggs to processor bowl. Process 30 seconds. Scrape down sides of the processing bowl. Add oil and honey. Process until well-mixed. Remove processor cover, scrape down sides and add all dry ingredients at once. Combine with 5 on/off pulses only until batter is mixed. Before last on/off, scrape down sides of processor bowl. Do not over-process.

Grease bottom and sides of a small foil dish 20×10cm (8×4in). Line bottom with wax paper. Pour in batter. Bake for 30 minutes. Reduce oven temperature to gas mark 3/160°C/325°F and bake an additional 20–30 minutes until a skewer inserted in the middle of the loaf comes out clean. Let cool in dish on a wire rack.

Preparation: 10 minutes
Baking: 50–60 minutes
Protein g/s: 8 slices–5.5
           10 slices–4.5

Bran Prune Muffins

12 Muffins

These are an especially nice accompaniment to a main-dish salad lunch or dinner. One 15ml tablespoon of baking powder is the minimum amount needed to raise the heavy bran batter.

250ml (10fl oz) milk
2×15ml (tbsp) oil
1 egg
250g (9oz) pitted prunes
1×15ml (tbsp) wholewheat flour
125g (4oz) wholewheat flour
40g (1½oz) bran
½×5ml (tsp) salt
1×15ml (tbsp) baking powder

Preheat oven to gas mark 5/190°C/375°F. In a measuring jug, stir together milk, oil and egg. Set aside.

METAL BLADE: Place the prunes and 1×15ml (tbsp) wholewheat flour in the processing bowl. Pulse on/off to chop prunes.

METAL BLADE OR PLASTIC MIXING BLADE: Add to the chopped prunes the wholewheat flour, bran, salt and baking powder. Pulse on/off to mix. Stop machine, remove cover and pour in liquid mixture all at once. Pulse on/off 3–4 times until flour is just moistened. Spoon batter into greased muffin tins filling each two-thirds full. Bake 20–25 minutes or until a skewer inserted in centre comes out clean.

Remove from muffin tins and serve hot or place on metal rack to cool.

Preparation: 5 minutes
Baking: 20–25 minutes
Protein g/s: 3

Rye Wheat Biscuits

6-7 5cm (2in) biscuits

Biscuits are quick to prepare. Larger biscuits can be shaped by doubling the recipe, rolling the dough to 2.5cm (1in) thickness and cutting with a 7.5cm (3in) cutter. Bake as directed, adding a few minutes to the baking time. Split and fill with sautéed vegetables.

50g (2oz) rye flour
50g (2oz) wholewheat flour
3×15ml (tbsp) dried milk powder
1¹/₂×5ml (tsp) baking powder
pinch salt
50g (2oz) butter, chilled, cut into small pieces.
1×15ml (tbsp) honey
60ml (2¹/₂fl oz) cold water

VARIATION: Cheese Rye Wheat Biscuits. Shred 25g (1oz) cheese and add to bowl with dry ingredients. Proceed as directed.

Preheat oven to gas mark 8/250°C/450°F

METAL BLADE: Place rye flour, wheat flour, milk powder, baking powder and salt in processing bowl. Pulse on/off to mix. Add butter, pulse on/off until mixture resembles crumbs. With machine running, pour in honey and cold water.

Stop machine as soon as a soft ball is formed. Do not overprocess.

Turn out dough onto a lightly floured board. Using a lightly floured rolling pin, roll the dough out to form a rectangle a little more

than 6mm (¼in) thick. Fold the dough over once. Cut straight down with a biscuit cutter, lightly dipped in flour. Be careful not to twist the cutter. Twisting may seal the cut edge and prevent rising. Place on an ungreased baking sheet. Bake on the middle shelf of the oven 10–12 minutes or until golden brown. Serve at once.

Preparation: 10 minutes
Baking: 10–12 minutes
Protein g/s: 3.5

Irish Soda Bread

1 loaf, 15 slices

No time for a yeast bread? This is a quick and easy bread you can make for any meal.

300-325g (11-12oz) wholewheat flour
1¹/₂×5ml (tsp) baking powder
1¹/₂×5ml (tsp) bicarbonate of soda
1×5ml (tsp) salt
2×15ml (tbsp) honey
about 250ml (10fl oz) buttermilk, at room temperature
1×15ml (tbsp) melted butter
75g (3oz) raisins (optional)

Preheat the oven to gas mark 5/190°C/375°F.

METAL BLADE: Place the wholewheat flour, baking powder, bicarbonate of soda and salt in the processing bowl. Pulse on/off to mix. Add the honey. With the machine running pour in sufficient milk to form a soft ball of dough. Remove the dough to a lightly floured surface; knead in the raisins. Shape the dough into a ball. Place on a greased baking sheet; flatten into a 16.5-18cm (6½-7in) circle approximately 4cm (1½in) thick. Press a large floured knife into the centre of the loaf halfway through to the bottom. Repeat, at right angles, to divide the loaf into quarters. Bake for 30 minutes or until the bottom crust of the loaf sounds hollow when tapped. Remove to a wire rack. Brush the top with melted butter and allow to cool.

Preparation: 10 minutes
Baking: 30 minutes
Protein g/s: 3.5

Fresh Mango or Peach Bread

1 loaf, 16 slices

Dozens of loaves of this bread are baked in homes throughout the Hawaiian Islands when the fruit is in season. Our version uses wholewheat flour and brown sugar. Substitute fresh firm peaches if mangoes are not available – the results are similar. Try to resist temptation and allow the loaf to 'age', well-wrapped, overnight so the flavours can blend.

1 loaf 23×12.5cm (9×5in)

225g (8oz) wholewheat flour
75g (3oz) brown sugar
2×5ml (tsp) bicarbonate of soda
good pinch salt
1×5ml (tsp) ground cinnamon
75g (3oz) walnuts
2 medium fresh mangoes or fresh peaches chopped
3 eggs
125ml (5fl oz) oil
2×5ml (tsp) vanilla essence

1 loaf 21.5×11.5cm (8½×4½in)

200g (7oz) wholewheat flour
50g (2oz) brown sugar
1×5ml (tsp) bicarbonate of soda, heaped
pinch salt
1×5ml (tsp) ground cinnamon
50g (2oz) walnuts
2 small mangoes or fresh peaches, chopped
2 eggs
80ml (3½fl oz) oil
1×5ml (tsp) vanilla essence

Preheat oven to gas mark 4/180°C/350°F

METAL BLADE: Place flour, brown sugar, bicarbonate of soda, salt and cinnamon in processing bowl. Pulse on/off to mix. Add walnuts, pulse on/off until coarsely chopped. Remove from bowl and set aside. Add mangoes, cut roughly into 4cm (1½in) pieces, to processing bowl. Pulse on/off to coarsely chop. Remove from bowl and set aside. Place eggs in processing bowl; process 30 seconds. With machine running, pour in oil and vanilla essence. Process until well-mixed, 15–20 seconds. Turn machine off and add flour mixture all at once. Combine with 3–4 on/off pulses. Add mangoes; pulse on/off until mangoes are just mixed in. Do not overprocess or you will have puréed mangoes. Scrape down sides of bowl and mix gently with the spatula, if necessary.

Grease the bottom of a loaf tin and line the bottom with waxed paper. Pour the batter into the tin. Bake for 55–60 minutes for a large loaf, or 45–55 minutes for a small loaf, or until a skewer inserted into the centre of the loaf comes out clean. Carefully turn out onto a wire rack to cool.

Preparation: 15 minutes
Baking: 55–60 minutes
Protein g/s: 3

Unleavened Breads

Chapatis

Serves 8

This unleavened wholewheat bread is quite similar to our wholewheat tortillas. The food processor is perfect for kneading this heavy dough. An excellent accompaniment to dal, a standard in Indian cuisine.

175g (6oz) wholewheat flour
½×5ml (tsp) salt
1×15ml (tbsp) oil
125ml (5fl oz) lukewarm water

METAL BLADE: Place the flour and salt in the processing bowl. Pulse on/off to mix. Add the oil and process until the mixture resembles crumbs. With the machine running, add sufficient water in a steady stream to form the dough into a ball. Process the dough for 20 seconds. Stop the machine and feel the dough – it should be smooth and elastic. If not, process for a further 10 seconds.

Divide the dough into 8 portions. Knead each portion for about 10 seconds, shaping into a ball. Roll each ball into a 18cm (7in) circle on a lightly floured board. If the dough is difficult to shape, allow to rest for a few minutes.

Heat an ungreased non-stick pan over a high heat. To test the pan, sprinkle with a few drops of water. If the droplets bubble and move around the pan, the heat is right. Bake the chapatis until the surface puffs with air bubbles and the bottom begins to brown. Turn and continue baking until cooked.

Preparation: 25 minutes
Cooking: 15–20 minutes
Protein g/s: 3

Lavosh

Serves 16

225g (8oz) wholewheat flour
1×5ml (tsp) salt
2×15ml (tbsp) dried milk powder
50g (2oz) butter
1×5ml (tsp) honey
1 egg, beaten
125ml (5fl oz) water
toasted sesame seeds
poppy seeds

METAL BLADE: Place the flour, salt, milk powder and butter in the processing bowl. Process until the mixture resembles breadcrumbs. Add the honey and egg. With the processor running, add sufficient water, in a steady stream, to form a ball. Stop processing as soon as the ball is formed. Wrap and allow to rest for 30 minutes. Prepare the oven. Place a pan of hot water on the lowest shelf. Preheat the oven to gas mark 6/200°C/400°F. Lightly grease a baking sheet and place in the hot oven briefly to warm.

Divide the dough into 8 portions. Roll out two portions at a time, keeping the remaining pieces covered to prevent drying. Dust the dough with flour and place on a floured pastry board. Roll out to a rectangle until 2mm (one sixteenth of an inch) thick. Sprinkle with the seeds during rolling to press the seeds into the dough. Set aside on a sheet of waxed paper.

Carefully transfer the dough to the hot, lightly greased baking sheet and bake for 8–10 minutes. Watch carefully as these brown quickly. Remove the lavosh to wire racks to cool. Break into pieces and store in an air-tight tin. The baking sheet does not require greasing after the first baking.

Preparation: 20 minutes
Standing: 30 minutes
Baking: 30–40 minutes
Protein g/s: 3

Wholewheat Flour Tortillas

Makes 12 tortillas

Essentially an unleavened bread, these tasty tortillas contain a small amount of baking powder to produce a light texture. A good accompaniment to most of our Mexican main dishes.

250g (9oz) wholewheat flour
½×5ml (tsp) salt
1×5ml (tsp) baking powder
2×15ml (tbsp) sunflower margarine, well chilled
200ml (8fl oz) warm water

METAL BLADE: Place the flour, salt and baking powder in the processing bowl; pulse on/off until mixed. Add the margarine and process until just blended. With the machine running, add sufficient water through the feed tube in a steady stream for the dough to form a ball. Stop processing as soon as the ball has formed. Remove from the processor and divide into 12 portions. Place in a plastic bag to prevent drying.

Work one piece of dough at a time and bake. Repeat until all are made. Form each piece into a ball and roll in additonal flour. Roll out to a circle 15.5–18cm (6–7in) in diameter. If the dough is difficult to work, leave for a few minutes, covered. Bake immediately.

Heat an ungreased non-stick pan over a medium high heat. Bake each tortilla until brown flecks appear, about 1½ minutes. Turn and cook the other side. Tortillas should puff up a little during baking. Stack and cover the tortillas, keeping warm until they are all cooked and ready to be served.

Preparation: 5 minutes
Cooking: 25 minutes
Protein g/s: 3

Pancakes and Waffles

Spiced Fruit Pancakes

12 pancakes

These light, mildly flavoured pancakes need no syrup. Try a different fruit each time you make them.

Any of these fresh or dried fruits:
125-225g (4-8oz) fresh whole berries
1 unpeeled apple, halved, cored and shredded
1 large banana, mashed
75g (3oz) raisins
75g (3oz) dates, roughly chopped
1-2 peaches, roughly chopped
2 eggs
2×15ml (tbsp) oil
2×15ml (tbsp) honey
250ml (10fl oz) water
150g (5oz) wholewheat flour
2 ×5ml (tsp) baking powder
1/2×5ml (tsp) ground coriander
1/2×5ml (tsp) ground cinnamon
1/2×5ml (tsp) ground nutmeg
pinch salt
15g (1/2oz) dried milk powder

SHREDDING DISC OR METAL BLADE: Shred or chop the fruit of your choice. Remove from the processing bowl and set aside. Wipe the processing bowl dry. In a jug, combine the eggs, oil, water and honey. Set aside.

METAL BLADE OR PLASTIC MIXING BLADE: Place the flour, baking powder, spices, salt and milk powder in the bowl; pulse on/off to mix. With the machine running, pour in the liquid. Stop the machine as soon as all the liquid has been added. Scrape down the sides of the bowl, add the fruit and combine with 2–3 pulses. Do not overprocess.

Heat a lightly oiled non-stick frying pan over a medium heat. Before baking, test the pan by adding a few drops of cold water to it. If the water bounces and bubbles, the pan is ready. Spoon a little of the mixture into the pan. Pancakes are ready to turn when bubbles appear on the top and the underside is light brown, 2–3 minutes. Turn the pancakes only once and continue baking until the second side is done. Cooking the second side takes about half as long as the first.

Preparation: 5–7 minutes
Cooking: 23–25 minutes
Protein g/s: 4 per pancake

Oven Pancakes

2 large pancakes

Fresh lemon juice and a light dusting of caster sugar top these puffy baked pancakes. Without a doubt, they are one of our all time favourites. Sprinkle the tops with cinnamon or serve with our Sautéed Apples (see index) for variation.

125g (4oz) butter or margarine
225g (8oz) wholewheat flour
2 eggs
125ml (5fl oz) milk
1/2×5ml (tsp) ground nutmeg
juice of half a lemon
caster sugar
cinnamon (optional)

Preheat the oven to gas mark 7/220°C/425°F. Place half the butter in each of two 23cm (9in) cake tins and heat briefly in the oven. Spread the melted butter over the bottom of the tins and set aside. When the oven has reached the required temperature, prepare the batter.

PLASTIC MIXING BLADE OR METAL BLADE: Place the flour, eggs, milk and nutmeg in the processing bowl. Combine with 3–4 on/off pulses. Do not overprocess. Immediately pour the batter into the centre of the prepared tins and bake for 10–15 minutes. The pancakes will puff and become golden brown. Carefully remove the pancakes to a serving dish and serve with lemon juice and sugar.

Preparation: 3–5 minutes
Baking: 10–15 minutes
Protein g/s: 13 per pancake

Wholewheat Pancakes

9 pancakes

This basic recipe calls for ingredients you will usually have on hand.

2 eggs
1×15ml (tbsp) oil
scant 250ml (10fl oz) skimmed milk
1×15ml (tbsp) brown sugar
1×5ml (tsp) baking powder
pinch salt

In a measuring jug, stir together eggs, oil and milk and set aside.

METAL BLADE OR PLASTIC MIXING BLADE: Place flour, brown sugar, baking powder and salt in processing bowl. Pulse on/off to mix, and with machine running, pour in liquid mixture. Stop machine as soon as all the liquid has been added. Do not overprocess. Scrape down sides of bowl.

Heat a lightly oiled non-stick frying pan over medium heat. Before baking, test the pan by sprinkling a few drops of cold water on it. If the water bounces and splutters, the pan is ready. Pour a little batter into pan. Pancakes are ready to turn when bubbles appear on top and the underside is light brown, 2–3 minutes. Turn pancakes only once and continue cooking until the second side is done. Cooking the second side takes about half as long as cooking the first side.

Preparation: 5 minutes
Cooking: 15 minutes
Protein g/s: 4 per pancake

Wholewheat Hazelnut Pancakes

9 pancakes

The food processor is ideal for grinding the hazelnuts into a flour for this recipe. We enjoy these on special occasions topped with a knob of butter and a little maple syrup.

2 eggs
1×5ml (tsp) vanilla essence
200ml (8fl oz) skimmed milk
50g (2oz) hazelnuts, shelled but not skinned
125g (4oz) wheatflour
1×5ml (tsp) baking powder
pinch salt
1×15ml (tbsp) brown sugar
25g (1oz) margarine

In a measuring jug, stir together eggs, vanilla essence and milk. Set aside.

METAL BLADE: Place the hazelnuts and 50g (2oz) flour in processing bowl. Process until nuts are ground to a consistency of coarse flour. Add remaining flour, baking powder, salt and brown sugar; pulse on/off to mix. Add margarine, cut into 4 pieces; pulse on/off to rub in. With machine running, pour in liquid

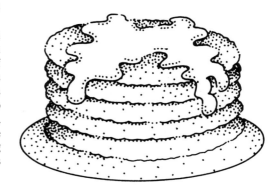

mixture. Stop machine as soon as all the liquid has been added. Do not overprocess. Scrape down sides of bowl.

Heat a lightly oiled non-stick frying pan over medium heat. Before baking, test the pan by sprinkling a few drops of cold water on it. If the water bounces and splutters, the pan is ready. Pour a little batter into pan. Pancakes are ready to turn when bubbles appear on top and the underside is light brown, 2–3 minutes. Turn pancakes only once and continue cooking until the second side is done. Cooking the second side takes about half as long as cooking the first side.

Preparation: 5–7 minutes
Cooking: 15 minutes
Protein g/s: 4.5 per pancake

Cinnamon Apple Pancakes

9 pancakes

Pieces of shredded apple are the surprise in these light and fluffy pancakes.

250ml (10fl oz) skimmed milk
2 eggs
1×15ml (tbsp) oil
125g (4oz) wholewheat flour
1×5ml (tsp) baking powder
pinch bicarbonate of soda
½×5ml (tsp) cinnamon
pinch salt
1 large apple, peeled and cored

In a measuring jug, stir together milk, eggs and oil. Set aside.

METAL BLADE OR PLASTIC MIXING BLADE: Place flour, baking powder, bicarbonate of soda, cinnamon and salt in processing bowl, pulse on/off to mix. With machine running, pour in liquid mixture. Stop machine as soon as all the liquid has been added. Do not overprocess. Carefully remove blade and insert shredding disc.

SHREDDING DISC: Quarter apple and insert vertically into feed tube; shred onto batter. Remove shredding disc and with a spatula or end of a wooden spoon, gently mix apple into batter.

Heat a lightly oiled non-stick frying pan over medium heat. Before baking, test the pan by sprinkling a few drops of cold water on it. If the water bounces and splutters, the pan is ready. Pour a little batter into pan. Pancakes are ready to turn when bubbles appear on top and the underside is light brown, 2–3 minutes. Turn pancakes only once and continue cooking until the second side is done. Cooking the second side takes about half as long as cooking the first side.

Preparation: 5 minutes
Cooking: 15 minutes
Protein g/s: 4 per pancake

Sunflower Seed Pancakes

Makes 10 pancakes

A delicious high protein breakfast with a crunch. Top with a knob of butter and maple syrup or honey.

2 eggs
2×15ml (tbsp) oil
1×15ml (tbsp) honey
1×5ml (tsp) vanilla essence
250ml (10fl oz) skimmed milk
125g (4oz) wholewheat flour
1×5ml (tsp) baking powder
½×5ml (tsp) salt
40g (1½oz) sunflower seeds

In a measuring jug stir together the eggs, oil, honey, vanilla essence and milk. Set aside.

METAL BLADE OR PLASTIC MIXING BLADE: Place the flour, baking powder, salt and sunflower seeds in the processing bowl. Pulse on/off to mix. With the machine running, pour in the liquid mixture. Stop the machine as soon as all the liquid has been added. Do not over-process.

Scrape down the sides of the bowl.

Heat a lightly oiled non-stick frying pan over medium heat. Before baking, test the pan by sprinkling a few drops of cold water on it. If the water bounces and splutters, the pan is ready. Pour a little batter into pan. Pancakes are ready to turn when bubbles appear on top and the underside is light brown, 2–3 minutes. Turn pancakes only once and continue cooking until the second side is done. Cooking the second side takes about half as long as cooking the first side.

Preparation: 5 minutes
Cooking: 15 minutes
Protein g/s: 6 per pancake

Bran Cheese Waffles

4-6 large waffles

Top with warm apple sauce, spiced with cinnamon. These freeze well; reheat in the oven at gas mark 4/180°C/350°F for about 10 minutes or until crisp and hot.

2 eggs, separated
60ml (2½fl oz) oil
375ml (15fl oz) water
75g (3oz) mature Cheddar cheese, well chilled
200g (7oz) wholewheat flour

1×15ml (tbsp) baking powder
40g (1½oz) bran
40g (1½oz) dried milk powder
1×5ml (tsp) salt

In a measuring jug, stir together the egg yolks, oil and water and set aside.

SHREDDING DISC: Cut the cheese to fit the feed tube; shred. Leave the cheese in the processor bowl.

METAL BLADE: Add the flour, baking powder, bran, milk powder and salt to the cheese and pulse on/off to mix. With the machine running, pour in the liquid mixture. Stop the machine as soon as all the liquid has been added. Do not over-process. Pour the batter into a medium mixing bowl. Wash and dry the bowl and metal blade.

METAL BLADE: Place the egg whites in the processor bowl. Process until stiff but not dry. Fold into the batter. Bake in a hot waffle iron according to the manufacturer's instructions. Thin the batter with milk if it becomes too thick.

Preparation: 10–15 minutes
Baking: 20–30 minutes
Protein g/s: 4–23 per waffle
6–15 per waffle

Desserts

Fruit Nut Squares

Makes 16 squares

A moist chewy topping on a shortbread-like crust. The processor takes the work out of chopping the prunes and mixing up the crust!

Crust

75g (3oz) wholewheat flour
2×15ml (tbsp) soft brown sugar
75g (3oz) butter or margarine, cut into 2.5cm (1in) pieces

Preheat the oven to gas mark 4/180°C/350°F.

METAL BLADE: Place the flour and sugar in the processing bowl; pulse on/off to mix. Add the butter and process until the butter is blended into the flour and the pastry just begins to form a ball. Turn into a 23×23cm (9×9in) square tin. Press down into an even layer and bake for 16–18 minutes, until lightly browned.

Filling

25g (1oz) wholewheat flour
1/2×5ml (tsp) baking powder
pinch salt
20 pitted prunes
75g (3oz) walnuts
2 eggs
40g (1½oz) soft brown sugar
few drops vanilla essence

METAL BLADE: Place the flour, baking powder and salt in the processing bowl; pulse on/off to mix. Add the prunes and walnuts and pulse on/off to roughly chop. Remove from the bowl and set aside. Place the eggs, sugar and vanilla essence in the processing bowl. Process for 10 seconds. Stop the machine and scrape down the sides of the bowl. Add the reserved flour and fruit mixture to the machine all at once. Combine with 3–4 on/off pulses until just mixed.

Carefully spread the filling over the hot crust. Return the tin to the oven and bake for a further 30 minutes. Place the tin on a wire rack to cool completely. Cut into squares. Store in an air-tight container in the refrigerator.

Preparation: 10 minutes
Baking: 45 minutes in total
Protein g/s: 2.5

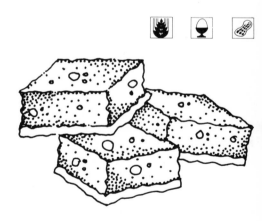

Apple Yogurt Muesli

Serves 1

Muesli, originally developed by Dr Bircher-Benner, is a fruit dish with a little cereal, milk and nuts. This dish is usually served at the start of breakfast or the evening meal, following the Bircher-Benner principle that 'the keenest edge should be taken off the appetite with fresh, raw food, before anything else is eaten.' We think that muesli makes a delicious anytime snack!

1×15ml (tbsp) rolled oats
3×15ml (tbsp) hot water
4×15ml (tbsp) yogurt
1×5ml (tsp) lemon juice
4 whole almonds
1 large apple, halved and cored

Place the oats in a small dish and pour in the hot water. Allow to soften for a few minutes then pour off the majority of the water. Add the yogurt and lemon juice.

METAL BLADE: Place the almonds in the processor bowl; pulse on/off until finely chopped. Remove from the bowl and set aside.

SHREDDING DISC: Cut the apple to fit the feed tube; shred. Remove the shredding disc. With a spatula push the apples to the sides of the bowl and insert the metal blade or plastic mixing blade.

METAL BLADE: Spread the apple evenly around the bottom of the processing bowl and pour in the yogurt mixture. Combine with 2–3 on/off pulses. Do not over-process. There should be shreds of apple in the mixture. Place in a serving dish, sprinkle with nuts and serve immediately.

Preparation: 5–7 minutes
Protein g/s: 3.5

Sautéed Apples

Serves 4

A simple and excellent topping for pancakes and desserts.

4 cooking apples
50g (2oz) butter or margarine
2×15ml (tbsp) honey
pinch ground cinnamon
60ml (2½fl oz) water

Peel, core and quarter the apples.

SLICING DISC: Stack the apple quarters in the feed tube horizontally. Slice 2 quarters at a time with the flat side on the disc. Melt the butter in a pan over a medium heat. Add the apple slices and cook until they are just cooked but still crisp. Add the honey, cinnamon and water and stir to mix. Reduce the heat and cook until all the water has evaporated and the apples are tender but not mushy.

Preparation: 5 minutes
Cooking: 15–20 minutes

Apple Pie

Serves 8

Only 1-3×15ml (tbsp) of honey are in this dessert. Do not substitute Golden Delicious apples – their flavour is simply not comparable. A pâté brisée crust is used because it does not absorb moisture as readily as other crusts.

2 quantities Wholewheat Pâté Brisée Crust (see index)
900g (2lb) tart cooking apples
1×15ml (tbsp) lemon juice
1-3×15ml (tbsp) honey
pinch salt
½×5ml (tsp) ground cinnamon
1 egg, separated

Preheat the oven to gas mark 5/190°C/375°F. Prepare the pâté brisée crust; wrap in two separate portions and refrigerate whilst preparing the apples. Peel, core and quarter the apples.

SLICING DISC: Stack the apple wedges in the feed tube vertically; slice. Remove to a mixing bowl and add lemon juice and honey. Toss to mix. Remove one portion of pastry from the refrigerator. Dust lightly with flour and place between two sheets of waxed paper. Roll into a circle 30.5cm (12in) in diameter. Line an oiled 25.5cm (10in) pie plate with the pastry; trim, leaving a 2.5cm (1in) overlap. Prick the bottom with a fork. Lightly beat the egg white and brush the bottom and sides of the pastry. Mix together the salt and cinnamon. Layer the apple on the pastry shell, occasionally adding a sprinkling of the cinnamon mixture.

Roll the remaining pastry. Place over the filling; trim edge leaving a 2.5cm (1in) overlap. Fold the overlap under and bring up over the edge of the pie plate. Flute with your fingers. Prick the top of the pie with a fork to allow the steam to escape. Decorate with leaves made from the remaining pastry. Brush with lightly beaten egg yolk. Bake for 40–50 minutes. Remove to a wire rack. Serve warm or cold.

Preparation: 20–30 minutes
Baking: 40–50 minutes
Protein g/s: 4

Sunflower Seed Carrot Bars

Makes 24

Moist bars loaded with sunflower seeds and raisins.

125g (4oz) wholewheat flour
1×5ml (tsp) baking powder
pinch salt
½×5ml (tsp) ground cinnamon
125g (4oz) sunflower seeds
140g (4½oz) raisins
2 medium carrots, peeled
2 eggs
2×15ml (tbsp) oil
150g (5oz) honey
1×5ml (tsp) vanilla essence

Preheat the oven to gas mark 4/180°C/350°F.

METAL BLADE: Place the flour, baking powder, salt, cinnamon, sunflower seeds and raisins in the processor bowl. Pulse on/off to mix. Remove to a medium mixing bowl and set aside.

SHREDDING DISC: Cut the carrots to fit the feed tube vertically; shred. Remove and add to the flour mixture, tossing to mix.

METAL BLADE: Place the eggs, oil, honey and vanilla essence in the processing bowl. Process for 10 seconds. Scrape down the sides of the bowl. Add the flour and carrot mixture all at once. Combine with 3–4 pulses – do not over-process. Spread the batter into a 20×20cm (8×8in) baking tin and bake for 30 minutes. Place the tin on a wire rack and allow to cool. Cut into bars.

Preparation: 10 minutes
Baking: 30 minutes
Protein g/s: 2.5

Carob Nut Bars

Makes 16 bars

Moist brownie-like bars.

125g (4oz) butter or margarine
225g (8oz) honey
50g (2oz) carob powder
75g (3oz) wholewheat flour
1×5ml (tsp) baking powder
pinch salt
2 eggs
1×5ml (tsp) vanilla essence
75g (3oz) walnuts

Preheat the oven to gas mark 4/180°C/350°F. Melt the butter in a small saucepan then add the honey and carob powder. Remove from the heat and set aside. Stir together the flour, baking powder and salt and set aside.

METAL BLADE: Place the eggs and the vanilla essence in the processing bowl; process for 5 seconds. Stop the machine and scrape down the sides of the bowl. With the machine running, pour in the honey and carob mixture. Process until well mixed. Scrape down the sides of the bowl. Turn the machine off. Add the flour mixture all at once then add the walnuts. Combine with 3–4 on/off pulses until mixed and the walnuts are roughly chopped.

Spread the mixture evenly in a greased 20×20cm (8×8in) baking tin. Bake for approximately 30 minutes or until a skewer inserted into the middle of the mixture comes out clean. Remove the tin to a wire rack and allow to cool completely. Cut into bars.

Preparation: 5–8 minutes
Baking: 30 minutes
Protein g/s: 2.5

Fresh Apple Sauce

Makes about 300ml (12fl oz)

This uncooked apple sauce is an excellent pancake topping. When prepared in advance, the apple sauce turns brown so it is best made just before serving.

2 large Golden Delicious apples, quartered and cored
1×15ml (tbsp) lemon juice
1-2×15ml (tbsp) honey

METAL BLADE: Place the apples, cut into 2.5cm (1in) pieces, lemon juice and honey in the processing bowl. Process until the apples are puréed. Stop the machine and scrape down the sides of the bowl occasionally. Serve at once.

Preparation: 2 minutes

Peanut Butter Sandwiches

Makes 20 biscuits

Homemade peanut butter is delicious as a filling for these crisp cookies.

150g (5oz) wholewheat flour
½×5ml (tsp) bicarbonate of soda
pinch salt
2×15ml (tbsp) dried milk powder
325g (12oz) roasted peanuts OR
225-275g (8-10oz) smooth peanut butter
50g (2oz) butter, cut into 2.5cm (1in) pieces
50g (2oz) soft brown sugar
1×15ml (tbsp) honey

Stir together the flour, bicarbonate of soda, salt and milk powder. Set aside.

METAL BLADE: Place the peanuts in the processing bowl; process until smooth. Stop the machine and scrape down the sides of the bowl as necessary. Remove about 125g (4oz) and reserve for filling. Add the butter, sugar and honey to the peanut butter in the processor; process until well mixed. Stop the machine, remove the cover and add all the dry ingredients at once. Process until just blended. The dough may be slightly crumbly.

Remove the dough from the bowl and form into a roll 18cm (7in) long and 6cm (2½in) in diameter. Wrap in waxed paper and refrigerate for at least 2 hours until firm enough to slice. Preheat the oven to gas mark 4/180°C/350°F. Remove the dough from the refrigerator.

With a sharp knife, cut half the roll into 3mm (⅛in) thick slices. Place 3cm (1½in) apart on a foil lined baking sheet. Place 1×5ml (tsp) peanut butter on each cookie. Slice the remaining dough and place over the peanut butter. Allow to stand for 2–3 minutes. Seal the edges of the biscuits by pressing together with the fingertips. The tops will crack slightly. Bake for 10–12 minutes. Allow to stand on the baking sheets for a few minutes then transfer to a wire rack to cool. Store in an air-tight container.

Preparation: 10 minutes
Chilling: 2 hours
Baking: 10–12 minutes
Protein g/s: 5

Carrot Cake

Serves 6-9

Your processor takes the work out of shredding the carrots for this popular, moist cake. Let the cake stand, well wrapped, overnight for the flavours to develop.

125g (4oz) wholewheat flour
2×5ml (tsp) ground cinnamon
1/2×5ml (tsp) ground nutmeg
1×5ml (tsp) salt
1 1/2×5ml (tsp) bicarbonate of soda
2 medium carrots, peeled
2 eggs
125ml (5fl oz) oil
150g (5oz) honey
1×5ml (tsp) vanilla essence
50g (2oz) walnuts

Preheat the oven to gas mark 4/180°C/350°F.

METAL BLADE: Place the flour, cinnamon, nutmeg, salt and bicarbonate of soda in the processing bowl. Pulse on/off to mix. Remove the metal blade; insert the shredding disc.

SHREDDING DISC: Cut the carrots to fit the feed tube vertically. Shred into the flour mixture. Remove from the processor and set aside.

METAL BLADE: Place the eggs, honey and vanilla essence in the processing bowl; process for 5 seconds to mix. Stop the machine and scrape down the sides of the bowl. Process for a further 10 seconds. Scrape down again. Add the dry ingredients all at once with the walnuts. Combine with 3–4 on/off pulses. Before the last on/off, scrape down the sides of the bowl. Pour into a greased 20×20cm (8×8in) baking tin. Bake for 30–35 minutes or until a skewer inserted into the centre of the mixture comes out clean. Cool completely.

Preparation: 10 minutes
Baking: 30–35 minutes
Protein g/s: 6 servings–6.5
         9 servings–4.5

200g (7oz) wholewheat flour
1/2×5ml (tsp) bicarbonate of soda
pinch salt
1×5ml (tsp) ground cinnamon
1×15ml (tbsp) soft brown sugar
2×15ml (tbsp) dried milk powder
50g (2oz) rolled oats
50g (2oz) butter or margarine
150g (5oz) peanut butter
75g (3oz) honey
1 egg
1×5ml (tsp) vanilla essence

In a mixing bowl combine the flour, bicarbonate of soda, salt, cinnamon, sugar, milk powder and rolled oats. Set aside.

METAL BLADE: Place the butter, peanut butter, honey, egg and vanilla essence in the processing bowl, process for 20 seconds, stopping to scrape down the sides of the bowl once. Add all the dry ingredients at once to the processing bowl and combine with 3–4 on/off pulses until well mixed.

Shape into two 13cm (5in) long rolls. Wrap in plastic or waxed paper and chill for several hours or overnight in the refrigerator. Preheat the oven to gas mark 5/190°C/375°F. Remove the dough from the refrigerator and cut into 8mm (1/4in) slices with a sharp knife. Place 1cm (1/2in) apart on foil lined baking sheets. These biscuits do not spread. Bake for 5–8 minutes, until the edges are browning. Cool on a wire rack.

Preparation: 10 minutes
Baking: 5–8 minutes
Chilling: 3–4 hours
Protein g/s: 2

Oatmeal Refrigerator Cookies

Makes 36 biscuits

An interesting pattern is produced when the knife slices through the rolled oats. These are crunchy cookies.

Almond Rounds

Makes 30 biscuits

A crunchy, slightly chewy biscuit delicately flavoured with almond. These biscuits travel well.

50g (2oz) whole almonds
150g (5oz) wholewheat flour
1×5ml (tsp) baking powder
pinch salt
75g (3oz) butter or margarine
6×15ml (tbsp) honey
1×5ml (tsp) almond essence
few drops vanilla essence
1 egg

Place the oven shelves towards the top of the oven. Preheat the oven to gas mark 4/180°C/350°F.

METAL BLADE: Place the almonds in the processor bowl; pulse on/off to chop finely. Add the flour, baking powder and salt. Pulse on/off to mix. Add the butter, cut into 2.5cm (1in) pieces; process until the mixture resembles breadcrumbs. Stop the machine and pour in the honey, almond essence, vanilla essence and egg. Process until well blended. The mixture will be soft.

Transfer the dough to a sheet of paper lightly dusted with flour. Pat the dough to a circle 1cm (½in) thick. Cut into 4cm (1½in) rounds. Gather the remaining dough and repeat until all the dough is cut.

Place the rounds on foil lined baking sheets about 4cm (1½in) apart. These do not spread. Bake for 20 minutes or until browned. Do not overbake or these biscuits will become dry. Remove to a wire rack to cool completely. Store in an air-tight container.

Preparation: 10–15 minutes
Baking: 20 minutes
Protein g/s: 1

Oat Peanut Butter Crunchies

Makes 26 biscuits

125g (4oz) butter, cut into 2.5cm (1in) pieces
50g (2oz) soft brown sugar
125g (4oz) peanut butter
75g (3oz) honey
1 egg

1×5ml (tsp) vanilla essence
75g (3oz) wholewheat flour
50g (2oz) rolled oats
2×15ml (tbsp) dried milk powder
½×5ml (tsp) bicarbonate of soda
pinch salt
50g (2oz) carob chips

Preheat the oven to gas mark 4/180°C/350°F.

METAL BLADE: Place the butter, sugar, peanut butter, honey, egg and vanilla essence in the processing bowl. Process for 5 seconds. Stop the machine and scrape down the sides of the bowl. Process for a further 10 seconds then scrape down again.

Stir together the flour, oats, milk powder, bicarbonate of soda, salt and carob chips. Add the dry ingredients all at once to the work bowl. Combine with 3–4 on/off pulses until just mixed. Do not over-process.

Line a baking sheet with foil. Drop the batter in heaped 5ml (tsp) spoonfuls onto the sheet, 5cm (2in) apart. Bake for 10 minutes. Remove to a wire rack to cool. Store in an air-tight container.

Preparation: 5–7 minutes
Baking: 10 minutes
Protein g/s: 1.5

Sunflower Seed Oatmeal Cookies

Makes 32 biscuits

As cookies go these are crunchy, extremely nutritous and high in protein.

125g (4oz) butter
150-175g (5-6oz) soft brown sugar
1 egg
1×5ml (tsp) vanilla essence
75g (3oz) wholewheat flour
50g (2oz) soy flour
½×5ml (tsp) bicarbonate of soda
125g (4oz) rolled oats
65g (2½oz) sunflower seeds

Preheat the oven to gas mark 4/180°C/350°F.

METAL BLADE: Place the butter, cut into 2.5cm (1in) pieces, sugar, egg and vanilla essence in the processing bowl. Process for 5 seconds. Stop the machine and scrape down the sides of the bowl. Process for 10 seconds until well blended and fluffy. Stir together the flours, bicarbonate of soda, rolled oats and sunflower seeds. Remove the cover of the processing bowl and add the flour mixture all at once. Pulse on/off 2–3 times until just mixed. The oats and sunflower seeds should remain whole.

Line a baking sheet with foil. Drop the cookie dough by the 15ml (tbsp) spoonful onto the sheet, 5cm (2in) apart. Flatten slightly – these cookies spread only a little. Bake for 10–12 minutes or until lightly browned on the edges. Remove to a wire rack to cool. Store in an air-tight container.

Preparation: 5 minutes
Baking: 10–12 minutes
Protein g/s: 2

Fresh Apple Cake

Serves 6

Shredded apple makes this spicy cake soft and moist. Serve it warm or cold.

125g (4oz) wholewheat flour
1×5ml (tsp) baking powder
³/₄×5ml (tsp) salt
pinch baking powder
1×5ml (tsp) cinnamon
¹/₂×5ml (tsp) ground nutmeg
1×5ml (tsp) grated lemon rind
50g (2oz) walnuts
1 Golden Delicious apple, cored and quartered
50g (2oz) butter
150g (5oz) honey
1 egg
2×15ml (tbsp) water
¹/₂×5ml (tsp) vanilla essence

Preheat the oven to gas mark 4/180°C/350°F.

METAL BLADE: Place the flour, baking powder, salt, cinnamon, nutmeg, lemon rind and walnuts in the processing bowl. Pulse on/off to mix. Remove the metal blade and insert the shredding disc.

SHREDDING DISC: Stack the apple quarters in the feed tube; shred into the flour mixture. Remove to mixing bowl and toss to mix.

METAL BLADE: Place the butter, honey, egg, water and vanilla essence in the processing bowl; process for 10 seconds. Stop the machine and scrape down the sides of the bowl. Process for an additional 15 seconds. Scrape down the bowl again. Add the dry ingredients all at once. Add the walnuts. Combine with 3–4 on/off pulses. Before the last pulse scrape down the sides of the bowl. Do not over-process.

Pour into a greased 20×20cm (8×8in) baking tin. Bake for 30–35 minutes or until a skewer inserted into the centre comes out clean. Cool slightly and serve warm or allow to cool completely.

Preparation: 10 minutes
Baking: 30–35 minutes
Protein g/s: 5.5

Appendix A – Amino Acids

Protein is found in all plant and animal tissue. Chemically it is made up of 22 amino acids, strung together in different sequences and different numbers depending on the type of protein. Each amino acid consists of a central carbon atom with a hydrogen atom attached, an amino or nitrogen group, and an acid group. Additional atoms (mostly hydrogen, oxygen and carbon) are attached in various patterns. Each variation in pattern constitutes a different amino acid.

It is nitrogen which makes the protein quite distinct from other classes of nutrients, such as fats and carbohydrates. When scientists measure protein they usually measure nitrogen and use a conversion factor to arrive at the amount of protein present.

Of the twenty-two amino acids, nine cannot be produced in the body. They must be present in the food we eat and are therefore referred to as 'essential amino acids'. The nine essential amino acids are: tryptophan, phenylalanine, leucine, isoleucine, lysine, valine, threonine, methionine, and cystine and histidine.

Methionine and cystine, the two sulphur-containing amino acids, are usually considered together because cystine is partially convertible into methionine. Sometimes tyrosine, a non-essential amino acid, is paired with phenylalanine because it has the capacity to spare this essential amino acid. The combination of phenylalanine and tyrosine is referred to as 'total aromatic amino acids' or TAAA, whereas the combination of the sulphur-containing amino acids is referred to as TSAA. Histidine has been established as essential for infants and may well be for children. It has not yet been established whether or not it is essential for adults.

Traditionally, the egg has been considered the one food which best approximates the ideal balance of essential amino acids needed by the human species. This is why the egg is used as 'reference protein', or the food against which the quality of all other proteins is judged. Recently the egg as a standard has been challenged as containing certain essential amino acids in excess of human needs.

However, no alternative food has gained wide acceptance as the 'ideal' protein. One difficulty in judging the quality of a plant protein diet against a fairly rigorous standard such as the egg, is that the quality of the protein will in many instances appear to be lower than it really is. This is particularly true of high quality vegetable proteins such as soy products.

It seems reasonable to consider not using a particular food as a standard at all and to base the composition of the 'ideal' protein on actual human requirements for individual amino acids. The table overleaf compares the amino acid patterns of the egg and milk with a proposed pattern based on human amino acid requirements in terms of milligrams per gram of protein.

Proteins approximating the ideal pattern are sometimes referred to as 'complete' proteins. This term is often used in a misleading way by people who view the animal sources as 'complete' and the vegetable sources as 'incomplete' proteins. To the nutritionist, however, an 'incomplete' protein is totally lacking in one or more of the essential amino acids, and few foods other than gelatine fall in that category. If animal and vegetable proteins are viewed in terms of usability, which is what is really important,

AMINO ACID PATTERNS PROPOSED FOR
EVALUATING THE NUTRITIONAL QUALITY OF PROTEINS

(Stated in milligrams per gram of protein contained)

Amino Acid	Egg	Milk	Proposed NRC pattern
histidine	24	27	17
isoleucine	66	65	42
leucine	91	100	70
lysine	66	66	51
total sulphur containing amino acids	55	34	26
total aromatic amino acids	101	100	73
threonine	50	47	35
tryptophan	18	14	11
valine	74	70	48

Source: National Research Council. Committee on Amino Acids. Improvement of Protein Nutriture, Washington, D.C. National Academy of Sciences, 1974.

the 'complete–incomplete' distinction is largely irrelevant. There is little difference in usability between a soy product, such as tofu, and beef.

When the proportion of essential amino acids deviates from the ideal pattern, the one in shortest supply proportionately determines the extent to which all of the others are utilised and is therefore called the limiting amino acid.

When we compute how well the individual amino acids in a food compare to the egg, or any other standard for that matter, we are computing a theoretical chemical score to predict how a protein should perform biologically, based on the effect of limiting amino acids. This score, in effect, amounts to a percentage of the limiting amino acid in the food compared to the same amino acid in the egg or other standard. When rated according to the egg standard, the chemical score of beef is somewhere around 67–69 because of its fairly low tryptophan content, which is only 67–69% of the tryptophan present in the egg per gram of protein.

It is possible to compute these theoretical values for individual foods or combinations of foods. These values generally correlate well with experimental measurements of protein quality, such as Net Protein Utilisation (NPU), which is the percentage of protein consumed that is actually retained and used in the body, and Protein Efficiency Ratio (PER), which is the amount of weight gain in growing laboratory animals per gram of protein consumed.

Chemical or amino acid scores, however, are not always exact predictors of PER and NPU. In some instances these values are far enough apart to cause puzzlement. Possibly the egg, our current reference protein, contains more of some amino acids than we need, thereby making chemical scores for other foods too low. This could be particularly true in the case of some of the pulses (beans, peas and lentils) which are deficient in the sulphur-containing amino acids, those amino acids which in the egg seem to exceed human requirements. To confound matters further, there is evidence to suggest that estimates based on experimental measurements of proteins on the lower end of the quality scale are far too high – particularly in cases where lysine is the limiting amino acid. A good example of this phenomenon is gluten, a poor quality wheat protein which is extremely low in lysine. It has a chemical score of approximately 26, but its experimentally determined usability is somewhere around 39.

The amount of protein the body can actually use is always less than the total amount of protein in the food because, in addition to the limiting amino acids, the digestibility of a food limits the availability of specific amino acids, or total protein. If a certain amino acid is concentrated in a less digestible part of the food, less of it will be absorbed.

Protein synthesis occurs in the body continuously. Therefore, for the most part, all essential amino acids should be present in nearly ideal proportions at the same time. But a bit of leeway is provided by a 'pool' of amino acids in the small intestine. This 'pool' consists chiefly of sloughed off cells from the intestinal lining, which are renewed every few days, but also contains amino acids from protein broken down in the tissues throughout the body and from digestive enzymes which are finally digested themselves. When you ingest a protein food, it is broken down, diluted with amino acids in the 'pool', and circulated through the bloodstream to the liver and other locations where protein synthesis takes place. However, not a great

deal is known about the relative contributions of 'pool' amino acids and 'food' amino acids to protein synthesis, although synthesis usually exceeds protein intake by a wide margin. What we do know suggests caution in placing too much reliance on this 'pool', because it has been shown that amino acid patterns in the food consumed are reflected in the blood plasma after digestion when the percentage of protein in the diet is over 10%. This suggests that deficiencies in the amino acid patterns of foods are only partially offset by this amino acid 'pool'. Recent research indicates that the 'pool' may not be as large as was once thought.

To be on the safe side, we recommend trying to obtain a reasonably good balance of amino acids at each meal, so that they will be in the system in adequate proportion to one another. This is extremely important because tissues and other body proteins are constantly being broken down and rebuilt and while some amino acids are recycled, others are lost in the faeces, urine, sweat, hair and fingernails, or are sloughed off in dead skin cells. In sum, a continuous supply of essential amino acids is required for maintenance and repair, for growth, and for the regulation of metabolic processes.

In addition to the essential amino acids, the body requires a sufficient amount of non-specific nitrogen, or protein in the form of the non-essential amino acids, so that it can synthesise those that it needs at any given time.

Appendix B

FOOD AND NUTRITION BOARD, NATIONAL ACADEMY OF SCIENCES—NATIONAL RESEARCH COUNCIL
RECOMMENDED DAILY DIETARY ALLOWANCES,[a] Revised 1980

Designed for the maintenance of good nutrition of practically all healthy people in the U.S.A.

	Age (years)	Weight (kg)	Weight (lb)	Height (cm)	Height (in)	Protein (g)	Vitamin A (µg RE)[b]	Vitamin A (IU)	Vitamin D (µg)[c]	Vitamin D (IU)	Vitamin E (mg α-TE)[d]	Vitamin E (IU)	Vitamin C (mg)	Thiamin (mg)	Riboflavin (mg)	Niacin (mg NE)[e]	Vitamin B-6 (mg)	Folacin[f] (µg)	Vitamin B-12 (µg)	Calcium (mg)	Phosphorus (mg)	Magnesium (mg)	Iron (mg)	Zinc (mg)	Iodine (µg)
Infants	0.0-0.5	6	13	60	24	kg × 2.2	420	1400	10	400	3	4	35	0.3	0.4	6	0.3	30	0.5[g]	360	240	50	10	3	40
	0.5-1.0	9	20	71	28	kg × 2.0	400	2000	10	400	4	5	35	0.5	0.6	8	0.6	45	1.5	540	360	70	15	5	50
Children	1-3	13	29	90	35	23	400	2000	10	400	5	7	45	0.7	0.8	9	0.9	100	2.0	800	800	150	15	10	70
	4-6	20	44	112	44	30	500	2500	10	400	6	9	45	0.9	1.0	11	1.3	200	2.5	800	800	200	10	10	90
	7-10	28	62	132	52	34	700	3500	10	400	7	10	45	1.2	1.4	16	1.6	300	3.0	800	800	250	10	10	120
Males	11-14	45	99	157	62	45	1000	5000	10	400	8	12	50	1.4	1.6	18	1.8	400	3.0	1200	1200	350	18	15	150
	15-18	66	145	176	69	56	1000	5000	10	400	10	15	60	1.4	1.7	18	2.0	400	3.0	1200	1200	400	18	15	150
	19-22	70	154	177	70	56	1000	5000	7.5	300	10	15	60	1.5	1.7	19	2.2	400	3.0	800	800	350	10	15	150
	23-50	70	154	178	70	56	1000	5000	5	200	10	15	60	1.4	1.6	18	2.2	400	3.0	800	800	350	10	15	150
	51+	70	154	178	70	56	1000	5000	5	200	10	15	60	1.2	1.4	16	2.2	400	3.0	800	800	350	10	15	150
Females	11-14	46	101	157	62	46	800	4000	10	400	8	12	50	1.1	1.3	15	1.8	400	3.0	1200	1200	300	18	15	150
	15-18	55	120	163	64	46	800	4000	10	400	8	12	60	1.1	1.3	14	2.0	400	3.0	1200	1200	300	18	15	150
	19-22	55	120	163	64	44	800	4000	7.5	300	8	12	60	1.1	1.3	14	2.0	400	3.0	800	800	300	18	15	150
	23-50	55	120	163	64	44	800	4000	5	200	8	12	60	1.0	1.2	13	2.0	400	3.0	800	800	300	18	15	150
	51+	55	120	163	64	44	800	4000	5	200	8	12	60	1.0	1.2	13	2.0	400	3.0	800	800	300	10	15	150
Pregnant						+30	+200	+1000	+5	+200	+2	+3	+20	+0.4	+0.3	+2	+0.6	+400	+1.0	+400	+400	+150	h	+5	+25
Lactating						+20	+400	+2000	+5	+200	+3	+4	+40	+0.5	+0.5	+5	+0.5	+100	+1.0	+400	+400	+150	h	+10	+50

[a] The allowances are intended to provide for individual variations among most normal persons as they live in the United States under usual environmental stresses. Diets should be based on a variety of common foods in order to provide other nutrients for which human requirements have been less well defined. See text for detailed discussion of allowances and of nutrients not tabulated.

[b] Retinol equivalents. 1 retinol equivalent = 1 µg retinol or 6 µg β carotene. See text for calculation of vitamin A activity of diets as retinol equivalents.

[c] As cholecalciferol. 10 µg cholecalciferol = 400 IU of vitamin D.

[d] α-tocopherol equivalents. 1 mg d-α tocopherol = 1 α-TE. See text for variation in allowances and calculation of vitamin E activity of the diet as α-tocopherol equivalents.

[e] 1 NE (niacin equivalent) is equal to 1 mg of niacin or 60 mg of dietary tryptophan.

[f] The folacin allowances refer to dietary sources as determined by *Lactobacillus casei* assay after treatment with enzymes (conjugases) to make polyglutamyl forms of the vitamin available to the test organism.

[g] The recommended dietary allowance for vitamin B-12 in infants is based on average concentration of the vitamin in human milk. The allowances after weaning are based on energy intake (as recommended by the American Academy of Pediatrics) and consideration of other factors, such as intestinal absorption.

[h] The increased requirement during pregnancy cannot be met by the iron content of habitual American diets nor by the existing iron stores of many women; therefore the use of 30-60 mg of supplemental iron is recommended. Iron needs during lactation are not substantially different from those of nonpregnant women, but continued supplementation of the mother for 2-3 months after parturition is advisable in order to replenish stores depleted by pregnancy.

Reproduced with equivalents added from: *Recommended Dietary Allowances*, Ninth Edition (1980), with the permission of the National Academy of Sciences, Washington, D.C.

Subject and Recipe Title Index

Aioli Mayonnaise, 38
Almond Rounds, 144
amino acids, 13, 147
appetisers, 27
Apple Bran Muffins, 126
Apple cake, fresh, 146
Apple Cinnamon Wholewheat
　Bread, 120
Apple Pie, 141
apple sauce, fresh, 143
Apple Yogurt Muesli, 140
apples, sautéed, 141
Apricot Yogurt Bran Muffins, 127
Arabic Musakka'a, 45
Aubergine Dip, 27
Aubergine Parmesan, 69
aubergines
　dip, 27
　stuffed, 50

Baked Green Fettucine, 66
bake
　broccoli rice, 48
　cauliflower basil
　　mushroom, 54
　cheese and broccoli, 54
　cheese scalloped potatoes with
　　mushrooms, 52
　green chilli and pepper, 49
　mushroom olive, 55
　Swiss 'n' broccoli, 51
baking
　food processor
　　techniques, 104ff
　ingredients used in, 102
　measuring ingredients, 104
Banana Nut Bread, 128
Banana Walnut Bran Muffins, 126
Banana Yoghurt Nut Bread, 130
bars
　carob nut, 142
　sunflower seed carrot, 142
Basic Marinara Sauce, 65
Bean and Chilli Cheese Pie, 87
Bean and Raisin Enchiladas, 90
bean curd, see tofu
beans
　as sources of protein, 13
　cooking ahead, 25
　limiting amino acids in, 148
　pressure cooking, 21

shopping hints for, 21
storage, 22
beans (recipes)
　For a complete listing of bean
　dishes by type of bean consult
　the Major Ingredient Index
Black Bean Soup, 31
Boston Baked Beans, 45
bran, in baking, 103
Bran Bread, 111
Bran Cheese Waffles, 139
Bran Pitta, 125
Bran Prune Muffins, 13
breads, quick (recipes), 126
　see also biscuits, muffins
　　and scones
　banana nut, 128
　banana yoghurt nut, 130
　carrot sesame, 131
　cheese and chilli corn, 130
　fresh mango or peach, 133
　Irish soda, 132
　pineapple bran, 129
　raisin spice, 129
breads, unleavened, 134
　chapatis, 134
　lavosh, 134
　tortillas, wholewheat, 133
breads, yeast, 104ff
　basic techniques for, 104ff
　coolrise method for, 108
breads, yeast (recipes), 110ff
　apple sauce cinnamon
　　wholewheat, 120
　bran, 111
　buckwheat, 123
　carrot, 111
　Christmas stollen, 118
　complementary, 110
　cottage wheat loaf, 122
　double cheese, 112
　herb buttermilk, 119
　honey wheat, 112
　Irish oatmeal, 114
　malted milk, 116
　molasses wheat, 124
　nut butter, 122
　oat bran, 113
　pitta, 125
　poppy seed, 119
　rye, 115

sunflower seed, 114
swiss and rye, 121
Wholewheat French, 116
yoghurt bran, 123
Broccoli Rice Bake, 48
Buckwheat Mushroom Pilaf, 100
bulgur, in baking, 102
burgers, lentil sunflower, 42
Buttermilk Pitta, 125

cabbage
　red, with apples, 97
Cacciatore Sauce over
　Noodles, 64
cake
　apple, 146
　carrot, 143
calcium
　sources of, 16
Carob Nut bars, 142
Carrot and Courgette Slices, 40
Carrot Cake, 143
Carrot Filled Courgettes, 27
Carrot Noodles, 60
Carrot Sesame Bread, 131
Carrot Wholewheat Bread, 111
Cashew Noodle Crunch, 71
Cauliflower Basil Mushroom
　Bake, 54
Cauliflower with Creamy
　Parmesan Dressing, 34
cereals, whole grain, 18
Chapatis, 170
Cheese and Broccoli Bake, 54
Cheese and Chilli Corn
　Bread, 130
Cheese and Onion Quiche, 79
Cheese Radish Salad, 39
Cheese Scalloped Potatoes with
　Mushrooms, 52
Cheese Soufflé, 56
chemical score, 148
Chick Pea and Cheese Salad, 40
Chinese cooking, staples for, 25
Chinese Style Fried Rice, 99
Chinese Stir-Fried Vegetables with
　Cashews, 97
Chinese Style Stir-Fried
　Noodles, 61
cholecalciferol, 150
Cinnamon Apple Pancakes, 138

coleslaw, red and white,   35
Complementary Bread,   110
complementary protein
    combinations and
        complementing,   13
    need for,   13
    tradition of,   13
cookies
    almond,   144
    Oatmeal Refrigerator,   144
    sunflower seed oatmeal,   145
cooking ahead,   25
Cottage Cheese Oil Pizza
    Crust,   73
Cottage Wheat Loaf,   122
Courgette and Green Chilli
    Quiche,   85
Courgette Lasagne,   55
Courgette Pancakes,   98
Courgette Parmesan,   69
Courgette and Tomato
    Quiche,   78
cracked wheat in baking,   102
crêpes
    feta spinach,   89
    sesame,   88
    wholewheat,   88
Cucumber Dip,   29
Curried Chick Peas,   43
Curried Lentils,   46
curry, vegetable tofu,   94
cystine,   147

Danish Feta and Spinach Tart,   83
desserts, *see* bars, cakes, cookies
    and pies
diet, suggestions for balanced
    diet,   17
Dilled Egg Salad,   35
dip
    aubergine,   27
    cucumber,   29
    guacamole,   30
    Parmesan herb,   29
Double Cheese Bread,   112

egg
    amino acid pattern of,   147
    as sources of protein,   12
    in baking,   104
    storage,   23
Egg Fu Yung,   50
Enchilada Sauce,   92

enchiladas
    bean and raisin,   90
    coloradas,   91
    fresh corn,   89
Enchiladas Coloradas,   91

fats
    excess,   18
    in baking,   103
    storage,   24
Feta Spinach Crêpes,   89
fettucine, baked green,   66
fibre, dietary,   11
filo dough, wholewheat,   76
flour, wholewheat
    in baking,   102
    general hints,   22
food processors
    hints for purchasing,   9
    tasks performed,   7
French bread, wholewheat,   116
Fresh Apple Cake,   146
Fresh Apple Sauce,   143
Fresh Corn Enchiladas,   89
Fresh Mango or Peach Bread,   133
fruit
    in a balanced diet,   19
    nutrients supplied,   19
Fruit Nut Squares,   140

German Potato Pancakes,   53
gluten,   149
Gnocchi Verde,   66
grains, whole
    as sources of protein,   18
    limiting amino acids in,   131
    main dishes,   42ff
    side dishes,   99
    storage,   22
Greek Chef's Salad,   36
Greek cooking, staples for,   25
Green Chilli and Pepper Bake,   49
Guacamole,   30

Harvest Vegetable Quiche,   83
Herb Buttermilk Bread,   119
honey
    in baking,   104
    general hints,   23
Honey French Dressing,   38
Honey Wheat Bread,   112
Hot German Potato Salad,   34
Hummus Bi Tahini,   100

Hungarian Paprika Noodles,   71

IU, *see* international units
Indian cooking, staples for,   25
international units,   150
Irish Oatmeal Bread,   114
Irish Soda Bread,   133
iron
    absorption,   15
    general information,   15
    requirements,   15
iron pots and pans,   16
Italian cooking, staples for,   25

Japanese cooking, staples for,   25

lactase,   17
lactose intolerance,   17
Lasagne,   62
    courgette,   55
    spinach,   68
    with aubergine mushroom
        sauce,   64
Lasagne with Aubergine
    Mushroom Sauce,   64
Lavosh,   134
leavening or raising agents,   103
Lentil Soup,   33
Lentil Spaghetti,   62
Lentil Sunflower Burgers,   42
lentils, curried,   46
Lentils Burgundy,   46
loaf, nut cheese,   52
    potato,   121

major protein sources,   12
Malted Milk Bread,   116
Mangetout with Bamboo
    Shoots,   96
maple syrup, storage,   23
margarine,   24
Mayonnaise,   37
mayonnaise, garlic (aioli),   38
menu planning,   26
methionine,   147
Mexican cooking,
    staples for,   25
Mexican Chef's Salad,   36
Mexican Salad,   36
Middle Eastern cooking,
    staples for,   25
milk and milk products
    amino acid, pattern of,   13

as sources of calcium, 16
as sources of protein, 18
in balanced diet, 18
general information, 18
miller's bran, *see* bran
minerals, recommended
allowances, table, 150
Minestrone, 32
Mini Pitta Pizzas, 73
molasses, storage of, 23
Molasses Wheat Bread, 124
Moussaka, 48
Mozzarella Cheese Quiche, 84
muesli, apple yogurt, 140
muffins
apple bran, 126
apricot yogurt bran, 127
banana walnut bran, 126
bran prune, 131
oat raisin, 128
prune, 127
Musakka'a, Arabic, 45
Mushroom and Broccoli
Tartlets, 28
Mushroom Cheese Tart, 82
Mushroom Olive Bake, 55
Mushroom Quiche, 78

natural foods, advantages of, 10
Net Protein Utilisation, 148
niacin, units of
measurements, 148
niacinamide, 148
nicotinamide, 148
nicotinic acid, 148
nitrogen balance studies, 14
noodles, *see also* pasta
cacciatore sauce over, 65
carrots, 60
Hungarian paprika, 71
parsley, 68
rich egg, 60
wheat germ, 68
wholewheat egg, 60
Nut Butter Bread, 122
Nut Cheese Loaf, 56
nutrients, recommended
allowances, table of, 150
nuts
as sources of protein, 12
general hints, 22

Oat Bran Bread, 113

Oatmeal Refrigerator
Cookies, 144
Oat Peanut Butter
Crunchies, 145
Oat Raisin Muffins, 128
oats, rolled, in baking, 103
oils
varieties, 24
general hints, 23
omelette, egg fu yung, 50
Onion Mushroom Pizza, 74
Oven Pancakes, 136
oxalate, 17
oxalic acid, *see* oxalate

PER, 148
pancakes
cinnamon apple, 138
courgette, 98
German Potato, 53
hazelnut, 137
oven, 136
spiced fruit, 136
sunflower seed, 138
wholewheat, 137
Parmesan Herb Dip, 29
Parsley Noodles, 68
pasta
basic techniques, 57
cooking, 59
cutting, 59
drying, 58
egg, 57
food processor techniques, 57
manual techniques, 59
mixing, 57
pasta machine tehniques, 57
problems and solutions, 58
rolling, 59
spinach, 57
storage, 59
pasta (recipes using)
cacciatore sauce over, 64
Chinese Style Stir-Fried
Noodles, 61
green fettucine, baked, 66
lasagne, 62
lasagne, with aubergine
mushroom sauce, 64
lentil spaghetti, 62
ravioli, 67
rustica, 70
with pesto sauce, 63

pasta machines, 57
pasta rack, 58
pasta sauces
basic marinara, 65
cacciatore, 64
pesto, 63
two-in-one tomato, 63
Pasta Verde, 61
pastry crust, *see also* quiche
shell, 76
pâté brisée crust, 77
Peanut Butter, 143
Peanut Sunflower Waldorf
Salad, 37
Pepper Olive Quiche, 85
Pesto Sauce Over Pasta, 63
phenylalanine, 147
phytase, 147
phytate, 147
phytic acid, *see* phytate
pie
apple, 141
bean and chilli cheese, 87
Pie Valasian, 80
tomato and mozzarella, 53
pilaf
buckwheat mushroom, 100
yellow rice, 99
Pineapple Bran Bread, 129
pitta bread, 125
bran, 125
buttermilk, 125
pizza
crust, cottage cheese oil, 73
mini pitta, 73
onion mushroom, 74
sauce, 65
Sicilian, 74
Poppy Seed Milk Rolls, 119
Potato Loaf, 121
potato salad, hot German, 34
potatoes, scalloped, 52
pressure cookers, 21
protein, *see also* amino acids
complete, 11
composition and quality of, 11
excess, 11
recommended allowances and
requirements, 12
table of, 20
sources of, 12
usable, 15
Protein Efficiency Ratio, 148

pulses
  as sources of protein,   12
  nutrients in,   19
  general hints,   21

quiche, *see also* pie and tart
  cheese and onion,   79
  courgette and green chilli,   85
  courgette and tomato,   78
  harvest vegetable,   83
  mozzarella cheese quiche,   84
  mushroom,   78
  pepper olive,   85
  sprout,   80
quiche shell
  wholewheat,   76
quick breads, *see* breads, quick

Raisin Spice Bread,   129
raisins, storage of,   23
Ratatouille,   96
ravioli, wholewheat,   67
Recommended Dietary Allowances,
  table,   150
Red and White Coleslaw,   35
Red Cabbage with Apples,   97
Rice and Vegetable Torte,   44
Rich Egg Noodles,   60
rolled oats, *see* oats, rolled
rolls
  poppy seed milk,   119
Rye Bread,   115
rye flour, in baking,   103
Rye Wheat Biscuits,   132

salad
  carrot and courgette slices,   40
  cauliflower,   34
  cheese radish,   39
  chick pea and cheese,   40
  dilled egg,   35
  Greek chef's,   36
  hot German Potato,   34
  Mexican,   36
  Mexican chef's,   36
  peanut sunflower Waldorf,   37
  tabouli,   39
salad dressing
  honey French,   38
  tart Greek,   38
  vinaigrette herb,   39
  yogurt herb,   38
salt, shopping hints for,   24

sauce
  enchilada,   12
  marinara,   65
  pasta, *see* pasta sauces
  pesto,   63
  tomato,   63
Sautéed apples,   141
Scrambled Tofu,   93
seasonings, types to have on
  hand,   24
seeds
  as sources of protein,   12
  general hints,   22
sesame seeds, hulled,   22
shopping, hints for,   26
Sicilian Pizza,   74
Soufflé, cheese,   56
soup
  black bean,   31
  lentil,   33
  minestrone,   32
soy flour in baking,   103
spaghetti, *see also* pasta
  lentil,   62
spaghetti sauce, Italian,   65
Spanakopita,   81
Spiced Fruit Pancakes,   136
Spinach Lasagne,   68
Spinach Noodles,   61
Sprout Quiche,   80
stollen, wholewheat,   118
Stuffed Aubergine,   50
sugar, *see* sweeteners
Sunflower Seed Bread,   114
Sunflower Seed Carrot Bars,   142
Sunflower Seed Oatmeal
  Cookies,   145
Sunflower Seed Pancakes,   138
Sunny Prune Muffins,   127
Sweet and Sour Tofu,   94
sweeteners
  in baking,   104
  general hints,   23
Swiss and Rye Bread,   121
Swiss 'n' Broccoli Bake,   51

Tabouli salad,   39
tacos, vegetarian,   42
tart, *see also* quiche and pie
  Danish feta and spinach,   83
  mushroom cheese,   82
Tart Greek Salad Dressing,   38

tocopherols,   150
tofu, general hints,   22
tofu (recipes),   9
  scrambled,   93
  sweet and sour,   94
  vegetable curry,   94
  with fresh mushrooms,   93
Tofu with Fresh Mushrooms,   93
Tofu Wheat Bread,   117
Tomato and Mozzarella Pie,   53
tomato sauce, Italian,   63
tortillas, wholewheat,   135
triticale flour in baking,   103
Two-in-One Tomato Sauce,   63
tyrosine,   147

Vegetable Tofu Curry,   94
vegetables
  as sources of protein,   18
  nutrients supplied by,   18
  general hints,   24
vegetables (recipes),
  For a complete listing of
  vegetable recipes by name of
  vegetable, consult the major
  ingredient index.
  Chinese, with cashews,   97
vegetarian cooking
  general hints,   21
vegetarian diets,   9
  balanced,   17
Vegetarian Tacos,   42
Vinaigrette Herb Dressing,   39
vitamin A
  allowances, table,   150
  units of measurement for,   150
vitamin B-12
  vegetable sources of,   17
vitamin D
  allowances, table,   150
  forms of,   17
  units of measurement for,   150
vitamin E
  allowances, table,   150
  units of measurement for,   150
vitamins, recommended
  allowances for, table,   150

waffles
  bran cheese,   139
wheat flakes, in baking,   102
wheat germ, in baking,   103
Wheat Germ Noodles,   68

whole grain cereals, *see* cereals,
  whole grain
Wholewheat Christmas Stollen, 118
Wholewheat Crêpes, 88
Wholewheat Egg Noodles, 60
Wholewheat Filo Dough, 77
wholewheat flour, *see also*
  flour, wholewheat, 22, 102
Wholewheat Flour Tortillas, 135
Wholewheat French Bread, 116

Wholewheat Hazelnut
  Pancakes, 137
Wholewheat Oil Crust, 83
Wholewheat Pancakes, 137
Wholewheat Pâté Brisée
  Crust, 77
Wholewheat Pitta Bread, 125
Wholewheat Quiche Shell, 76
Wholewheat Ravioli, 77
Wholewheat Sesame Crêpes, 88

yeast
  general hints, 103
yeast-risen breads, *see* breads,
  yeast
Yellow Rice Pilaf, 99
Yoghurt Bran Bread, 123
Yogurt Herb Dressing, 38

zinc, sources of, 16

Major Ingredient Index

This index lists our recipes by major or distinctive ingredients. It will help you find dishes that can be prepared with the food that you have on hand, items that are on special offer at your supermarket, or vegetables that are plentiful in your garden. This index excludes wholewheat flour, butter, margarine, ordinary quantities of eggs, most fluid milk, and all oil except olive oil. Small amounts of honey and brown sugar are also omitted, as are most herbs and seasonings.

Aioli Mayonnaise
  Dilled Egg Salad, 35
  Red and White Coleslaw, 35
almonds
  Almond Rounds, 144
almonds, blanched
  Wholewheat Christmas
  Stollen, 118
apple sauce
  Apple Sauce, Cinnamon
  Wholemeal Bread, 120
  Fresh, 143
apples
  Apple Bran Muffins, 126
  Apple Pie, 141
  Apple Yogurt Muesli, 140
  Cinnamon Apple
  Pancakes, 138
  Fresh Apple Cake, 146
  Fresh Apple Sauce, 143
  Spiced Fruit Pancakes, 136
apples, Red Delicious
  Peanut Sunflower Waldorf, 37
apples, tart (cooking)
  Pie Valasian, 80
  Red Cabbage with Apples, 97
  Sautéed Apples, 141
apricots, dried
  Wholewheat Christmas
  Stollen, 118
Apricot Yogurt Bran Muffins, 127
aubergines
  Arabic Musakka'a, 45
  Dip, 27
  Moussaka, 48
  Parmesan, 69
  Ratatouille, 96
  Rice and Vegetable Torte, 44
  Stuffed Aubergine, 50
avocados
  Guacamole, 30
  Mexican Chef's Salad, 36
  Mexican Salad, 36

bananas
  Banana Nut Bread, 128
  Banana Walnut Bran
  Muffins, 128
  Spiced Fruit Pancakes, 136
Basic Marinara Sauce
  Lasagne, 62
  Lentil Spaghetti, 62
  Mini Pitta Pizzas, 73
  Onion Mushroom Pizza, 74
  Wholewheat Ravioli, 77
basil, fresh
  Gnocchi Verde, 66
  Minestrone, 32
  Pesto Sauce over Pasta, 63
  Pie Valasian, 80
  Yogurt Herb Dressing, 38
bean curd, fresh, see tofu
bean sprouts
  Chinese Style Stir-Fried
  Noodles, 61
  Egg Fu Yung Omelette, 50
  Sprout Quiche, 80
beans, black turtle (dry)
  Black Bean Soup, 31
beans, green
  Minestrone, 32
  Vegetable Tofu Curry, 94
beans, haricot
  Boston Baked Beans, 45
beans, kidney (cooked)
  Bean and Chilli Cheese Pie, 87
  Mexican Chef's Salad, 36
beans, kidney (dry)
  Minestrone, 32
beans, pinto (cooked)
  Bean and Raisin
  Enchiladas, 90
  Vegetarian Tacos, 42
berries
  Spiced Fruit Pancakes, 136
bran
  Apple Bran Muffins, 126

Apricot Yogurt Bran
  Muffins, 127
Banana Walnut Bran
  Muffins, 126
Bran Bread, 111
Bran Cheese Waffles, 139
Bran Pitta Bread, 125
Oat Bran Bread, 113
Pineapple Bran Bread, 129
bread, wholewheat
  Stuffed Aubergine, 50
broccoli, fresh
  Broccoli Rice Bake, 48
  Cheese and Broccoli Bake, 54
  Mushroom and Broccoli
  Tartlets, 28
  Swiss 'n' Broccoli Bake, 51
  Vegetable Tofu Curry, 94
buckwheat kernels
  Buckwheat Mushroom
  Pilaf, 100
Burgundy
  Basic Marinara Sauce, 65
  Lentil Spaghetti, 62
  Lentils Burgundy, 46
buttermilk
  Buttermilk Pitta Bread, 125
  Wholewheat French Bread, 116
cabbage, red
  Red and White Coleslaw, 35
  Red Cabbage with Apples, 97
cabbage, white
  Minestrone, 32
  Red and White Coleslaw, 35
carob chips
  Oat Peanut Butter
  Crunchies, 45
carrots, fresh
  Carrot cake, 143
  Carrot and Courgette
  Slices, 40
  Carrot Noodles, 60

Chinese Stir-Fried Vegetables
   with Cashews, 97
Filled Courgettes, 27
Lentil Soup, 33
Lentils Burgundy, 46
Minestrone, 32
Sunflower Seed Carrot
   Bars, 142
Sweet and Sour Tofu, 94
Tofu with Fresh
   Mushrooms, 93
Vegetable Tofu Curry, 94
cashew nuts, raw
   Chinese Stir-Fried Vegetables
   with Cashews, 97
cashew nuts, roasted
   Cashew Noodle Crunch, 71
   Yellow Rice Pilaf, 99
cauliflower, fresh
   Cauliflower Basil Mushroom
      Bake, 54
   Cauliflower with Creamy
      Parmesan Dressing, 34
   Vegetable Tofu Curry, 94
celery
   Chinese Style Stir-Fried
      Vegetables, 97
   Egg Fu Yung Omelette, 50
   Mexican Salad, 36
   Red and White Coleslaw, 35
   Sweet and Sour Tofu, 94
Cheddar cheese
   Cheese Scalloped Potatoes with
      Mushrooms, 52
   Cheese Soufflé, 56
   Danish Feta and Spinach
      Tart, 83
   Double Cheese Bread, 112
   Enchiladas Coloradas, 91
   Mexican Chef's Salad, 36
   Sprout Quiche, 80
   Vegetarian Tacos, 42
Cheddar cheese, mild
   Fresh Corn Enchiladas, 89
Cheddar cheese, strong
   Bean and Raisin
      Enchiladas, 90
   Broccoli Rice Bake, 48
   Cauliflower, Basil Mushroom
      Bake, 54
   Cheese and Broccoli Bake, 54
   Chick Pea and Cheese
      Salad, 40

Green Chilli and Pepper
   Bake, 49
Nut Cheese Loaf, 52
Courgette and Tomato
   Quiche, 78
Bran Cheese Waffles, 139
cheese, *see* types of cheese
chick peas (cooked)
   Arabic Musakka'a, 45
   Curried Chick Peas, 43
   Hummus Bi Tahini, 100
chillis, green, canned (mild)
   Bean and Raisin
      Enchiladas, 90
   Fresh Corn Enchiladas, 89
   Green Chilli and Pepper
      Bake, 49
chillis, red, dried (mild)
   Enchilada Sauce, 92
chives, fresh
   Hot German Potato Salad, 34
   Yogurt Herb Dressing, 38
coriander, fresh
   Chinese Stir-Fried Vegetables
   with Cashews, 97
corn (sweetcorn), fresh or frozen
   Fresh Corn Enchiladas, 89
cottage cheese
   Cheese and Broccoli Bake, 54
   Cottage Cheese Oil Pizza
      Crust, 73
   Courgette Lasagne, 55
   Danish Feta and Spinach
      Tart, 83
   Double Cheese Bread, 112
   Enchiladas Coloradas, 91
   Feta Spinach Crêpes, 89
   Fresh Corn Enchiladas, 89
   Green Chilli and Pepper
      Bake, 49
Cottage Cheese Oil Pizza Crust
   Onion Mushroom Pizza, 74
courgettes
   Carrot and Courgette
      Slices, 40
   Carrot Filled Courgettes, 27
   Courgette and Green Chilli
      Quiche, 85
   Courgette Lasagne, 55
   Courgette Parmesan, 68
   Courgette and Tomato
      Quiche, 78
   Chinese Stir-Fried Vegetables

   with Cashews, 97
   Minestrone, 32
   Ratatouille, 96
   Rice and Vegetable Torte, 44
   Sicilian Pizza, 74
   Vegetable Tofu Curry, 94
cucumbers
   Cucumber Dip, 29
curd cheese
   Gnocchi Verde, 66
   Lasagne, 62
   Moussaka, 48
   Mushroom Cheese Tart, 82
   Spanakopita, 81
   Wholewheat Ravioli, 77
Currants
   Irish Oatmeal Bread, 114

dates, dried (pitted)
   Spiced Fruit Pancakes, 136
dill pickles, mild
   Dilled Egg Salad, 35

eggs
   Cheese and Onion Quiche, 79
   Courgette Pancakes, 98
   Dilled Egg Salad, 35
   Egg Fu Yung Omelette, 50
   Green Chilli and Pepper
      Bake, 49
   Moussaka, 48
   Mushroom Quiche, 78
   Nut Cheese Loaf, 56
   Spanakopita, 81
   Sprout Quiche, 80
   Swiss 'n' Broccoli Bake, 51
Enchilada Sauce
   Bean and Raisin
      Enchiladas, 90
   Enchiladas Coloradas, 91
   Fresh Corn Enchiladas, 89

feta cheese, Danish
   Danish Feta and Spinach
      Tart, 83
   Greek Chef's Salad, 36
   Spanakopita, 81

green beans, *see* beans, green
Gruyere cheese
   Cheese Radish Salad, 39
   Courgette and Tomato
      Quiche, 78

Harvest Vegetable Quiche, 83
Mushroom and Broccoli
Tartlets, 28
Pie Valasian, 80
Stuffed Aubergine, 50
Swiss and Rye Bread, 121
Swiss 'n' Broccoli Bake, 51

hazelnuts
Wholewheat Hazelnut
Pancakes, 137
honey
Almond Rounds, 144
Carrot Cake, 142
Raisin Spice Bread, 129
Sunflower Seed Carrot
Bars, 142
Honey French Dressing
Mexican Chef's Salad, 36

leeks
Lentils Burgundy, 46
Minestrone, 32
lemons, fresh
Black Bean Soup, 31
Guacamole, 30
Hummus Bi Tahini, 100
Oven Pancakes, 136
Tart Greek Salad Dressing, 38
lentils, cooked
Curried Lentils, 46
Lentil Spaghetti, 62
Lentil Sunflower Burgers, 42
lentils, dry
Lentil Soup, 33
Lentils Burgundy, 46
lettuce
Greek Chef's Salad, 36
Mexican Chef's Salad, 36
Mexican Salad, 36
lettuce, iceberg
Vegetarian Tacos, 42
limes
Yogurt Herb Dressing, 38

mayonnaise
Dilled Egg Salad, 35
milk powder
Bran Cheese Waffles, 139
German Potato Pancakes, 53
mozzarella cheese
Aubergine Parmesan, 69
Courgette Lasagne, 55

Courgette Parmesan, 68
Lasagne, 62
Lentil Spaghetti, 62
Mini Pitta Pizzas, 73
Mozzarella Cheese Quiche, 84
Onion Mushroom Pizza, 74
Rice and Vegetable Torte, 44
Tomato and Mozzarella Pie, 53
mushrooms, fresh
Cauliflower Basil Mushroom
Bake, 54
Cheese Scalloped Potatoes
with Mushrooms, 52
Chinese Style Stir-Fried
Rice, 99
Mini Pitta Pizzas, 73
Mushroom and Broccoli
Tartlets, 28
Mushroom and Olive Bake, 54
Mushroom Cheese Tart, 82
Mushroom Quiche, 78
Nut Cheese Loaf, 56
Onion Mushroom Pizza, 74
Scrambled Tofu, 93
Sicilian Pizza, 74

noodles, wholewheat, see pasta,
wholewheat

oats, rolled
Irish Oatmeal Bread, 114
Oat Bran Bread, 113
Oat Raisin Muffins, 128
Sunflower Seed Oatmeal
Cookies, 145
olive oil
Greek Chef's Salad, 36
Ratatouille, 96
Tart Greek Salad Dressing, 38
olives, black
Greek Chef's Salad, 36
olives, black (pitted)
Enchiladas Coloradas, 91
Mexican Salad, 36
Sicilian Pizza, 74
onions
Basic Marinara Sauce, 65
Cheese and Onion Quiche, 79
Onion Mushroom Pizza, 74
onions, salad
Cheese Scalloped Potatoes
with Mushrooms, 52
Chinese Style Stir-Fried

Noodles, 61
Chinese Style Fried Rice, 99
Enchiladas Coloradas, 91
Mushroom Quiche, 78

Parmesan Cheese
Aubergine Parmesan, 69
Baked Green Fettucine, 66
Cacciatore Sauce over
Noodles, 65
Cauliflower with Creamy
Parmesan Dressing, 34
Courgette
Parmesan, 69
Gnocchi Verde, 66
Lasagne, 62
Lentil Spaghetti, 62
Minestrone, 32
Moussaka, 48
Mushroom and Broccoli
Tartlets, 28
Mushroom Quiche, 78
Parmesan Herb Dip, 29
Rice and Vegetable Torte, 44
Scrambled Tofu, 93
Sicilian Pizza, 74
Stuffed Aubergine, 50
Tomato and Mozzarella Pie, 5
Wholewheat Ravioli, 77
Yogurt Herb Dressing, 38
parsley, fresh
German Potato Pancakes, 53
Minestrone, 32
Parmesan Herb Dip, 29
pasta, wholewheat (homemade)
Baked Green Fettucine, 66
Cacciatore Sauce over
Noodles, 65
Carrot Noodles, 60
Cashew Noodles Crunch, 71
Chinese Style Stir-Fried
Noodles, 60
Hungarian Paprika Noodles, 7
Lasagne, 62
Lentil Spaghetti, 62
Pasta Rustica, 70
Rich Egg Noodles, 60
Spinach Noodles, 60
Wholewheat Egg Noodles, 60
pasta, wholewheat (purchased)
fettucine, 66
Pesto Sauce over Pasta, 63
Lasagne, 62

Lentil Spaghetti, 62
Minestrone, 32
Peanut Butter
  Oat Peanut Butter
    Crunchies, 145
peanuts, raw (unsalted)
  Peanut Butter, 143
peanuts, roasted (unsalted)
  Peanut Sunflower Waldorf
    Salad, 37
peas, frozen
  Chinese Style Fried Rice, 99
peppers, green
  Bean and Raisin Enchiladas, 90
  Mexican Salad, 36
  Mini Pitta Pizzas, 73
  Onion Mushroom Pizza, 74
  Pepper Olive Quiche, 85
  Ratatouille, 96
  Sicilian Pizza, 74
pine nuts, shelled
  Pesto Sauce over Pasta, 63
pineapple, dried (unsugared)
  Wholewheat Christmas
    Stollen, 118
pineapple juice
  Pineapple Bran Bread, 129
pistachio nuts,
  Yellow Rice Pilaf, 99
pitta bread, wholewheat
  Mini Pitta Pizzas, 73
potatoes
  Cheese Scalloped Potatoes
    with Mushrooms, 52
  German Potato Pancakes, 53
  Minestrone, 32
  Mexican Salad, 36
  Potato Loaf, 121
  Tomato and Mozzarella Pie, 53
potatoes, new
  Hot German Potato Salad, 34
prunes, pitted
  Bran Prune Muffins, 131
  Fruit Nut Squares, 140
  Sunny Prune Muffins, 127

radishes
  Cheese Radish Salad, 39
  Hot German Potato Salad, 34
  Red and White Coleslaw, 35
raisins
  Bean and Raisin
    Enchiladas, 90

Irish Oatmeal Bread, 114
Peanut Sunflower Waldorf
  Salad, 37
Raisin Spice Bread, 129
Spiced Fruit Pancakes, 136
Sunflower Seed Carrot
  Bars, 142
Wholewheat Christmas
  Stollen, 118
Yellow Rice Pilaf, 99
rice, brown (cooked)
  Broccoli Rice Bake, 48
  Chinese Style Fried
    Rice, 99
  Moussaka, 48
  Nut Cheese Loaf, 52
  Rice and Vegetable Torte, 44
rice, brown (long grain)
  Yellow Rice Pilaf, 99
rye flour
  Rye Bread, 115

sesame seeds, hulled (white)
  Wholewheat Sesame
    Crêpes, 88
Sesame Tahini
  Hummus Bi Tahini, 100
spinach, fresh or frozen
  Danish Feta and Spinach
    Tart, 83
  Gnocchi Verde, 66
  Spanakopita, 81
  Spinach Lasagne, 68
  Spinach Noodles, 61
spinach, frozen
  Wholewheat Ravioli, 77
sugar, brown
  Banana Nut Bread, 128
sunflower seeds, unroasted
  Lentil Sunflower Burgers, 42
  Peanut Sunflower Waldorf
    Salad, 37
  Sunflower Seed Bread, 114
  Sunflower Seed Carrot
    Bars, 142
  Sunflower Seed Oatmeal
    Cookies, 145
  Sunflower Seed Pancakes, 138
  Sunny Prune Muffins, 127

taco shells
  Vegetarian Tacos, 42
tahini, *see* sesame tahini

Tart Greek Salad Dressing
  Greek Chef's Salad, 36
tofu
  Chinese Style Stir-fried
    Noodles, 61
  Scrambled Tofu, 93
  Tofu Wheat Bread, 117
  Tofu with Fresh
    Mushrooms, 93
  Vegetable Tofu Curry, 94
tomato paste, canned or bottled
  Basic Marinara Sauce, 65
  Bean and Raisin
    Enchiladas, 90
  Courgette Lasagne, 55
  Enchilada Sauce, 92
  Enchiladas Coloradas, 91
  Honey French Dressing, 38
  Moussaka, 48
  Ratatouille, 96
  Two-in-One Tomato Sauce, 63
  Vegetarian Tacos, 42
tomatoes, canned
  Arabic Musakka'a, 45
  Minestrone, 32
  Two-in-One Tomato Sauce, 63
tomatoes, fresh
  Courgette and Tomato
    Quiche, 78
  Greek Chef's Salad, 36
  Ratatouille, 96
  Rice and Vegetable Torte, 44
  Scrambled Tofu, 93
  Stuffed Aubergine, 50
  Tomato and Mozzarella Pie, 53
  Vegetarian Tacos, 42
tortillas, corn
  Bean and Raisin Enchiladas, 90
  Enchiladas Coloradas, 91
  Fresh Corn Enchiladas, 89
turnips, 18
Two-in-One Tomato Sauce
  Nut Cheese Loaf, 56
  Sicilian Pizza, 74

walnuts
  Banana Nut Bread, 128
  Banana Walnut Bran
    Muffins, 126
  Carrot Cake, 143
  Fresh Apple Cake, 146
  Nut Cheese Loaf, 52
Wholewheat Buttermilk Pizza

Bread,   125
Onion Mushroom Pizza,   74
Wholewheat Crêpes
Feta Spinach Crêpes,   89
Wholewheat Pâté Brisée Crust
Danish Feta and Spinach
Tart,   83
Mushroom Cheese Tart,   82
Pie Valasian,   80

Wholewheat Quiche Shell
Cheese and Onion Quiche,   79
Courgette and Tomato
Quiche,   78
Mushroom Quiche,   78
Sprout Quiche,   80
Wholewheat Sesame Crêpes
Feta Spinach Crêpes,   89

yogurt
Apple Yogurt Muesli,   140
Apricot Yogurt Bran
Muffins,   127
Cucumber Dip,   29
Raisin Spice Bread,   129
Vegetable Tofu Curry,   94
Yoghurt Bran Bread,   124
Yogurt Herb Dressing,   38